RUSH

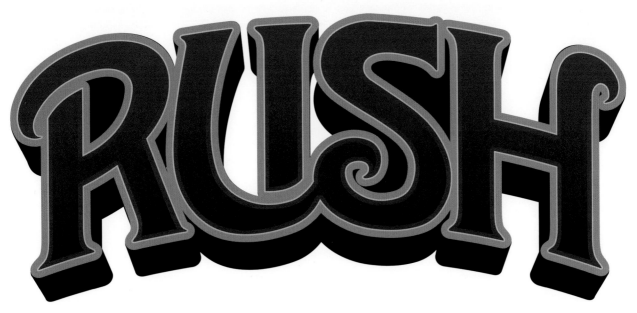

ALBUM BY ALBUM

MARTIN POPOFF

with

RALPH CHAPMAN | PAUL GILBERT | IAN GRANDY

KIRK HAMMETT | CHRIS IRWIN | SEAN KELLY

PETE KOZA | MICHEL LANGEVIN | DOUGLAS MAHER

JILLIAN MARYONOVICH | JIM MATHEOS | EDDY MAXWELL

CHRIS NELSON | MARY JO PLEWS | JASON POPOVICH

MIKE PORTNOY | CHRIS SCHNEBERGER | ROBERT TELLERIA

JEFF WAGNER | RAY WAWRZYNIAK

VOYAGEUR
PRESS

Quarto is the authority on a wide range of topics.

Quarto educates, entertains and enriches the lives of
our readers—enthusiasts and lovers of hands-on living.

www.quartoknows.com

First published in 2017 by Voyageur Press, an imprint of Quarto Publishing Group USA Inc., 400 First Avenue North,
Suite 400, Minneapolis, MN 55401 USA. Telephone: (612) 344-8100 Fax: (612) 344-8692

quartoknows.com
Visit our blogs at quartoknows.com

Voyageur Press titles are also available at discounts in bulk quantity for industrial or sales-promotional use. For details contact
the Special Sales Manager at Quarto Publishing Group USA Inc., 400 First Avenue North, Suite 400, Minneapolis, MN 55401 USA.

10 9 8 7 6 5 4 3 2 1

ISBN: 978-0-7603-5220-5

Library of Congress Cataloging-in-Publication Data

Names: Popoff, Martin, 1963- author.
Title: Rush : album by album / Martin Popoff.
Description: Minneapolis, Minnesota : Voyageur Press, 2017. l Includes index.
Identifiers: LCCN 2016039073 l ISBN 9780760352205 (hc w/jacket)
Subjects: LCSH: Rush (Musical group)—Criticism and interpretation.
l Rock music—History and criticism.
Classification: LCC ML421.R87 P65 2017 l DDC 782.42166092/2—dc23
LC record available at https://lccn.loc.gov/2016039073

Acquiring Editor: Dennis Pernu
Project Manager: Jordan Wiklund
Art Director: Cindy Samargia Laun
Cover and Book Design: Brad Norr Design

Front cover: *(top) All the World's a Stage* tour, Civic Center, Springfield, Massachusetts, December 9, 1976; *(bottom) All the World's a Stage* tour, Aragon Ballroom, Chicago, May 20, 1977. *Both Fin Costello/Redferns/Getty Images*

Title pages: Recording *Permanent Waves* at Le Studio, Morin Heights, Quebec, October 1979. *Fin Costello/Redferns/Getty Images*

Back cover: *Clockwork Angels* tour, Bridgestone Arena, Nashville, Tennessee, May 1, 2013. *Frederick Breedon/Getty Images*

Printed in China

Contents

VIP

TORONTO, JUNE 17 - 20, 2015

RUSHCON

FIFTEEN

MARTIN POPOFF

Introduction

n the immortal words of Yngwie Malmsteen, "Who says less is more?! *More* is more!" Or, you know, something to that effect.

Yngwie, who loves Rush and has covered them on record, said this to Sam Dunn during the making of *Metal Evolution*, a project that I worked on with Banger Films. Banger, of course, produced the award-winning film *Rush: Beyond the Lighted Stage*, which I also worked on full-time for like a year.

But I was pondering the Swede's words of wisdom as I walked to work one morning listening to an old Rush bootleg on my iPod (by the way, Geddy was *not* a ducker of the notes live—holy crap). A debate among me and my music buds, and indeed a point of conjecture in the progressive metal episode of *Metal Evolution*, is that very concept, "more is more," which I basked in like a figurative tub of baked beans as I sprung-step to intimate versions of "La Villa Strangiato," "The Trees," and "Something for Nothing," striding to the office in my yellow and green Soulfly shirt (always a nod-getter).

So yes, where were we? As our cast of characters know all too well, the snobby rock cognoscenti has always put down Rush because, of course, they believe less is more. Punk rock, folkies, music for airports, old blues sides from the '30s . . . we're supposed to find the art in the spaces, in what is left unsaid, and project our own interpretations onto lyrics because we're so smart and it's all about us. Well, the Rush philosophy was, why not just try harder? And guess what? You can still do all that other reflection about the spaces. Why start on the bottom shelf and have to stack everything on top of it until it breaks?

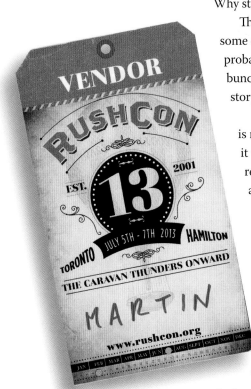

The idea with Rush is, let's start on the top shelf together, let's give you a lot of music, some of the chords are a little weird, you might twist an ankle dancing to it, and you'll probably look goofy trying. And if you've got any reflecting gray matter left, here's a bunch of lyrics, which likely together combust up synergistically to make even more story, because, like, more is more.

Oh sure, Rush tried to play the game, positing with a witch cackle, "Our more is more is even more, because we're even going to include less is more!" But alas, it wasn't in their nature, and so the point I'm trying to make is, '80s and '90s records included, Rush and their substantial music and lyrics and productions and album covers made it pretty darn easy to build this book and to have it be relentlessly interesting.

Somewhat to my surprise, for a couple things were happening here. Number one, this is only the second book in this series, the first of which was on friggin' Bob Dylan. Talk about stacking up a challenge with harmonica dents to the head. I knew we'd have no problem killing Bob Dylan on the music. It would take some sky-high Lower Eastside air of condescension to get most people to believe his version of less is more trumps Rush when it comes to the music. There's no way I'm buying that. I knew this book would kill Bob Dylan on the music, meaning, logically like Spock, there's more to talk about here. That's just a fact. We can talk about good taste and bad taste until we're blue bloods in the face, but the harder objective surface of craft will always win out in the end. That's why all those old Vertigo Records albums are so collectible.

I was a little more apprehensive on philosophies, concepts, themes, and lyrics, but I soon found out I shouldn't have been. Because, again, even if you don't believe more is more, any open-minded person can believe that more *can be* more, and Neil has always provided more. And he certainly provided more than enough to engage all these smart people you're about to meet. It's a fast canon of lyrics, and as with his charted and then replicated fills, well, Neil tries harder. And so, bloody 'ell, halfway through this process I was about ready to concede no ground to Bob Dylan, widely considered rock music's greatest poet, although, screw it, does he even play rock music?

Second, I was apprehensive of having people from all walks of life expound on Rush, and have it be not only engaging but stacked with enough new provocative ideas to make this gorgeous book useful. It's not that I was worried about these people more so than my long bias about having the band themselves be the main speakers in the books I do. Again, my fears were quickly allayed through the pile of completely engaging, fun, thought-provoking conversations I had across this catalog and across a wide swath of humanity parachuting in to breathe life into often ignored corners of the catalog.

And I think that was the key, that we strived for and built a perfect balance in the cast of people, including those who could technically analyze music (in composite and isolating guitar, bass, and drums), complementing those who could place Rush smartly within the pop culture and the music industry of each specific album's launch date, buttressed by those who most deeply felt the lyrics on any number of intellectual and emotional levels.

And I must admit, again, from a base of thinking, "How do we match the quality of the Bob Dylan book?" to "I love this damn book—this is awesome!" Well, it was bloody effortless in the baking and the making. The long and short of it, I have every confidence in the fact that after reading this book, you will be able to look at each and every one of these at times contentious Rush records in completely new rainbows of refracted light, and you will join me in now and forever defending the likes of Rush (and yes, I don't mean just Rush, I mean all of our prog heroes) against the barbs of the Rock Hall tastemakers who think Yngwie is yucky.

Martin Popoff

Tools of the trade: a quiver of Alex's axes at a shoot for *Total Guitar* magazine, May 22, 2011 (*Gavin Roberts/* Total Guitar *magazine via Getty* *Images*); Geddy's pedals at Alsterdorfer Sporthalle, Hamburg, Germany, September 27, 2004 (*Malzkorn/Getty Images*); and Neil's kit at the Austin360 Amphitheater, Austin, Texas, May 16, 2015. (*Gary Miller/Getty Images*).

CHAPTER 1

RUSH

**with Paul Gilbert, Ian Grandy,
Chris Irwin, and Kirk Hammett**

*Geddy Lee: lead vocals, bass
Alex Lifeson: guitars, backing vocals
John Rutsey: drums, percussion, backing vocals
Released March 1, 1974
Recorded at Eastern Sound, Toronto, and Toronto Sound
Studios, Toronto
Produced by Rush*

**(opposite)
Canuckleheads in the washroom. Neil
Peart replaced John Rutsey in the drum
chair some five months after the March
1974 release of the band's debut.**
© *1974, Bruce Cole/PlumCom Inc.*

know because I was there. All too much is made of the comparison of brash young upstarts Rush to legends Led Zeppelin. Although on the other hand—again, because I was there—about the right amount of (or even not enough) hand wringing took place over *that voice*. Seriously, as kids, although we loved Rush instantly, they had verged on novelty band due to Geddy's inhuman birdlike chirp.

Of course, any surly '70s teen of a heavy-rock disposition quickly turned around and learned to love it, but the nagging fact in the back of the metal mind remained that due to those odd pipes, the regular rules of singing probably didn't apply, that the band was almost instrumental with an extra instrument no one else could claim.

But here's the thing: most definitely not enough was made of the fact that, with record one, Rush were an act bounding in a professional slab of product better than the first from Aerosmith or Kiss (but not Montrose), and admirably, even bravely, heavy for the day.

Let's not forget that 1974 was yet another dreary year for North American metal, in fact the fifth dreary year in a row, while the UK was forging hard rock—and prog—anew seemingly on a quarterly basis. Yes, Genesis, Sabbath, Zeppelin, Heep, Purple, Budgie . . . we had Cactus, Mountain, the Amboy Dukes, BTO, and April Wine, and not a single prog band yet, with Kansas still a year away.

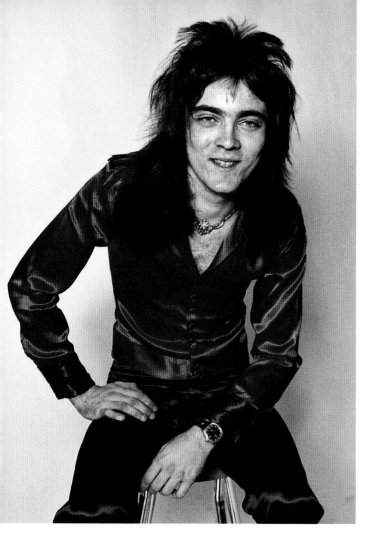

John Rutsey, like many other musicians of his generation, was under the spell of the mighty Led Zeppelin. © 1973, Bruce Cole/ PlumCom Inc.

So to get *Rush* in gargantuan pink and black letters, with "Finding My Way," "What You're Doing," "Working Man," and instant BTO-beater "In the Mood," this was something to be proud of in Canuckleheadland, that a band could emerge fully formed and rocking hard, self-aware, givin' 'er. And most importantly, the band were for the most part post–blues boom, crowding around riff, although down a whole different road than the classical gas of Heep Purple and more toward Kiss and where Aerosmith and Ted Nugent would be from '75 on (by which point Rush had evolved to a higher state).

But beyond the underground (and concert) hits and the doomy drone of "Working Man," which is every kind of hit, let's hear it for the deep tracks as well. There is actually quite a lot going on in "Need Some Love" and "Take a Friend," including layers of guitars, vocals, interesting flashes of prog and sophisticated arrangements, while "Here Again" contains a pile of Geddy's best blues wailing, over mellow doom, to match "Working Man"'s Sabbatherian version of six-string fatalism. Left among the tunes that no one dare mention is "Before and After," which begins folk and then rocks out as hard as anything on this road-ready album.

Ultimately, the math is inescapable: there's one non-rocker on the whole damn *Rush* album, and even that turns into an electricity-drenched power ballad for much of its duration, Geddy matching Alex screech for screech, as soon-to-depart timekeeper John Rutsey cranes around and sees two shooting superstars who are about to leave him in their cosmic dust.

POPOFF: So what was your assessment of this first Rush album against the others, and how much credence should be put in the "next Led Zeppelin" talk?

GILBERT: Actually, I got this record as part of a three-record set called *Archives*, because I think the first album that I had for them was actually *All the World's a Stage*, the live one, and then I went back and got *Archives*. So that got me into the first album and *Fly by Night* and *Caress of Steel*. But I loved it. Alex's guitar sound and guitar playing was real fiery and strong, and Geddy's screamin' away. And John Rutsey, he did the job, he made it work. Great songs and riffs on there, and sure, at the time they were accused of being very influenced by Led Zeppelin. But to me, whenever I hear people say a band sounds like other bands, it never bothers me, because it's always a good band. Like when Frank Marino is accused of sounding like Hendrix, yeah, that's great, more Hendrix! And obviously Rush evolved in all sorts of directions since then. But to me, that's a great place to start to pick a band to sound like—Led Zeppelin is a pretty good one.

HAMMETT: Yeah, it's funny. Recently I was in a very popular grocery store that had a lot of organic food and whatnot, and they had the stereo on, and they were playing the Doobie Brothers or something, and then all of a sudden I heard "Working Man," and I thought, well, times have definitely changed. So I'm going through the produce or whatever and listening to the song, and I was remembering that exact thing, that when that album came out, everybody was saying, "Rush, yeah, they're the new Led Zeppelin! They're just like Led Zeppelin!" And I would hear people say, "You gotta hear this band—they sound just like Led Zeppelin!" And in retrospect, you say "Huh?" Rush is nothing like it.

But when you listen to the first album, the guitar tone is like straight Les Paul/Marshall. It sounds like a Zeppelin tone that you would hear on the second album, *Zep II*. You listen to Geddy's singing, and it's high-pitched like Robert Plant might've done at any given time. And so sure, I started to hear some Led Zeppelin comparisons. Then when you hear "Working Man," that riff could be like some faraway distant cousin to "Heartbreaker" or something—it had some of the same elements "Heartbreaker" had. But then when they go into the verse, then it gets a little heavier and darker, and starts going into Black Sabbath territory for a second.

POPOFF: Ian, you were there doing sound for them. What's the connection there with Zeppelin?

GRANDY: Well, John Rutsey went and saw Led Zeppelin the first night they were ever in Toronto. He absolutely flipped, and then the next day or two they had the first album . . . I'm going to say there were three or four songs off that album that [Rush] played live. You know, you're playing a high school and you can pull off a Led Zeppelin song, that's where we were at there, five hundred bucks for a high school. So they played a few Zeppelin songs. And the boys could play them. Whatever song that is, Alex was pretty good with the violin bow. I'm kind of surprised he never kept that up. And it's well documented that I think the second time they went to see Zeppelin, Alex tells the story of sitting right in front of Jimmy Page, jumping up, and Jimmy Page looked at him and gave him kind of a head nod. Yeah, they were fans. So, sure, they did some Zeppelin songs, and I guess people thought "Working Man" was a Zeppelin song originally. Yeah, I say, there was some influence.

POPOFF: There were people who were under the impression, however briefly, that *Rush* was the new Led Zeppelin album.

IRWIN: Yes, well, "Finding My Way" was a second very Zeppelin-y sounding one, that opening riff especially, and Geddy's *ooh yeah*'s. When Donna Halper debuted the album on radio down in Cleveland, listeners were thinking it was a Led Zeppelin

While North American hard rock stagnated in 1974, UK metal and prog forged ahead.

album. Of course, Alex Lifeson's guitar god is Jimmy Page, and he talks about, many years later, when they were backstage at the Page-Plant show in Toronto in '98, he was just terribly nervous. Alex at the time was an established guitar god himself, but here he was. He said he felt like a little boy meeting Jimmy Page.

POPOFF: You mention Cleveland, which in Rush lore is the city where the album broke, thanks to "Working Man." Why did that song connect with people?

IRWIN: "Working Man" hit so well in the Cleveland area because Cleveland was the stereotypical factory town. And that song really resonates with the working man. It's got that great, heavy, heavy opening, and great playing throughout. Lyrically, you go, yeah, that's me. And if it's not them, it's someone that they know, absolutely.

HAMMETT: Like I said, "Working Man" does sound like Zeppelin, and from far away, it sounds like "Heartbreaker." And possibly people were just hungry for that back then—if there was anything that had that sound, they would just jump on it. But it's a cool song with a great riff, and the subject matter makes sense, you know? It's like, all us hard rock and heavy metal people, we were all working men at one point or another.

GILBERT: When I heard it, I was too young to really relate to the lyrics. But it's a great riff, with a great jam in the middle, and Geddy's voice is just incredible on that song. It surprises me so much as the years go on, how Geddy has gotten criticism for either his style or the tone or the range of his voice. I always loved Geddy's voice. He really established himself as an extremely powerful and versatile singer, if you look at that first album. He comes out of the box just full speed, and everything is just on fire. Obviously they had something to prove and they proved it.

GRANDY: "Working Man," you know, is such an anthem for them. You can hardly not like it. I heard Geddy a little while ago. "So, if there's one ultimate Rush song, what is it?" "It's 'Working Man.'" The first album, a song that you're still playing forty-five years later, and the crowd still loves, and people can still relate to. I get up at six-thirty and I go to work at eight-thirty. So, they can understand.

POPOFF: At the other end of the emotional spectrum is "In the Mood."

HAMMETT: Yeah, the party song! *Hey, baby, it's a quarter to eight. / I feel I'm in the mood. / Hey, baby, the hour is late. I feel I've got to move.* It's funny, because that was pretty much the beginning and the end of that sort of lyrical matter [laughs]. I think that was the first and last time they actually sang about females. To me, it's pretty fun to listen to. It's a great rocking song. Why not?

IRWIN: Love the guitar riff on it, and it's actually a pretty heavy tune. The lyrics, of course, were kind of juvenile, about chicks and beer and working—basic stuff. At least that one I don't cringe when I listen to it. Great title, but people used to confuse it with that old Glenn Miller hit. And you could tell even on that song that Geddy and Alex are

John Rutsey flipped over Led Zeppelin's first Toronto appearance, at the Rockpile in 1969. Three or four songs from Zep's first LP found their way onto Rush's early setlists.

superior musicians to John Rutsey. But at least on the *Rush* album, they're not that much superior to him. I've heard his drumming described as pedestrian, but Rutsey was solid for what they needed at the time.

POPOFF: Ian, you have some insight into how the album came to be in the first place.

GRANDY: Do you know what CanCon is? Well, about '72 or so, that came in, and . . . radio stations had to play thirty percent Canadian music, and they were scrambling. They had this thirty percent block to fill, and when that happened . . . a guy I knew was running a bar, and suddenly every band that came in there had an album. Whereas before, none of them had an album. You'd be hearing, "Hey, you're number five in Thunder Bay."

At Toronto's Piccadilly Tube, circa 1973. Manager Ray Danniels is standing, second from left. © 1973, Bruce Cole/PlumCom Inc.

Anyway, so the guys at least had been writing their own songs; it wasn't like we were doing all covers or anything. And they had this group of songs and mostly what I remember about it is that a lot of it was recorded after bar gigs. We would play the Gasworks 'til one o'clock, strike the stage gear and the drums, drag them over to the studio, which was only three or four blocks, start recording about two until about seven, and then get home about eight thirty and crash all day, come back, set up at the Gasworks, do another gig. So most of my memories are crawling in a corner and going, I don't care. It was pretty primitive, that's for sure. That's how that album got made, really low budget.

Terry Brown came in to rescue it after they weren't happy with the original sessions. But we were thrilled to be in the studio putting down tracks. I remember later Geddy coming to me, with various albums, going, "Can you believe we have seven albums?" [laughs] But the first one, the first time you heard something on the radio, it's like, wow. You gotta understand, I started out with them in the basement, so if you would've told me that "You were lucky to work with this band . . ." Well, I was lucky, and I helped, and we all worked together, but the truth is, you work for a band in the basement, and then to get to where Rush did, it's pretty unlikely. People tell me I was lucky . . . well, maybe a little hard work too.

But John was the one that really, really wanted it. Geddy and Alex were on the same course too, but John did all the band business and dealt with the managers and promoters, stuff like that, and did the announcing. If the drumming hadn't have fallen apart, who the hell knows? But John, you know, liked to party, and he was a true diabetic. You really can't combine those two things. I love the guy, he was a friend of mine, and rest in peace and all that, but his drumming was slipping, and the band knew that, and I knew that too. You can't do cymbal crashes for everything.

The only thing that bothered me was the whole fallacy that, "Oh, he left because he wanted to do this and that." And for years I'd be going, they fired him. "No, no, they

Promo copy of "Finding My Way," the first single from the debut.

Beginning the long climb to the top. © 1974, Bruce Cole/ PlumCom Inc.

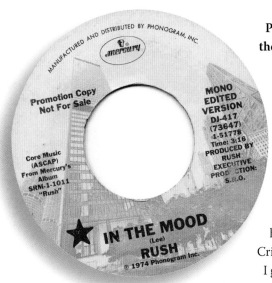

Promo copy of the second single, "In the Mood"—the beginning and the end of Rush's foray into dumb rawk lyrics.

didn't." Don't tell me what happened, because I was there and I know what the hell happened. I know what the story is. And now when it finally came out, I'm going, yeah, like I've always been saying.

But I tell you what, when the first album first came out, it was horribly pressed, and everybody I knew who got one, it skipped and skipped and skipped and skipped. Glad they fixed that, but the first run was embarrassing, really. And then it was great that you had an album out, but you're still playing the Piccadilly Tube and still playing these places. You had an album for people to buy, and your mom and dad hear a couple of Rush songs on the radio and that helps. My mom and dad are thanked on the first album, on the Moon Records one anyway. They rehearsed in my basement, and my parents parked outside in the snow while their equipment was in our garage [laughs].

But they had all committed very early. You've seen that documentary, *Come on Children.* Alex wanted to be a guitar player, and he's talking to his parents. I knew him when he was probably thirteen, and he was in a band with my brother. His father was a plumber, he didn't want to do that. He wanted to be guitar player, and even at thirteen, you're going, this guy can play. Not like he can now, but for a thirteen-year-old kid . . . and my brother was three chords on the rhythm guitar, and he'd just be looking at Alex going, I'm so far outclassed [laughs]. Geddy, same thing. I see him now with his mom and all that, but she was just so dead-set against it. And so they all wanted it, they really did. And John really wanted it too. He ran out of steam physically, and those guys didn't.

POPOFF: Even though *Rush* is not progressive metal yet, you can hear that these guys can play.

HAMMETT: Definitely. The amazing thing about "Working Man" and "Finding My Way" and "What You're Doing" is that they had these kind of basic heavy blues rock elements, but you could see a level of musicianship that was breaking through, or that was trying to break through, in all of those songs. You could see that there was a level of aggressiveness that was infused into these songs that set them apart from what anyone else was doing back then.

"Working Man" has that whole guitar solo section, which speeds up. "Finding My Way" is pretty high-energy. I love that song. Maybe it's because of that shining guitar part, but I like the fact that it's a real upbeat kind of high-energy song. "What You're Doing" has kind of like progressive King Crimson–ish tendencies.

I guess my point is, you can hear the influences, and you can hear them trying to be progressive. In retrospect, looking back, you can hear what they're shooting for and what they're trying to do. And you can see how logical the evolution is from album to album—it just makes total sense. There are steps that they took, chances that they took, that totally worked for them, so that by the time *2112* came out, they had their sound;

they'd figured it all out. But that first album shows a lot of glimpses of what was to come.

GILBERT: I actually played those in cover bands. But listening to that album, we played the whole thing. That was the cool thing about the vinyl days, is that, physically, it was inconvenient to skip around on the record. You had to go over, pick up the needle, and try to get it at the right place. So a lot of times, the listening style in those days was album sides. And the way that a band would sequence a record was really significant, because you wouldn't skip around the way you would now. So it wasn't just the songs, it was the whole record. And that first album just had a great vibe and made you want to rock. And really, as much, again, as people were trying to say, oh, it sounds like Zeppelin, it didn't. It sounded like Rush, and they were their own thing right off the bat.

IRWIN: Just a note on one of those. "What You're Doing," absolutely love that heavy riff and it rocks, but the lyrics on that song are probably the most intelligent on the album in that it's almost like a protest song of some sort. They're speaking out to someone, some sort of authority figure, but I'm not sure who or what it's directed at. But at least it gets my mind working, to try to figure it out. Whereas a lot of the other songs, it's just kind of like, "Hey baby, I wanna be your man," that sort of thing.

But as for its heaviness, and I guess the heaviness of the whole album, I know that the first show that Geddy went to was to see Cream at Massey Hall. And I know that he was influenced by heavier music. Jack Bruce was one of his earliest idols, as was John Entwistle and also Jack Casady of the Jefferson Airplane, who was an innovative player. And I just think with the music progressing and getting heavier at that time . . . that [first album] was just a couple years after the birth of heavy metal, because, as I recall, in your *Who Invented Heavy Metal?* book, you say that the first true heavy metal record was the first Black Sabbath album.

POPOFF: But in the end, there was a sizable number of potential fans, as heavy as *Rush* was, that couldn't get past Geddy's voice.

GRANDY: I went out with a girl who said I respect that you work for Rush, but I hate that voice. She was a singer and a vocal coach. She says, "I hate his voice, it's terrible." It's an acquired taste, I guess.

HAMMETT: A lot of people couldn't take it. You know, a lot of people weren't having it, and were just like, how can you listen to that? Funny thing, I always thought that I could hear Geddy's Canadian accent. But I think that was pretty much my imagination. But you have to understand that we were listening to stuff because we wanted to listen to it. Big difference. If you want to listen to something, you learn to like it. And we wanted to listen to it. Just like we wanted to listen to Mercyful Fate and to Motörhead and to punk rock music—because we wanted to. That was our attitude. And if people didn't get it, that was their tough luck and their loss.

Cleveland DJ Donna Halper was instrumental in breaking Rush in the US. She's seen here working at Northeastern University's radio station in 1968. *Courtesy Donna Halper*

Trade ad promotes the debut and autumn 1974 US tour dates.

CHAPTER 2

Fly by Night

with Chris Schneberger
and Jeff Wagner

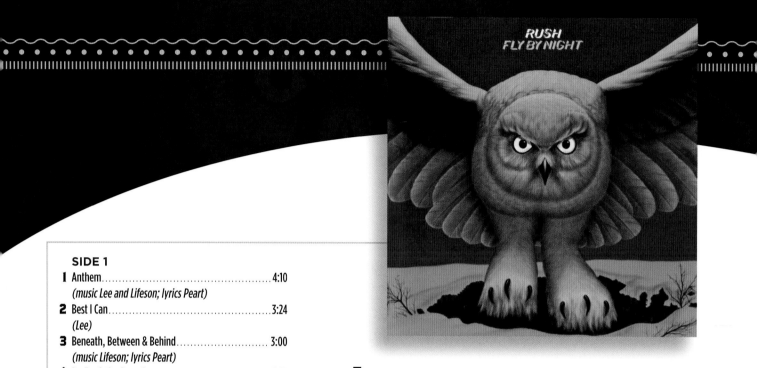

Geddy Lee: lead vocals, bass, classical guitar
Alex Lifeson: guitars
Neil Peart: drums, percussion
Released February 15, 1975
Recorded at Toronto Sound Studios, Toronto
Produced by Rush and Terry Brown

t's hard to imagine an example in which hiring on a new drummer transformed a band as much as it did Rush. Previously a spirited Led Zeppelin–loving band harder than almost anybody in 1974, Rush found themselves the following year pretty much inventing a new genre of music—namely progressive metal— amusingly, right around the time that heavy metal itself was getting branded as such.

And much of the credit goes to the band's well-traveled and professionally scarred young drummer Neil Peart, head in the upper echelons of rock, feet planted firmly behind the counter of the parts department at his father's farm equipment dealership in St. Catharines, Ontario.

Once the "bit of a rube" (as Alex recalls) was hired, Neil got himself a set of chrome Slingerlands that he played with fury at his first gig, opening for Uriah Heep in Pittsburgh before a crowd of eleven thousand punters who could not have known rock history was in the baking.

But it was Rush's second record, *Fly by Night*, that cemented the legend of Peart, who set about drumming up a storm on "Anthem," "Beneath, Between & Behind," "By-Tor & the Snow Dog," and even the band's poppy FM rock staple, "Fly by Night," which didn't ask for the man's thespian flair yet received it just the same, much to the chagrin of rock cred gatekeepers all over the US press.

Serendipitously, both Alex and Geddy were similarly enamored with the fussy rock of the progressive aristocracy and were swept right along with Neil, forcing them to get better overnight as the three dove headlong into their Zeppelin- and Who-charged take on ornate structures favored by the likes of Genesis, Yes, and King Crimson. And double serendipitously, Alex and Geddy, for whom lyrics were a necessary evil at best, found in Neil a reader of actual books who was all too happy to take over the literary helm, perfectly pleased to mine the same fantastic themes as prog bands, with some ambitious philosophizing thrown in to boot.

Vaulting this already charged situation even further upon high was the full-on production handled by the pedigreed Terry Brown, from the land of their favorite bands (England), mere fixer and mixer of the band's debut but now knob-twiddling as fast as he could, capturing the action.

The result was a bright and brisk record, snow-blind (but not in the Black Sabbath manner), sequenced to eventful perfection, and fortunately propelled further than should have been possible even on paper, through the poignant strains of modest hit single "Fly by Night," on which Neil reminisces about how a hopeful trip toward fame and fortune in London, England, nearly destroyed his spirit before it could fly.

Geddy rocks a Fender Precision Bass prior to the period when he became synonymous with Rickenbacker. *Fly by Night* tour, April 1975. *Fin Costello/Redferns/ Getty Images*

POPOFF: Rush welcomed a new drummer and lyricist into their wee fold on *Fly by Night*. **What does Neil "The Professor" Peart bring to the party?**

WAGNER: Dexterity and intelligence. Not that they were unintelligent on the first album. But there was some caveman rock, some barroom boogie, and that kind of went out the door. Musically, you just have to listen to "Anthem," the first song, and it's obvious there's a new drummer in town. I'm sure Lifeson and Lee became better players, sitting down with Neil for the first few times. But he brings this kind of dexterity and attention to percussive detail that made Rush a lot more colorful. And lyrically, those guys were not great writers on the first album. Neil's bringing in Ayn Rand, obviously, with "Anthem," and fantasy topics, plus he's using allegory and infusing various kinds of general philosophy. It made them a different and better band, there's no doubt about it.

SCHNEBERGER: What I heard in that record were a lot of the things that are quintessentially Rush, but it was from an earlier raw period. There was still some of that

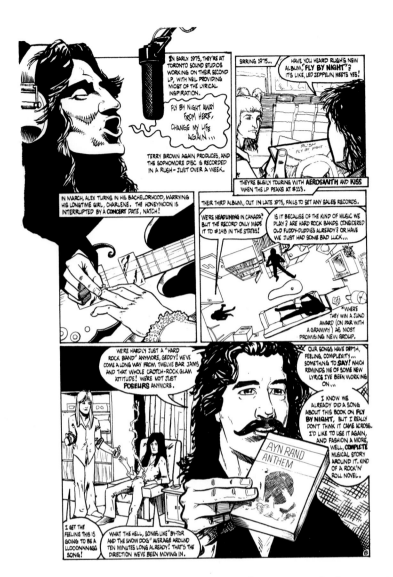

The addition of Neil in mid-1974 spurred the band to move beyond twelve-bar crotch rock, as detailed in this brilliant page from Rock 'N' Roll Comics. © *Rock 'N' Roll Comics/Revolutionary Comics. Courtesy Jay Allen Sanford*

bar rock/Zeppelin influence in there, although not quite as bluesy as it had been on the first record. And then, yes, you had Neil, who I think was playing balls-out. I mean, he was announcing his presence. As Jeff says, just the opening figure of "Anthem," with this crazy, furious snare drum intro, and building with every measure or section of that intro, more and more all the time, Neil flexing. You knew he replaced the previous drummer and he was showing as much as he could, announcing, "I'm here, look at what I'm bringing."

POPOFF: Since you both brought up "Anthem," let's address the record's sort of only controversy, this idea that Neil, through that lyric, was exposing himself as some sort of heartless libertarian, or worst, as the press called him, a fascist!

WAGNER: The book *Anthem* . . . I'm not a huge Ayn Rand follower, but I have read her stuff, and I think that there's something really important about "Anthem." Kind of staking your individuality and not making excuses for being an individual and not making excuses for how good you might be or how talented you might be. It's not boastful, but it's like, for me, them drawing a line in the sand. Like, "You know what? We're really good at it, and we're going to continue to be even better each time out." And I think you can see that coming to fruition on all the rest of the albums that came after this one. So I think that's a really important lyric. It's probably my favorite. There's a parallel to some of the optimism in "Making Memories," like where they're singing *Our future still looks brighter than our past.* I thought that was a pretty cool idea.

But, yeah, Neil got some blowback on that, but I think it's because people don't understand true selfishness. Selfishness is not meanness . . . Just because you're selfish, it's not that you feel superior or better than anybody else. I think it means indulging in the self, taking matters into your own hands, not letting anybody else steer you off the paths that are available to you. I don't think people understand the nature of selfishness. I think selfishness has a bad name. Because we've all seen people act selfishly, and it's really not all that attractive. But I think at the same time, one can act for the self, you know, to better themselves, right? And so I don't think that people who criticized Neil for that understood that, and I don't think they read the book *Anthem*.

SCHNEBERGER: I'm still undecided. The title is the title of the Ayn Rand novella. A lot of the lyrics are about, don't get brought down by the masses, hold your head above the crowd, look out for yourself. He is also announcing his presence. He is bringing to this band this very philosophical point of view, which is, I mean, it's one that I've come to disagree with greatly [laughs]. And to be honest, when I listen to, you know, *Live for yourself, there's no one else / More worth living for,"* I kinda think it's one of the most damaging lyrics in their catalog. And I think he gave rise to a legion of fans that are libertarian and conservative and felt like that justified them being greedy assholes [laughs]. And I would love to sit with Neil and ask him sometimes, like his opinions on those ideas and those lyrics. He probably doesn't really oppose them completely, but I don't think he'd be as favorable to those ideas now. And sure, it's an anthemic song and there are aspects of that that are empowering. But it's also like, you know, "They've always told you selfishness is wrong . . ." Well, it *is* kind of wrong, you know? It certainly is. And I don't like lyrics where the message is the idea that selfishness is right.

On a lighter note, there are a couple on this record that were written prior to Neil joining the band and taking over as a lyricist. I like "Best I Can"; it's a rocking number for sure, and there's great playing by Neil. But lyrically, it's laughable, because it's got this like slangy rock 'n' roller content. One lyric I always laugh at is *Rock and rollin's a scream / Making millions my dream.* It's almost like a gangsta rap lyric. Making millions, yeah, we're just gonna say that in a song, I guess. And then Geddy calls himself "an impatient cat." So at the same time, I think he's being very direct about who he is. You know, he doesn't like a long rest, he's an active guy, he wants to get at it. But lyrically, it's just such a different kind of attitude or vocabulary than what Neil brought to the band.

POPOFF: The entire range of sounds on *Fly by Night* is excellent, but particularly fine is Neil's drum sound. Chris, what was Neil using for a kit on this album?

SCHNEBERGER: Well, I know very much what Neil was playing, because I play it from time to time, which is the '74 chrome Slingerland kit, now affectionately referred to as "Chromey." My friend Dean Bobisud owns it, and I'm kind of the drum tech for that kit, so I'm quite familiar. He didn't have quite as many pieces as he did later, but he bought that kit with his first advance checks from the band after joining, and he had it with him when they hit the stage in Pittsburgh and played that for a number of tours. The first four albums or so, he played those.

With Neil forcing them to get better, the revamped trio dove headlong into structures favored by the likes of Genesis, King Crimson, and Yes.

Promo copy of "Anthem," the song inspired by Ayn Rand's novella of the same name.

Fly by Night tour, April 1975. *Fin Costello/Redferns/Getty Images*

Neil had Chromey right up to just two months before they left for Europe on the *All the World's a Stage* tour, which is really a continuation of the *2112* tour. So at some point, it just got bashed-up, banged-up, and he got a black chrome kit from Slingerland, and played that on the remainder of that tour, and recorded *Hemispheres* with it.

I think early on he didn't have the four concert toms. So in its complete form, Chromey would be two kick drums, a snare drum, four concert toms, three rack toms, and a floor tom—so eleven pieces, just for the drums. I couldn't remember how many cymbals, but it's probably about six, seven different cymbals. And then he added things like temple blocks, bell tree. Eventually for *A Farewell to Kings* he had the tubular bells, which were so great in "Xanadu." Probably some other things I'm forgetting—glockenspiel.

POPOFF: And I suppose just as important to Neil's drum sound is the work of Terry Brown, beginning his reign as producer. What does he bring to the band?

WAGNER: All you have to do is listen to the first album versus the second, and you hear the amount of depth he brought in to the sounds. That soundscaping that they do on "By-Tor," he probably helped direct those guys toward that, I would think. And so the great thing about Terry Brown in this album particularly is that he helps them develop, he lets them do their thing, but he's a guide as well.

Plus there's just a clarity to the instrumentation and equipment that they are using. There's a clarity and a punch to it, but it's never too overdone or overproduced. It's clear as a bell, never antiseptic, always very earthy and organic. He was a master of making something sound both studio-created and simultaneously kind of off-the-floor live. You kinda got the sense that they were playing live, but the stuff sounded sharper than that. He struck a cool balance to everything that made all of those songs sparkle. So *Fly by Night* does not sound like a band that just changed membership and brought in a new producer. It sounds like they'd all been working together forever.

SCHNEBERGER: You can definitely hear in "By-Tor & the Snow Dog" a lot of auditory, supplementary kind of sounds. Did Terry bring that to the band? Did the band come up with it? I really don't know. But I imagine that'd be a place where Terry is having an influence. But they were already, in the first album, exploring stereo space and sounds that would happen on just one side or pan back and forth between two ears, which is a little '70s conceit. But no question, at this point he is becoming the fourth member of the band.

POPOFF: The new Rush can be heard on "Anthem" and "By-Tor" for sure, but it's also there in spades on "Beneath, Between & Behind," no?

SCHNEBERGER: Yeah, for sure. I just love that opening guitar figure, that kind of descending three-note or three-chord figure. That song is very bright, and that's another thing about *Fly by Night* . . . it's overall a bright record. It's musically fairly major and upbeat. And even though "Beneath, Between & Behind" has much darker and critical lyrical content, the music is bright and kind of romping. I don't know what the time signature is—it might be like a 12/16—but it's a kind of loping, galloping rhythm that Iron Maiden would use extensively later on with this kind of very fast triplet feel.

And, you know, I've got to be honest, I was too young to grasp what the lyrics were about when I first heard this record. It wasn't until years later I went back and went, "Oh, he's really ripping on the United States and the crumbling of the ideals that the country originally stood for. And he's writing in 1975, the time of the Vietnam War." Neil had a great affinity for the United States, but he could see the problems happening with it. And so its darker lyrical content contrasted with a brighter, rocking musical thing— a great combination.

WAGNER: I think if that song was played by three other musicians, it just wouldn't sound as cool as it does—there's just so much playfulness and fun. You can hear the chemistry really starting to develop in that song. I don't think it's an immediate favorite of anybody—nobody really talks about that song—but I think it's a highlight on the album for sure.

POPOFF: And *bam*! Right after that song, the prog-fest really kicks into gear with "By-Tor & the Snow Dog," not heavier than the song before it, but longer and more fanciful.

WAGNER: "By-Tor"—that's just the new Rush. Because otherwise you're getting "Best I Can," which really could've come from the first album, with its like boogie-down foundation. "Making Memories" could've fit on the first album. But on "By-Tor" they were showing their Yes influence quite directly, because if you listen to Yes's "The Gates of Delirium" from '74, that had basically a battle between instruments. And I guess Rush didn't really care if people heard them taking that influence, because they did the same thing shortly after. They always said they were pretty heavily influenced by that band, but they took it into their own, they made it heavier, darker, made it their own. And it's where they went—they weren't just dabbling on this album, which is proven by the next half dozen albums.

So I think for me it's "By-Tor," which kicks off the Rush that I like the most: that run from *Fly by Night* all the way up into the early '80s. But how can a Rush fan not love "By-Tor?" [laughs] It's got everything you like about Rush. But this is an album that demonstrates a lot of diversity too, which is also what they were known for. They were never a one-mood sort of band. Elsewhere you've got "Fly by Night," kind of this cool FM radio rocker; "Making Memories," which sounds like Southern rock or something; and then you've got "Rivendell," which kind of paves the way for some of the more fantasy-oriented Hobbit rock stuff that they were doing.

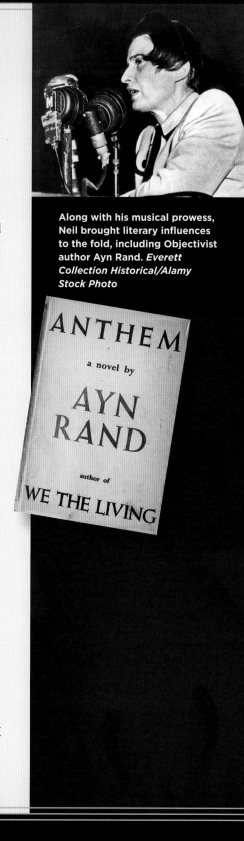

Along with his musical prowess, Neil brought literary influences to the fold, including Objectivist author Ayn Rand. *Everett Collection Historical/Alamy Stock Photo*

全米がその超ヘヴィーなサウンドに驚嘆、そしてダウン。

カナディアン・ロック・シーンが生んだ本格的ヘヴィー・メタル・バンド、ラッシュの閃光第2弾。

夜間飛行/ラッシュ

心の賛美歌／ベスト・アイ・キャン／メイキング・メモリーズ 他全8曲

●RJ-7012 ¥2,500 7月25日発売

Print advertisement for *Fly by Night*, Japan's *Ongaku Senka* magazine, August 1975.

SCHNEBERGER: My understanding of "By-Tor" is that it's about Herns, Howard Ungerleider, the band's tour manager and lighting guy, encountering their manager Ray Danniels' dogs. And one was really snappy, and he called him the biter, which became By-tor, and there was another one that I guess was maybe white and they called it the Snow Dog. And Neil thought it was kind of funny and made it into characters, tossed them into this kind of Tolkien-ish, slightly Greek mythology world of Hades and whatever.

But what was great in that song was, first of all, here's the first time that they're really going for an epic, and with multiple chapters. And as a twelve- or thirteen-year-old listener, looking on to the song list on the back of the album and seeing chapters, I was like, oh, this is developed and intelligent. This is like a symphony, like a Wagnerian opera with these different movements. It had these titles that were really intriguing and had a mythology about it.

And "The Battle," if you look on the interior lyric sheet, it even had subsections. Like the battle movement had four different parts. And then there were these other little epic-like mysteries, like The Sign of Eth. Well, what is The Sign of Eth? It seems that I should know what that is. And I thought that was really intelligent to lay down these things and make us think about how they apply to a much greater narrative or saga.

I very clearly remember listening to that song on cassette, on a Walkman, on a road trip with my parents, and thinking, well, the song is really good . . . and it's still going on! I can't believe how long this song is going, but it's still really good [laughs].

POPOFF: The album certainly has a heavy side and a light side, especially with "Rivendell" and "Making Memories" sequenced to the middle of side two.

SCHNEBERGER: I don't know if I want to rip on my favorite band, but "Rivendell" is one of my least favorite Rush songs. And I think the band themselves don't feel too fondly about it now, in retrospect. "Rivendell" is like they're trying to evoke some aspects of Zeppelin, but in kind of a wrong way. It's this kind of quiet, maudlin Tolkien-ish ballad without percussion. I don't know if it's worth it.

And "Making Memories" doesn't seem to be a favorite among Rush fans, but I've always enjoyed it. It's got the very strummy intro and it's almost like a country song. It's got this great syncopation from Neil. It's ironic to me that Neil is writing the song kind of nostalgically and complimentary about life on the road, when we know that even from those early days, he wasn't crazy about being on the road and touring. And later on in the career that became one of the hardest things for him to keep doing. But, yeah, to hear them saying maybe road life is not so bad [laughs], it's kind of ironic. Because he never was crazy about it. And then there's this fantastic solo from Alex, his one and only slide solo, where you can hear some of his Jimmy Page influence.

In 1976 the band would trot out a live version of their modest 1975 hit "Fly by Night" backed with 1974's butt-rockin' "In the Mood," also live.

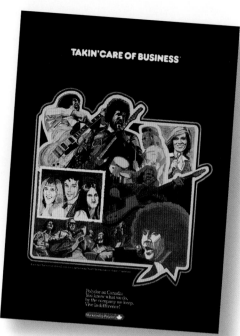

A Polydor print ad trumpeted the label's top Canadian acts, including Rush and Bachman-Turner Overdrive.

POPOFF: I suppose it makes sense to end with "In the End," which, Jeff, you say makes perfect sense as album-closer beyond simply the title.

WAGNER: Great song, yeah, that's what makes a great album, leaving on a higher note. If they went out with "Making Memories" or the title track, it might not have been so strong, but this is like a big, slow-burning ending—it just cycles. I always picture like some concert hall clearing out slowly, the lights going up slowly. It's a pretty cinematic song for being as simple as it is. Neil isn't credited on that one, and you can hear this is part of their past. It doesn't sound like a track from the self-titled, but it does sound like it could've come from that era.

SCHNEBERGER: It's got this kind of similar start to "Fly by Night," melodically, on the twelve-string, if I'm correct. It's got this really bright feel on this long acoustic intro, with Geddy singing the first verse, and then they kick into the heavier guitars and the drums. I'm not really sure what the message of the song is. It's sort of like, you're better than this other person, you feel things more intensely, you don't feel things more intensely. I like singing it, but I'm really not all that clear on the message. Geddy has a fantastic vocal performance in it. If you listen to the last verse, there's this combination of nearly kind of a scream but with a full-throated melody, which shows what a great vocalist he is. It's similar to what Chris Cornell did years later with Soundgarden, that kind of full-throated belting out. To me, Cornell wasn't quite as high-pitched, but he could do a similar growl in the middle of hitting a good high note.

WAGNER: "In the End" is great. It kind of eases you down. I read a modern-era review once that called it a sort of proto-doom metal track. It's not quite that slow or evil-sounding, but it does have that sort of languishing, down-wound vibe. It's a hard song to really put your finger on, but it's a perfect ending, hence the title, "In the End."

POPOFF: And then of course, next time out Rush delivered _Caress of Steel_, which, now that some time has passed, is considered the evil twin of the friendlier _Fly by Night_. Would you agree with that perspective?

WAGNER: Sure, yeah. And yet personally, I don't think they bit off more than they could chew on _Caress of Steel_. It's one of my favorite Rush albums. But comparatively, _Fly by Night_ is very song-based. Even "By-Tor" is only nine minutes. So I think it was a bit shocking for people coming off of this album to get like a twenty-minute song, and I think "The Necromancer" is twelve minutes. And it's not their best song in "I Think I'm Going Bald." It was an uneven, darker, muddier album, just not as accessible or approachable. _Fly by Night_ is so easy to get into. You have such variety on the album, and you don't have to think too hard about it, whereas _Caress_ is pretty dominating, a sledgehammer of an album, really. It's not attractive—it's an ugly thing. As for Geddy there, you get that screech, a forbidding kind of approach from him, while on _Fly by Night_ he sounds totally ready for FM radio rock. And I don't mean that in a dumbed-down way. It's very approachable and fun, and you don't get that on _Caress of Steel_. There you get the wizard—you get the angry wizard.

CHAPTER 3

Caress of Steel

**with Michel Langevin
and Jim Matheos**

Geddy Lee: lead vocals, bass
Alex Lifeson: guitars
Neil Peart: drums, percussion
Released September 24, 1975
Recorded at Toronto Sound Studios, Toronto
Produced by Rush and Terry Brown

t only sticks out because Rush are viewed as harmless, straight-laced Canadians, but Geddy's comment that the guys were "smoking a lot of pot" when they came up with *Caress of Steel* is indeed amusingly deprecating and so telling.

Put down as half-baked, Rush's third album is really also the world's first progressive metal album. And even if you don't buy that, *Fly by Night* is probably a better second candidate than fancy-pants answers like *In the Court of the Crimson King.*

Perhaps the reason *Caress of Steel* gets overlooked is that the band themselves are none too chuffed with it, as well as the fact that it's quite foreboding, from the ancient intrigue of the cover art on down through Terry Brown's constrictive production. On top of the record scaring people, its fate as obscure and marginal is sealed for many by that maniac at the mic, shrieking away everywhere—on the resident pop song, on the heavy metal barnstormer, on the loping boogie rocker recalling the Rutsey-era band, and on the two massive prog-metal epics, one of which is so befuddling only its pieces are named on the back cover.

But Rush would have the last laugh. Almost killed by *Caress of Steel*'s lack of fans at the time, both in the head shops selling records and the venues selling tickets to heads, the band would bounce back with *2112*, tacitly putting forth the idea that a record "like" *Caress of Steel* is indeed what they intended both this time and last time.

Neil digs in somewhere in Toronto, circa 1976. © 1976, Bruce Cole/PlumCom Inc.

And then, of course, the penultimate victory is that many a Rush fan loves the album for its dark prog-rock audacity. Fortunately for the music industry, many of those fans went on to form thought-provoking bands themselves, vaulted into action through the alchemical reactions conducted upon their impressionable minds through the wizardly deeds of The Necromancer.

POPOFF: Okay, so set up for us what kind of record the "new" Rush is making the second time out.

MATHEOS: I guess you have to look at the record previous and the one that comes after it. It's really the bridge record between those two records, I think. They started to dabble a little with the prog side on *Fly by Night*, and I think *2112* is pretty much all the way prog. So this is the missing link for me. It's got some of the more straightforward songs—"Bastille Day," "Lakeside Park," which is one of my favorites—and then their first real attempt at lengthy prog pieces with "The Necromancer," which is probably my all-time favorite Rush song, and then "Lamneth," of course. So you can see them starting. It's obviously a bit . . . I don't want to say immature. It's early in their career, but they're just dabbling with it. I'm sure they don't really know where they're going with it—and I like that. I like the rawness of the whole thing.

LANGEVIN: Compared to *Fly by Night*, I think it's a little more atmospheric, maybe toned down, more acoustic. It's their Led Zeppelin *III*. It starts with a classic Rush rock song, "Bastille Day," about the French Revolution. And then there's a little bit of silliness in "I Think I'm Going Bald," which Geddy says is pointed at Alex. And then it turns into this very dark, atmospheric album. I mean, "Lakeside Park" is sort of gentle, but then it's "The Necromancer" and then "The Fountain of Lamneth" on the whole of side two, which was like a long journey, a bit like Yes or Genesis would do. It's a lot more progressive rock, although to me they were always prog rock. But this one's a bit like the dark side of Tolkien. The vibe is epic and like Dungeons and Dragons. It's a different album and I really, really like it.

"Lakeside Park" was one of the poppier, quieter numbers where Neil really took over.

RUSH'S NEW ALBUM,
"CARESS OF STEEL"

Mercury SRM-1-1046
8-Track MC8-1-1046
Musicassette MCR4-1-1046

The more you hear it...

the more you hear in it.

Rush takes you on an incredible 43 minute sentient, mental journey. And each time you retrace your tracks, new images materialize. From the shadowy depths of the Necromancer to the Fountain of Lamneth's sunlit heights, "Caress of Steel," for a trip of ceaseless discovery.

Mercury began to play up
the band's increasingly
cerebral qualities.

POPOFF: Is Rush making history here? Is *Caress of Steel* the first progressive metal album of all time?

MATHEOS: Well, you're right, it is groundbreaking. I had heard things that were more prog, if you want to think strictly in terms of prog, when you're talking about Genesis, Emerson, Lake & Palmer, Yes, that kind of thing. But to kind of meld it with . . . I wouldn't say metal, because it wasn't really called metal at the time—hard rock? I can't think of anybody else who was doing that at the time, and so I think that's what really drew me in. I was a fan of heavy stuff— Sabbath, UFO, Deep Purple—and I was a fan of a lot of the prog stuff like I just mentioned. But I can't think of anybody at the time who was really putting the two together.

So I guess, yes, they were inventing prog metal. And I would say, again, this one more than *Fly by Night*. On *Fly by Night* they dabbled in it with "By-Tor" and perhaps parts of "Anthem," but this one was more blatant. Nobody had done a sidelong song in this kind of vein, as more of a rock thing. There are many groundbreaking moments on this record.

LANGEVIN: Even though Rush were like precursors of metal, I always put them in the Yes camp. To me, they were just a heavy prog-rock band, and so they were, in my head, up there with Genesis and Pink Floyd and all the bands that I loved.

POPOFF: Each of you has had Terry Brown produce records for your bands. What does he do special on *Caress of Steel* and, indeed, what did Terry do that made you want to tap his powers?

MATHEOS: Not being there at the time, I don't know what he brought to the table for Rush. I know what he brought to the table for us [Fates Warning], but that was twenty years later or more. So it's hard to say. I do love the sound of *Caress of Steel*, particularly the guitar sound. "The Necromancer"'s backward guitar parts just totally captivated me when I was kid listening to that. I didn't know what the hell they were doing. That was probably Terry's idea. I know that he brought that up when he was doing our record, so I can't claim to know exactly who came up with it, but I know that Terry likes to do that.

But I'd say it was the production especially on the mid-period records, *Permanent Waves* and *Moving Pictures*—the drum sound was something that made us really want to work with Terry, and a lot of guitar sounds on *Caress*. It was really intimidating for me, working with him for the first few weeks. I remember just sitting there recording at the console thinking, my God, this is the guy who recorded "The Necromancer," which is one of my favorite songs of all time.

LANGEVIN: I've always loved Terry Brown; I always loved his production. In the case of *Caress of Steel*, it was very different than the other ones in terms of his production. Definitely more of a softer sound, a bit obscure, but very atmospheric. I was hoping he would go for something like that for our [Voivod's] *Angel Rat* record and he did, so I was very happy. But the other Rush albums had a very crisp sound that you could hear with, let's say, the Ted Templeman productions or Boston, something very hi-fi. Rush always sounded amazing.

Piggy [late Voivod guitarist Denis D'Amour] introduced me to *Caress of Steel*, and at first I was taken aback, because I thought it was not heavy like *Hemispheres*. But I understood after a few listens that this was more of a dark approach. And as I said, we sort of wanted that to happen to *Angel Rat*. And Terry Brown did a good job of building that album into an atmospheric album instead of a thrash metal album.

POPOFF: Speaking of thrash metal, *Caress of Steel* opens with one of the fastest and heaviest songs of Rush's career, "Bastille Day."

LANGEVIN: A great rock song, with cool riffs. Geddy's voice is really an acquired taste. I remember that he drove some people crazy. But other people would find it interesting, like Robert Plant or other high-pitched voices like Ian Gillan. But I don't remember people saying bad stuff about Rush, really, in high school, even among my punk rock friends.

MATHEOS: I'm trying to transport myself back to 1975. I don't think I ever viewed it as being an odd voice, or being different. And some of his strongest vocal performances are on this record. Looking at it now, I can see how people would find it perhaps unpleasant. But to me, I thought it was just beautiful, the way he interpreted the lyrics, came up with the melody lines. A song like "Lakeside Park" is just beautiful to me. It doesn't sound odd to me at all.

But yeah, "Bastille Day" is definitely more towards metal—it's not very progressive at all. It stays to the script of a hard rock song from the time. Great opening riff; it's one of

Alex with his Marshall heads (background), by then de rigueur gear for any discerning rock guitarist. © 1975, Bruce Cole/ PlumCom Inc.

Geddy performing in Toronto, 1975. © 1975, Bruce Cole/ PlumCom Inc.

those where as the first thing they put on the record, it grabs your ear. It's one of the first songs that I played with my first band back in the day, so it has special meaning for me. And it's still something we toy around with at sound checks now and then, which goes to show you that all the rest of the guys think of that song as being one of the early seminal points for Rush. I don't know if it was particularly inventive, but it was a great song. It's just a great riff, one of those riffs that you can't really explain scientifically why it grabs you. It just feels really good, and the open choruses open it up and give it that majestic feel.

POPOFF: But then all the drama peels away for "I Think I'm Going Bald."

LANGEVIN: Definitely more of a straightforward riff to that one. I was a bit surprised about that song because I thought it was a bit silly compared to all the rest [laughs].

MATHEOS: To me, that doesn't fit. I would say that's the one oddball. To me it fits maybe more on the first Rush record, at least musically and not so much lyrically. I think the lyric's a bit tongue-in-cheek and that's okay. But musically, it's more in that kind of Led Zeppelin, rock 'n' roll type thing. I like it more now. I can listen to the whole record and enjoy it, but certainly to me, it stands out as not as strong as the rest of the record.

POPOFF: And I suppose "Lakeside Park" is the record's most enduring song on rock radio. Is this one of those poppier, quieter numbers where Neil really takes over to the point of perhaps overplaying?

MATHEOS: You know, it could be a little bit of all that. I think he does overplay, but he overplays in the sense of what you were hearing at the time from most drummers. But it's always tasty and doesn't get in the way. To me, it's hard to listen to with nonmusician ears, but it's very fitting, it makes you listen to the drums a lot more than you would on a normal song, but it never gets in the way, to me. It never gets in the way of the vocals or the lyrics. It's always subtle, him showing off his technique, within the context of the song and not taking over. I love the lyrics on that song. It's probably one of the first ones . . . where he started getting more introspective and away from the fantasy or sci-fi-type lyrics. It's really just about him, and I love that about the song.

LANGEVIN: He's not overplaying. Everything is very catchy and encapsulated, and it's not improvised. You can tell he rehearsed it. Dave Grohl is a bit like that, where he will play a roll that you think is a traditional roll, but if you notice, it's an innovation

Label for Mercury's Japanese pressing of *Caress of Steel.*

on a classic roll. And Neil was really good with that—totally innovative. If you wanna be a nerd and study drumming, you realize that there was no one like him before him. If he built on somebody's shoulders, I'm not aware of it.

POPOFF: And then we're into the dark lord of the record, "The Necromancer."
MATHEOS: Yes, "The Necromancer" is just one of those songs that hit me, I guess, at the right time as a kid growing up, and opening all kinds of doors, with the production of the song, the lyrics, and Geddy's amazing vocals. As I've said, a lot of people are turned off by his vocals, but I think his vocals on that song are just absolutely stunning all the way through.

The heavy section in the middle is probably one of the heaviest things they've ever done. Just the whole piece put together—you know, it brings you through those three movements, which is not something that I've heard at all, maybe, at least not up to that point. So it's very creative, and all the guys on their instruments are showing off, but restrained at the same time. A lot of different things came together, and then I also saw them on the tour, which again, was a perfect time for a twelve- or thirteen-year-old kid to just be blown away by them.

POPOFF: Tell me a bit about that show. Where was it?
MATHEOS: It was in Seattle at the Paramount Theatre. I was lucky enough to live in Seattle at that time, and they played there often. I got to see them on *Fly by Night*, *Caress of Steel*, and on *2112.* And the first one was opening for Kiss, if I remember right, and the two following shows were headlining, if I remember correctly, Styx and Rush, and Tommy Bolin and Rush on *2112.* Small venues at the time, it was a theatre—two thousand, three thousand people and old festival seating, so me and my friends would get there at nine o'clock in the morning and wait all day so we could get front row. And I thought, unless it's just selective memory, that on that *Caress of Steel* show, they did "The Necromancer."

So add all those things in there, a young guy just learning guitar, and you find these musicians who were relatively unknown. That was part of the charm of it, too, of discovering something that not too many people know of and seeing these guys challenging their instruments, showing me that there are all kinds of new things you can do on your instrument and still be very melodic at the same time.

LANGEVIN: I just remember the darkness of "The Necromancer," and it was epic and it had a Tolkien vibe. And I was really into *The Hobbit* and *Lord of the Rings* at that time, and it was also informing my concept of Voivod. Because I wanted to do comics for the magazine called *Heavy Metal*, I had created a world based on Tolkien, so I really connected to it.

And that song connected with the album cover. It was intriguing and solemn. I don't know who was represented. It looks like an alchemist to me, and that was the first time they used graphic artist Hugh Syme. I really like that cover. It had a biblical vibe; sometimes Rush could have an Armageddon feel to their imagery and music, a bit like

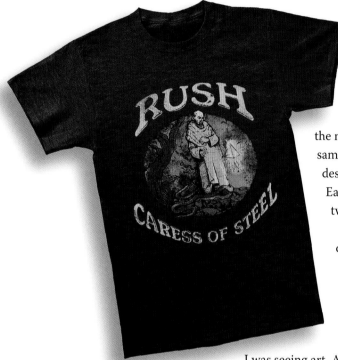

"Cygnus X-1: Book II" on *Hemispheres*. And so I was always attracted to that visually, and conceptually. They were always positive messages, but sometimes environmental messages, through sci-fi tales. So they had a strong impact on me and my Voivod world.

I mean, this was also a big influence on Voivod, the way the messages are put across, sort of folktales, in a way. Magma did the same to me, where they had their own world, discussing the destruction of a planet somewhere that is very reminiscent of the Earth. I really loved this concept, and so I really took from these two bands, Magma and Rush.

And it's also because both drummers are the writers of the concepts, and that was a huge influence. Both Neil and Christian Vander showed me that it could be done, for sure. Vander was the main driving force in Magma, and the only constant member, I think. So, and he had created a concept that was concerned with technology going awry and very apocalyptic. Being raised in the fear of nuclear war and all that, it really changed the way I was seeing art. And I saw the same parallels with Neil, as I said, in the idea that a drummer could be the conceptual guy in the band.

POPOFF: Where does Alex fit in all this? What are his particular charms on this record?

LANGEVIN: I remember him for his chords. I mean, he was very unique. He had his signature and he influenced so many people in the '80s and across different scenes. I mean, Robert Fripp and Alex Lifeson really changed things in terms of inventive chords.

According to Piggy anyway. Piggy loved Alex Lifeson. Piggy had five favorite guitar players: Jimmy Page, Jimi Hendrix, Alex Lifeson, Robert Fripp, and David Gilmour, and Piggy was really influenced by Alex's chords. Although I thought the solos on *Caress of Steel* were more floaty and progressive and David Gilmour–oriented.

MATHEOS: *Caress of Steel* and *Grace Under Pressure* are two of my favorite Rush records for guitar solos. As I say, the backward soloing in "The Necromancer" blew me away, hearing that for the first time. But also his use of chording on that song, on the first part and the last part . . . there's some incredible open flowing chords. Alex introduced me to a whole new palette of sounds when I was just learning how to play guitar.

POPOFF: What do you hear in terms of influence? Is he a Jimmy Page guy?

MATHEOS: I don't really hear a lot of Jimmy Page. I know the band in those early days did have a lot of Zeppelin influence. I know people have heard that in some of their songs. I don't hear that in his playing. I think his playing, especially from *Caress* on, is really hard to pin down. He's mentioned [Genesis's] Steve Hackett, and I do hear that somewhat. I don't know if he's a fan of Ritchie Blackmore; I hear that in the way he does a lot of pull-off-type runs. But it's really hard for me to pinpoint. He's an original guitarist, which is another thing that really drew me to him.

POPOFF: And then we arrive at the daunting and dark second side of the record, which is not really so intimidating when you realize that it's quite purposefully banded into discernable songs.

LANGEVIN: I love "The Fountain of Lamneth" because it's a long journey by somebody through some very obscure land. It reminded me of the darker side of some Genesis albums and Yes's *Tales from Topographic Oceans*. I always liked albums that made me travel to a darker place because that kind of music will make me draw something with a dark mood. I always draw when listening to music. It was hard for me to pay attention to lyrics, actually, because being French-Canadian, they were not in my main language. So I would often draw while listening to these albums instead of watching the lyrics on the sheet. And so playing this again made me flashback on the drawing.

POPOFF: As a drummer, you must have appreciated "Didacts and Narpets."

LANGEVIN: Yeah, I love it, because it sounds like an argument. And there is something very dualistic about Rush. There always seems to be some order versus chaos, light versus darkness, good versus evil, and this sounded like a discussion, almost like avant-garde music, Max Roach, you know? Avant-garde jazz.

MATHEOS: "The Fountain of Lamneth" has got some really strong elements in it. It's hit-and-miss for me, to be honest. The high moments are really high for me on the whole record, and there's a few of the lower moments—like we talked about, "Going Bald," and probably the drum solo [on] "Didacts and Narpets" [seems] a little out of place. But "In the Valley," "Bacchus Plateau," and especially "No One at the Bridge"—that's one of my favorite Rush songs and absolutely one of my favorite Alex solos. So these elements more than make up for any kind of failed experiments on the record.

"No One at the Bridge" . . . I can only describe it in terms of how it affected me as a kid, spending hours learning that song and that solo, discovering all kinds of new chords. I guess I look at it more through a guitar player's lens, but those chords, the production, the guitar sound on that solo, and the solo itself are just remarkable for me. Even to this day, listening to it again, it's just a beautiful solo, well-constructed, not overplayed, not shreddy whatsoever.

POPOFF: But in the end, all of this high-minded conceptualizing almost killed the band.

MATHEOS: Yeah. I've seen the videos and heard them talk about it. It was called the "Down the Tubes" tour or something, wasn't it? I guess I could see it from a record company's point of view. If you handed this into the record company, they're going to say, "Well, what are we going to do with this?!" Outside of, maybe, "Bastille Day." So, yeah, I could totally understand it from the record company's point of view [laughs].

CHAPTER 4

2112

with Ralph Chapman, Paul Gilbert, and Kirk Hammett

Geddy Lee: lead vocals, bass
Alex Lifeson: guitars
Neil Peart: drums, percussion
Hugh Syme: synthesizer on "2112," mellotron on "Tears"
Released April 1, 1976
Recorded at Toronto Sound Studios, Toronto
Produced by Rush and Terry Brown

f you look at the trajectory, it's easy to understand the panic. Over at the Mercury offices in Chicago, bearded wonder hippie Cliff Burnstein takes a flyer on this Canadian band, who promptly fire one-third of the band after the balls-to-the-wall buffalo-burger boogie rock record he liked so much is still arriving in shops. Then they make an album that is half fancy-pants progressive metal before such a thing ever existed, plus a few songs like those on the first album, and (fortunately) one minor hit single with the title track. Then comes the sullen King Crimson–like record *Caress of Steel*, and even if sales of each consecutive record didn't taper, affection and excitement did exactly that.

When it came time, hats in hand, fingers crossed behind the brims, for Rush to deliver their next record, the directive was that it better have some radio songs on it. Instead, Rush constructed an aural labyrinth as dark and progressive as the last, and, miracles of miracles, there was such an uptick in quality that rock fans still on the sidelines could not hold out any longer—Geddy's hair-whitening shriek be damned.

Indeed, *2112* is testimony to what rock fans in the mid-'70s were willing to accept, willing to digest, and willing to make their

(opposite) Shreddin' and thumpin', *All the World's a Stage* **tour, May 1977.**
Fin Costello/Redferns/Getty Images

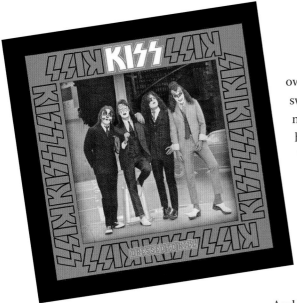

own. The continuing health of prog, and the understanding of it by a large swath of music buyers, was a conditioning factor, but surely what also must've helped Rush was the mini hard-rock earthquake of 1976, one that heavily featured American bands, with the British on the wane. Ergo, Kiss, Ted Nugent, Aerosmith, Blue Öyster Cult, Foghat, and Heart opened the door for a Canadian band, Rush, because they were just so darned polite. Supporting the US wave were hard rock–friendly magazines like *Circus*, *Hit Parader*, and *Creem*. The time was right for Alex to stack up his biggest, most tooth-rattling power chords, with Geddy howling away Neil's futuristic side-one sci-fi tale. On side two, to reign in the last stoner that might not be paying attention, an exotic song about drug tourism, which I don't think is a thing even now, let alone in 1976.

And so *2112* would prove the naysayers wrong. The band had indeed reversed its downward trajectory, but they wouldn't ring up RIAA gold status until the release of the album's follow-up, *A Farewell to Kings* (both being certified two months after that record's September 1977 release). In the interim, aiding and abetting the band's arrival from the lightless underground of trolls that was *Caress of Steel* was the issuance of a robust double live album in September 1976 called *All the World's a Stage*. With this stratagem, Rush could claim entry to '70s rock adulthood, driven home with a triple-gatefold one flap greater than that of Kiss *Alive!*

(above and opposite)
The American hard-rock earthquake of 1976 opened doors for the polite Canadians in Rush.

POPOFF: So what were your impressions when you heard *2112* for the first time?

HAMMETT: Well, it's actually the first Rush album I ever heard. I had gone over to my friend's house, who had a pretty extensive record collection. It was much more sophisticated than mine—I was only like thirteen years old at the time—and he put on

All the World's a Stage tour, 1977. Fin Costello/Redferns/ Getty Images

2112, and he said, "This is my favorite band. They're way better than UFO." And I said no way. And I heard it and was blown away. And my friend, who played guitar at the time, was playing along with it. And so I grabbed a guitar and watched him and started following him. And, you know, the amazing thing about the song, the whole suite, "2112," by the time I heard it for like the third or fourth time, I could play almost half of it [laughs]. Because my friend knew the whole thing, and he played the whole thing on guitar, and I was just a sponge back then. I just grabbed the guitar and started following him, and before you know it, I knew how to play "Temples of Syrinx" and all the different intros and outros and whatnot.

Neil and his incredible expanding kit, *All the World's a Stage* tour, 1977. *Fin Costello/Redferns/ Getty Images*

And I learned a lot about just how you can take a basic theme, a basic riff or a chord progression, and stretch it out over various beats and variations on the riff and on the notes, and that's what "2112" is. There's a chord—a theme—that runs all the way through it. It's in the key of B, as in boy, and I learned how to do that, pretty much exclusively from playing along to "2112." So that was pretty huge thing. I saw how all those riffs were interconnected thematically. I saw how they would bring in other elements to bridge them together. It was pretty amazing.

Then you had the musicianship itself. Neil's drums on the piece "2112" are just phenomenal. And then to turn the album over and hear *We're on the train to Bangkok*, with all the little [sings the "Oriental riff"], it was cool and a totally different vibe to what side one was all about.

GILBERT: When I first heard *2112*, that was one of the first times I'd heard these long album-side songs. And as a listener, you would almost congratulate yourself for making it through. Because I think most people start off with liking three-minute, or two-and-a-half-minute, pop songs on the radio. And if you could listen to a song and have the mental endurance to make it through a whole album side, it says something for the ability of the listener and also the ability of the band to write something interesting enough to hold somebody's attention for that long.

Also, obviously, the drumming was amazing. And I must admit, I used to audition drummers when I was a kid by just saying, can you do those fills? [sings the "Presentation" fill]. And if you could do that fill, you were in the band. That was the litmus test of whether somebody could play.

But that aside, Neil's lyrics were really captivating as well. You know, for a long time, that sort of sparked my interest in Ayn Rand . . . Ayn Rand's objectivism. So that was an inspirational record. And also, when I listen to it in retrospect, I can hear the influence they had from The Who. It's interesting, because at the time, I never would've put Keith Moon and Neil Peart in the same category. I mean, Keith was really kind of a loose cannon and very unbridled and very untethered, where Neil was very mature and was thought-out and almost like an intellectual drummer. But when I heard it in retrospect, and I've heard Neil talk about Keith Moon, I hear

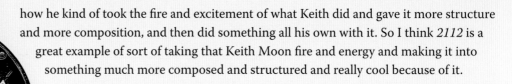

how he kind of took the fire and excitement of what Keith did and gave it more structure and more composition, and then did something all his own with it. So I think *2112* is a great example of sort of taking that Keith Moon fire and energy and making it into something much more composed and structured and really cool because of it.

POPOFF: You bring up Ayn Rand. Of course Neil found himself having to defend his views in the press. So it's just not a sci-fi tale with guitars, is it?

CHAPMAN: No, definitely not, and it begins with Neil's dedication, which said, "With acknowledgment to the genius of Ayn Rand" . . . I think there's been a dash of revisionism, because at the time, the band was criticized for honoring someone like Ayn Rand, because rock music wasn't usually the place to embrace libertarian ideas or the defense of capitalism or the virtue of selfishness or any of those philosophies that Neil seemed to be a student of.

If anything, what I think Neil was responding to in Ayn Rand's work is idealism—the youthful idealism of being able to overthrow the powers that be, to assert yourself as an individual with new ideas. And freedom, also. It's about the freedom to do what you want. A big tenet of Rand's philosophy is this idea of taking care of yourself first. And I think he responded to those ideas, and I think that was a big part of why he wanted to do what Terry Brown said, this sci-fi story. It appealed to him as an intellectual and as someone who believed in freedom, and he went on to write about it.

I mean, even "Something for Nothing" on side two has those themes: freedom and free will. So that became a theme in Neil's work. The problem was, at the time, a writer for the *NME* [Barry Miles] alluded to Rush as "crypto-fascist." So they took a lot of hits. So years later, when we were doing the Rush doc, *Beyond the Lighted Stage*, [director] Scot McFadyen asked Neil about the criticism that *2112* came under at the time, and he just completely blocked the question. Next thing you know, there's this new narrative that is being proposed in the film that this was a record about anger and if we are going to go down, we're going to go down in flames, we're gonna do it our way, we're going to assert ourselves. And that other side of the story, about Neil's interest in those types of philosophies and ideas, did not get a mention. So it was reframed.

But it doesn't mean that there isn't a lot of truth in that, and everyone is allowed hindsight forty years later. But I thought, okay, they don't want to talk about that. So it was reframed as Mercury was pressuring us and the management was pressuring us. Which I thought was laughable, because, there's no way that manager Ray Danniels was pressuring Geddy Lee [laughs]. It just wasn't happening. He was always a subordinate, as far as I could tell, to the band. But I really do think it's about Neil in the thrall of Ayn Rand and wanting to talk about self-determinism and going your own way and fighting back against the man. The man just happened to be—when we reframe it in the twenty-first century—the record company. But I think back then, it was a broader. We were living in the Cold War and under a very different set of political circumstances.

GILBERT: Well, you'd have to ask Neil about the specifics, but the story promotes individualism and the power of the individual. And to me that's the nice thing about that—everybody's an individual. I think some people think individualism is something that pushes people away. But I sometimes think of the phrase, "Individuals unite!" [laughs] We're all individuals; that's something that everybody has in common. So that's one way to look at it. The characters in Ayn Rand's fiction, they're all unstoppable in their pursuit of goals.

And in my own pursuit of being a musician, that was very inspiring. Just the unwillingness to give up, the unwillingness to compromise, the unwillingness to do anything but be true to your art. And I think when Rush did *2112*, that was very much on their minds, because the record company was putting pressure on them to do something more pop or something that would be more successful. And they made the choice, no, we're going to do it the way we want, we'll deal with the consequences, and they were fortunate enough to have their audience really respond positively to that. And they're a force to this day because of it.

The Twilight Zone host Rod Serling. Neil clearly leaned on childhood memories of the show, which dealt with serious topics through allegory.

POPOFF: On a lighter note, the band got some stick as well for that picture on the back, where they're wearing these robes. I guess the underlying criticism, also with the pentagram and the naked man, is the pomposity of prog.

HAMMETT: Well, for me, and I say this with all due respect and all due apologies, but the packaging of the album reminds me of Black Sabbath's *Paranoid* [laughs]. It's a really grand concept, but maybe they're not quite pulling it off, in a cheesy, low-budget '70s kind of way—which is highly forgivable. I never understood why the naked guy was there. You know, I got the pentagram, because I love pentagrams. I loved them back then and I love them now. After seeing that picture on the back cover and all those crazy clothes, I thought, well, those guys look like they raided their moms' closets too, like I was doing [laughs]. But I did like the look that Neil Peart had back then with the long hair and the semi-handlebar moustache. I thought that was very distinguished-looking and very appropriate for the image I had of him.

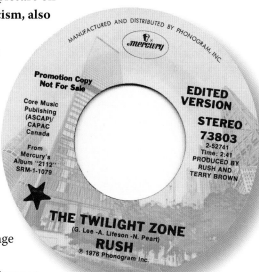

GILBERT: Oh, at the time it was all cool. I mean, everybody's wearing kimonos. To look at the other bands that were contemporary to Rush at that time, you can look at photos of Neil Schon from Journey in the mid- to late '70s, he's got the kimono too. He's got the handlebar moustache like Neil had. I mean, Rush never had afros, so I guess that was the only thing they were missing. But, you know, I wanted an Alex Lifeson perm and I think I had one for a while, although Def Leppard, the whole band had Alex Lifeson perms.

Somewhere in the American Midwest on the *All the World's a Stage* tour, May 1977. *Fin Costello/Redferns/Getty Images*

"The Temples of Syrinx" was the second single from *2112*. Kirk Hammett states the song and album taught him how to adapt a basic riff to various beats.

POPOFF: How about some of the deeper album tracks? "The Twilight Zone" always creeped me out.

CHAPMAN: Sure, well, "Twilight Zone," to me, is atmosphere. I like the idea that Neil is leaning on his childhood in invoking *The Twilight Zone*, which at that point had only been off the air about a decade and was science-fiction and very articulate, and through allegory dealt with very serious topics, antiwar themes, antiestablishment themes, antiauthoritarian themes. So I think that was the attraction. But from a musical standpoint, to me, Alex's solo is just superlative. Again, not just his technique but the sound that he is getting.

Elsewhere, it's odd, but to me "Tears" and "Lessons" are the highlights of the record. I think "Tears" is one of the great under-recognized Rush tunes. I remember when we were shooting *Rock Icons*, I asked Geddy about that, and you could tell that he hadn't thought about that song in thirty-five years. But to me, it's got his first great vocal. It's a very moving vocal. And "Lessons," that one, thematically, is not so distant from "2112," except "Lessons" seems to be about growing up with a father who maybe wasn't too crazy about the direction his son was going. I'm not sure. They both seem to be personal stories.

But what I find interesting about those two songs is it really puts a lie to the idea that Rush's music was predominantly sterile and nerdy, this sci-fi drudge and drivel. When I put on "Tears," to me it's just as moving as "Levon" by Elton John or "Fire and Rain" or "Ten Years Gone." It's enhanced by the Mellotron, which is beautifully done by Hugh Syme. So, I don't find them odd. I think at that point there are still aspirations—though not spoken about—by Geddy and Alex to still occasionally write lyrics. They still had something to say lyrically, I think, back then. They make a joke that, well, they let Neil do it because they didn't want to do it, or he was obviously the best. But I always thought that was a bit disingenuous. Those two are both good sets of lyrics.

GILBERT: I remember, as a kid, when you're a testosterone- and adrenaline-filled teenager, it's harder to really appreciate the ballads. And so I remember, with the ballads, I would actually go over and kind of pick up the needle and skip over those. But I spent a lot of time in my teenage bands covering the entire side one of *2112*. You know, it made me buy gear. I had to go out and get an analog delay so I could get Alex's echo sound. I was buying phase shifters and flangers. That album was really a litmus test of, not only if the drummer could play, but if the whole band could do it. And then the most difficult thing was finding a singer to sing the stuff. We never could, so we'd just do it instrumentally and hope.

POPOFF: No doubt the record is known more so for its rockers. Like "A Passage to Bangkok" and "Something for Nothing."

CHAPMAN: Well, I love "Something for Nothing," but it feels lyrically like it's not breaking any new ground. These themes of personal freedom, for me, are much more eloquently put on side one. Musically, it seems like a throwback to "Bastille Day," with that kind of straight-up hard rock. Aggressive track, great riff tune, but it's the one where I think, "Oh, that's the filler song." Musically it's treading old ground and lyrically it's not doing something as well as what's already been said.

HAMMETT: The riff on "Something for Nothing," I love so much and that guitar solo is crazy. I love how it builds—just fantastic [sings the solo]. It doesn't get much heavier [laughs]. And what I really love is that part just before the chorus. They're playing some pretty mellow chords, slightly arpeggiated, and then they go into those stop/start chords—so friggin' heavy and so light to dark, feathers to anchors—I just love it.

POPOFF: And then there's the debate over whether Neil overplays. It's one thing that put Rush at odds with the rock critic elite in the '70s.

HAMMETT: Personally, I never ever had a problem with his playing. I never ever felt that he overplayed. In fact, you know, I'm probably in praise of his technique and his decisions and his aesthetic absolutely. I never felt that he got in the way. If someone says, "Well, don't you think he overplays?" I might've thought about it for maybe two or three seconds, and thought, it doesn't even bother me. Because I've always enjoyed listening to him. There's never been a time when I didn't enjoy listening to Neil, or any of them. There was a time when I thought they were too synthesizer-heavy, around *Signals*. But I eventually came back, you know? Because I just love them so much and loved what they did and what they stood for, and eventually, I'm just like, "Yeah, okay, I'll just hit next track."

A live version of "A Passage to Bangkok," with its Middle Eastern Ritchie Blackmore vibe, would later become a single from *Exit . . . Stage Left.*

Print advertisement for *2112*, Japan's *Music Life* magazine, July 1976.

Some record label ads referred to *2112* as a "rock opera."

POPOFF: My favorite was always "A Passage to Bangkok" with that Middle Eastern Ritchie Blackmore/Rainbow vibe.

CHAPMAN: Well, I guess I'm a fan of the riff and that song, but what I like about that song is not so much the riff but the melodic chorus, and also the fact that Neil, I would say, is taking the piss out of himself; it's Neil writing something that is not so serious. So there's a real levity to that song. It's, you know, about traveling and getting high. And I think, similar to "Lakeside Park," there's a line of sentimentality and fun that runs through that song. The other appealing part to me is the solo on "Bangkok" that goes right into the chorus. You don't attribute Rush to a band that makes you—this is going to sound cornball—but it makes you groove. You listen to that moment and you're just floating.

POPOFF: Didn't that one help their reputation with the stoners?

CHAPMAN: Well, you could say that, but that implies that it was conscious. And I can't imagine Neil saying, "Hey man, we gotta write a song for the stoners." I just don't think he ever operated that way.

POPOFF: But he would want to write a song about travel.

CHAPMAN: Well, yeah, because he has a long history of that. I think, at the time, they were pot smokers. Rush has always had, to their credit, a sense of humor that has run through their music. And I think that on *2112*, that's where you'll find it. But I think that's just a happy byproduct, that the stoners, went, "Alright, Bogota."

GILBERT: I've always liked the quirky side of Rush, too, and this one is in that category. Like when they did "I Think I'm Going Bald" on *Caress of Steel*. I always loved that riff and those funny lyrics. And "Passage to Bangkok" is an unusual song—it's got that little [sings the "Oriental riff"], and at the same time it's got a great heavy riff, and it's got a heavy vibe to it.

Alex with his beloved Gibson ES-355, *All the World's a Stage* tour, 1977. *Fin Costello/Redferns/Getty Images*

But it's really unique. They were a very, very creative band. You know, being a guitar player, it's funny, but in my own evolution, I quickly got into the single-note *widdly widdly* kind of thing. And it took me a long time to really understand the sophistication of the chord playing of guys like Pete Townshend and, of course, Alex. And when I listen to it now, I think what were they thinking? How did they know this stuff? Because it seemed really inaccessible to me as a kid. My ears weren't sophisticated enough to hear chords that had sevenths in them and ninths in them and all these inversions that they we're doing.

I could hear punk rock—I could figure out Ramones songs [laughs], which is because it was based on your open cowboy chords. But Alex was really, you know, a little more sophisticated than a lot of what was going on with his writing, and certainly with his playing. And so, when I went back and played a lot of the *Hemispheres* album with Mike Portnoy when we did a tribute band to Rush, it was great, with the trained ear that I have now, to go back and finally get the chords right.

POPOFF: *2112* **really is a guitar-centric Rush album, and I'd say Terry Brown's production makes sure Alex is heard front and center.**

CHAPMAN: Sure, I'd buy that. For me, *2112* is where Alex really defined himself as a Canadian Jimmy Page in his ability to seamlessly and beautifully weave these electric and acoustic guitar parts. His playing had an extraordinary amount of power on that record, but it was also incredibly tasteful and melodic. And it always had a satisfying visceral tone to it. I love the guitar work on that record. And of course, it's one of the great riff records, and aside from the Mellotron on "Tears" and the opening ARP Odyssey, which is an early analog synthesizer, both played by Hugh Syme, there are no keyboards on the record. So it was the last great guitar statement, in my mind, from Alex. So throughout that record—be it the solo on "Twilight Zone;" be it the pastoral acoustic work on "Discovery" in the "2112" suite; the driving, tuneful, Townshend-esque acoustic stuff on "Lessons," or the hard riffing of "Overture" and "Finale," it was just an incredible palette Alex utilized, and to me, he's the star of that record from a musical point of view.

One last thing I want to say about *2112*. I called Alex the Canadian Jimmy Page. And as I'm older now, when I listen to that record, it reminds me of—and you will think this is hilarious—some of the layering that Page does on *Houses of the Holy*, particularly "The Song Remains the Same," which was this extraordinary example of a guitarist who knew how to layer different guitars onto one song and create this feast of guitar sounds that were so rich and so melodic and so interesting. And I swear that Alex was listening to Led Zeppelin for the production and sound of the guitars and what you could do. With *2112*, they truly left the rawness behind. And that's not a pejorative statement. They may have had ambitions to be a prog band, but on *2112*, that's where they pulled that off.

CHAPTER 5

A Farewell to Kings

with Ralph Chapman and Chris Schneberger

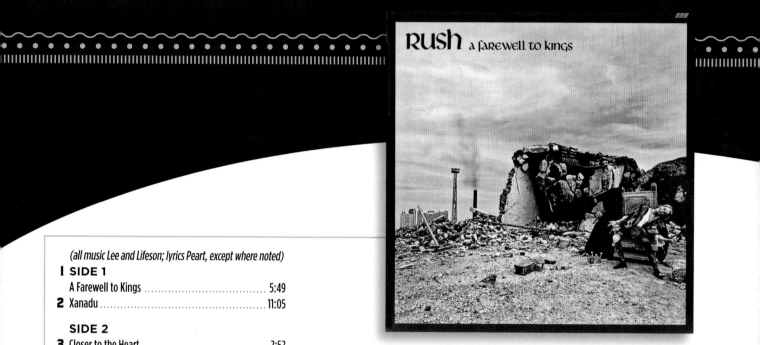

(all music Lee and Lifeson; lyrics Peart, except where noted)

SIDE 1

1 A Farewell to Kings 5:49
2 Xanadu 11:05

SIDE 2

3 Closer to the Heart 2:52
(music Lee and Lifeson; lyrics Peart and Talbot)
4 Cinderella Man 4:19
5 Madrigal 2:33
6 Cygnus X-1 .... 10:21
(music Lee, Lifeson, and Peart; lyrics Peart)

Geddy Lee: vocals, bass, twelve-string guitar, Minimoog, bass pedal synthesizers
Alex Lifeson: electric and acoustic guitars, classical guitar, bass pedal synthesizers
Neil Peart: drums, orchestra bells, wind chimes, bell tree, vibraslap, triangle, tubular bells, temple blocks
Terry Brown: spoken word on "Cygnus X-1"
Released September 1, 1977
Recorded at Rockfield Studios, Wales
Produced by Rush and Terry Brown

R ush had spent the latter half of 1976 arriving as a bona fide concert act, having had their *2112* album effusively received by their cult following—and ridiculed loudly by detractors. That classic rite of passage, double live album, *All the World's a Stage*, arrived later in the year, with Rush looking to close one chapter and begin another.

Recording in England for the first time, the band set up shop at the storied Rockfield Studios in rural Wales and set about building what would be their fussiest, most progressive set of songs, even if nods to other progressive rock tropes, such as the dominance of concept, would, in fact, mathematically fall short of *2112*, which offered a whole side dedicated to one tale.

Fortunately for the band's career arc, in among *A Farewell to Kings'* swooping sense of time-travel from past to far-flung future and all dream states in between, there would be a hit single in "Closer to the Heart." At barely three minutes of buoyant and brisk balladry, and given its bells and seasonal timing, "Closer to the Heart" would give Canadians as well as the band's loyal Rust Belt American fans a carol for their Christmas of '77. As a result, November 16, 1977, *A Farewell to Kings* was certified the band's first US gold record, with *2112* reaching the same gleaming plateau that same day.

Indeed, it's difficult to gauge whether the usual pathway of a pop single was in fact the real reason Rush finally went gold. Fact

Farewell to kings from Parliament Hill, Hampstead Heath, London, circa 1978. *Fin Costello/Redferns/Getty Images*

is, this was the most consummate of album bands operating in an album-length milieu (that of progressive rock), even if Rush had been fortunate enough to also command the attention of almost any proud member of Aerosmith's "blue army" or the Kiss Army, for that matter. In essence, the time was right for Rush, and it's a testimony to the pimply teens and the still-stoners-past-twenty of the day that a record as challenging and, yes, considerably less proto–heavy metal than its predecessor could have been purchased and assimilated without any sense of outcry. It's also to the credit of the band that they propelled themselves forward, one senses with the knowledge that their base could handle all these acoustic guitars, synthesizers, and percussion bells and whistles from their fathers' records, and reinterpretations of poetry from their English classes.

As history would have it, Geddy, Alex, and Neil would immerse themselves in this flagrantly progressive garden of Eden for but two records before reining it in. However, millions of Rush fans are glad they were taken on this trip, consistently citing *A Farewell to Kings* as one of the top handful of Rush albums of all time, arguably because of its daring to reach boldly for allegiance with the English art rock greats presumed untouchable by a next generation, much less by a trio of young and plucky suburban Canucks.

POPOFF: How does recording at Rockfield inform the vision of *A Farewell to Kings*?

CHAPMAN: Well, Rush were always chasing Englishness. And what's more British than going to Monmouth, Wales, into this absolutely pastoral setting and this renowned studio to record this new album? And to actually have the money to do so, which says a lot about the success of *2112*. So I think that was a huge moment for them, and then mixing it at Advision . . . certainly, when I've spoken to Terry Brown, when I was working on the *Beyond the Lighted Stage* Rush documentary, he talked about that as a high point in their career, and his favorite record. So part of it is this absolutely perfect setting. You hear that bucolic sound. They would never have done this for the first three records. All of a sudden they're recording in the courtyard of Rockfield, where you're hearing the birds and the wind and you're getting that type of decay you get when you record outside.

SCHNEBERGER: Yes, well, didn't they always want to go to England and record in some kind of stone mansion? They were in their Anglophile phase, where the goal was to be like Genesis or Yes and do these long conceptual albums. And it's a complex record, sonically, definitely the type of record you want to listen to on headphones. There's so much done on that album with acoustic guitars, twelve strings, often as intro instruments with a kind of Baroque feel at times, things you can almost imagine hearing on a harpsichord. The intro to the song "A Farewell to Kings" is kind of like that, as is "Madrigal" and the intro to "Closer to the Heart."

POPOFF: I've always maintained that songs like "Closer to the Heart" are distinguished by being up-tempo ballads that are drummed to a level of excess few other percussionists would dare. Bad taste or brilliance?

A Farewell to Kings tour, Birmingham, England, April 12, 1977. *Fin Costello/Redferns/ Getty Images*

CHAPMAN: Well, maybe this is heresy, but to me that's the only song in the Rush catalog where I wish instead of Neil, John Rutsey had played it. I've never enjoyed that drum track, other than his sweeping drum fill at the end; I've always thought it plodded along. It's like listening to Keith Moon try to play "905" on *Who Are You*. The guy just doesn't know how to play that. You can tell by the guys Neil was loving. He was loving Billy Cobham, Phil Collins, prog drummers, plus Keith Moon. He wasn't saying, "I want to play like Ringo." But if any track needed a guy like Ringo, it was "Closer to the Heart." "Cinderella Man" would be another one where he overplays, but because it's got that driving Townshend acoustic guitar, it doesn't chafe as much.

Having said that, it's "Closer to the Heart"! I put it on and I love everything about it [laughs]. But it's funny, if I was to hold up why Neil Peart is the greatest drummer in the world, I would hold that album up, specifically the title track, "Xanadu," and "Cygnus X-1." If someone was to say, give me an example of why he's not the greatest drummer ever, I would hold that album up, specifically "Closer to the Heart."

SCHNEBERGER: Okay, so I think it's actually an unfair knock about Neil that he overplays. He's a busy drummer, for sure. But one of the great things about Neil that isn't mentioned enough is that he's a master of creating rhythmic hooks, or rhythmic events, I would say. These are things that are not necessarily virtuosic or complicated to play, but just fit exactly right . . . "Fly by night away from here—*bam bam!*" Simple but effective. And I think oftentimes the focus on Neil is that he does a million beats thrown into two seconds, and double kicks and cymbals hit in the middle of fills, but I think it belies his really masterful compositional sense, creating those rhythmic hooks in songs, those little moments.

CHAPMAN: Sure, and having said that, "Closer to the Heart" represents Rush evolving as pop—meaning popular, for the people— songwriters, meaning the ability to write something that is infinitely catchy and stirring. "Fly by Night". . . it's an ear worm, very catchy riff. It's a pop song dressed up, but it's a pop song. Something like "A Passage to Bangkok" has this incredible chorus that allows you to float, and "Lakeside Park" would be another one. But "Closer to the Heart" is the most earnest, most successful take on a single. I'm not saying that was their intention, but that's the end result. It's also a really successful take on how to layer a three-minute song, how to create dynamics in such a short song, as it does have, again, a very pastoral opening, strummed guitars, a measured and yet inspired vocal from Geddy. Lyrically, it's about searching, so it's very enticing and inquiring that way, but it also has guts.

POPOFF: At the other end of the spectrum we have the sweeping and epic prog of "Xanadu," all eleven minutes of it. What does this song represent in terms of the band's evolution?

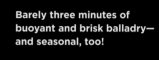

Barely three minutes of buoyant and brisk balladry— and seasonal, too!

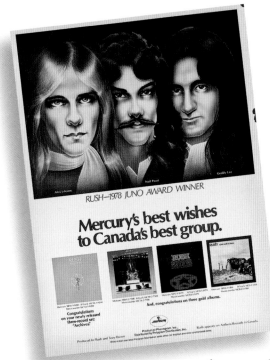

Farewell-era print ad. The album found the band in their Anglophile phase.

English poet Samuel Taylor Coleridge, whose poem "Kubla Khan" inspired Peart's "Xanadu" lyrics. *Pieter Van Dyke / National Portrait Gallery*

CHAPMAN: Well, there's an expansion of instrumentation. Neil had greatly expanded his percussion arsenal, and started to freely experiment with all sundry of woodblock, bell trees, different types of tubular bells. I think his kit got bigger again, where he was using these things called gong drums, these massive oversized floor toms you eventually saw on stands in the *Exit . . . Stage Left* video. I believe he increased his battery of cymbals. He was a one-man percussion orchestra now, as opposed to being a drummer. This was the debut of the double-necks. I mean, it was the age of the double-necks, but now Rush seemed to need them. When I think of "Xanadu," it feels like they were writing songs that demanded things like double-necks. Geddy, for example, plays rhythm guitar on "Xanadu," both live and in the studio. You see it on *Exit . . . Stage Left*. This was the idea of Geddy pushing their sound. This is right at the very end where he's just doing a very aggressive strumming on the bottom part of that double-neck. On the top is the bass, and on the bottom is a six-string guitar.

It's well-known that Geddy started to explore monophonic synthesizers, synthesizer lines, melody lines, but he was also generating on "Xanadu" sound effects, white noise, to create an atmosphere. What Hugh Syme started with on the beginning of "2112," they were now introducing as part of their palette. You know, spinning the modulators on the dial and looking for different sounds with the Moog. So *A Farewell to Kings* to me is such a crucial record because, for better or worse, they would never have gotten to, sonically, on the upside—records like *Moving Pictures* and *Signals*—and on the downside for some—*Power Windows* and *Hold Your Fire*—which are really . . . their lives started with *A Farewell to Kings*.

SCHNEBERGER: Right, well, first, I'd say "Xanadu" is absolutely my favorite Rush song of their entire catalog. The thing I love about "Xanadu" first is that long intro, first with the birds and the wind chimes and a little bit of wind sound. And then all these little swells from Alex as he builds up this long compositional figure with the soft attack amidst the bells, the Taurus pedals. And then finally, like after a few minutes, Alex kind of creeps in with that little figure—it's in 7/4, and then *boom*, that first big chord, which is so majestic.

And when I hear that, I connect it to the lyrics, and I think of a moment like this explorer has come over the top of the hill and gazed down into Xanadu, into the paradise. Maybe the sun is setting or rising. It evokes that moment of discovery of something majestic. And then it just builds from there. Neil has these increasingly complex accents before every big strike of the guitar chords, and then the fill, and then you're into the song. And I think, again, it's like three minutes into the song before there's an actual beat, a groove happening, which is amazing.

But they felt the luxury to take the time and build that composition. That's what I love about that song. And then it's still another couple of minutes before the first lyrics come in. And then you've got the main scene, with sort of the drone melody and rhythm, but then those runs that happen every fourth time [sings it]. And then at the end of that four cycle, there's the big, long extended run that goes further down and drops you into the verse.

And so, like I said, it's probably five minutes before Geddy is even singing. And I just love that they had the ambition, the wherewithal, the luxury to allow the thing some space and spread out and let this long passage develop. And I think in later years, in the live show, they were self-conscious about that, and they were often editing that down to a much shorter intro. This [R40 Live] tour, I think they played it pretty full, and it was so great to hear it, because to me, that's as good as any part on any album they've done.

Lyrically, of course, it's the Samuel Taylor Coleridge poem, and . . . I don't know [laughs]. What I get out of that lyrically is this classic thing of Neil kind of seeing the good and then the bad of something, both sides of the coin. And it's about this guy who's sought this thing out, and pursued it and pursued it, and he got there, and then he couldn't escape it. And I always wonder if in some ways that's reflective of Neil's view on the whole touring experience. Like he pursued and pursued and pursued this thing, finally got with this great band, they get on tour, and now he feels like he can't get out of it. And forevermore he's got this love/hate relationship with the touring experience.

Enter . . . stage door. *A Farewell to Kings* tour, The Odeon, Birmingham, England, April 12, 1977. *Fin Costello/Redferns/ Getty Images*

POPOFF: I remember as a young metalhead being a bit perturbed at how much lighter this record was than *2112*, and "Madrigal" is certainly the most egregious example of that.

SCHNEBERGER: You know, so, I think it's the weakest song on that album—and I think it's a pretty perfect album. To me it's a passing interlude between "Cinderella Man" and "Cygnus," kind of setting up "Cygnus." It's philosophical, but I don't think it's reaching any great insights, personally. It's doing something similar, sonically, to "Rivendell," which is one of my least favorite songs of the catalog. I will say also that I

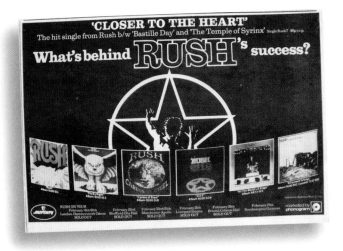

Farewell ad cross-promoting the band's growing backlist.

think it's the only song in Rush's catalog that actually mentions dragons, right? Because they always get that critical rip of like, "Oh yeah, they're the band that sings about swords and dragons." No, no [laughs]. So it's the only time dragons are mentioned—and they're not literal dragons.

And just before it is "Cinderella Man," which was kind of an overlooked song when they toured. Odd song. It's great, but I'm not sure, really, what the message is in that song. You know, there's this lyric about holding up his riches to challenge the hungry. Like, is he helping the hungry or is he challenging them to do better? Is it a charitable thing? I'm always thinking about this stuff through Neil's lens, back then, this idealistic Ayn Rand, you know, selfish libertarianism, denial of charity. And yet he himself is a very charitable-minded person. And so that's a song where I've been curious, like, what is this guy doing with his wealth? I don't know. Musically, it's got this fantastic outro that starts in eleven, and then it drops into a seven groove, and it's got a great flow, which is a characteristic of Rush, because they could take all those odd time signatures and make them not feel odd, make them feel like they flow where you could bop your head to it.

CHAPMAN: I agree with you about "Madrigal"—it's one of my least favorite songs for a variety of reasons. But I do love the bass playing on that song. Not just the fact that it's flanged, but that Geddy recognized that the song didn't need a bass part that was rhythm, but was melody. So he was doing these beautiful slides, these kind of glissandos, or he was dropping notes. Still covering the bottom, but he was just weaving, as opposed to landing on the beat. All that along with the flanging effect, and you've got a Geddy Lee bass performance that I'd never heard before. It's so tasteful and, dare I say, McCartney-esque. Geddy was known for being a very busy player, an aggressive player. So when we were doing *Beyond the Lighted Stage*, I cornered Geddy and asked him about that song. He didn't say much about it, other than it was an example of him going against his nature, that bass part, which made complete sense to me. He talked about how he would somehow paint pictures with his bass parts, and that, to me, is a better example of that than anything.

Alex and soldering iron dig into one of his Gibson Les Pauls backstage at the Odeon, Birmingham, England, April 12, 1977. *Fin Costello/Redferns/ Getty Images*

POPOFF: Chris, explain to Ralph and me this interesting connection you draw between the title track and "Cygnus X-1."

SCHNEBERGER: Well, "A Farewell to Kings" is a favorite song of mine that I wish they would have played on tour in recent years. But one thing I love in that song is the very, very end. So it's got this outro, which I think is also in 7/4 like the intro, and then the acoustic guitar comes back in, and you deal with this unresolved minor ending. And it's like it's not going to quite be okay. There's a darkness at the end of it, and there's more to come.

And then when you think about it, that's how "Cygnus X-1" also ends. Okay, I can understand ending the first song on the album like this—now I'm interested in what comes next. But to end the whole album like that? With a song that is already labeled "Book I?" You think there might be more to come . . . we're not sure where we're leading you, but we're not concluding, it's not the end. What's also amusing about that is that you had bands with multichapter songs, but you hadn't, that I know of, had an epic kind of track like that that wasn't even done at the end of the album. That it was to be continued because it was Book I. You knew there was going to be a Book II. And then there was this little cliffhanger, a minor and unresolved thing, with the guitar at the end.

Of course the next song in their catalog is "Hemispheres," and you know, "Cygnus X-1 Book II." And when you hear those played back to back, which they would do live for a number of years, you could tell, like that first big chord of "Hemispheres" was the next logical note in that progression. You play them back to back, and it sounds like one continuous composition.

POPOFF: Ralph, "Cygnus X-1" is an entirely different beast on this record from what came before, correct? It pretty much had to serve as the record's finale, for the reasons above, sure, but also for its choice of subject matter.

CHAPMAN: Sure, well, at lot that leads up to that song is a continuation of the atmosphere of the last record. It really started on "2112," with the "Discovery" section. But you get, with "Xanadu," that long introduction, this ethereal

Infamous February 25, 1978, cover of UK's *Sounds* magazine, an unabashed champion of punk rock.

Artist's rendering of the black hole Cygnus X-1, a well-known source of X-rays, and its blue companion star. Apt inspiration for eerie music. *M. Weiss/NASA*

introduction of bird sounds and just mystery. But "Cygnus X-1" is something ultimately far more foreboding. Terry Brown once told me that he would often experiment with microphones with Geddy, and obviously different EQ settings, and Geddy's voice on "Cygnus" represents, again, new ground, unlike anything we'd heard. The type of reverb he's got on his voice and the way he seems to be squeezing some of those . . . what's the expression? It's like he's compressing it.

And even the bass, the way it builds, to me, that's all about atmosphere as well. We have the first side, epic song, beginning with atmosphere, and then you have the second song, almost the flip of that. Side one is ethereal, necessarily mirroring the ethereal

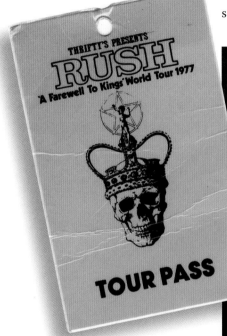

Alex and his Gibson EDS-1275, *A Farewell to Kings* **tour.** *Fin Costello/Redferns/Getty Images*

lyrics, the Coleridge poetry, while "Cygnus X-1" is all about mystery. In many ways, it's more successful as a sci-fi piece than anything on *2112*, as far as capturing that atmosphere of distance and deep space and coldness without sounding cold.

And as Chris says, it's continued on *Hemispheres*. But on this record, as you say, it's set apart and rightly so. One of the things I love about side two of that record is its sequencing. And that's something that isn't often talked about. You could say with *2112*, forget that it's a suite of music . . . but a great record is often a great record because of how you sequence it, what comes next, how you continue the journey. What I love about side two of *A Farewell to Kings* is that it's quite buoyant; it's acoustic, it's magical in parts, you get a sense of movement. And then at the end, you come to stasis. You're dropped in the middle of airless, soundless space with these sort of otherworldly sounds.

Adding to the effect, I think that's Terry Brown's voice tuned down, that ominous spoken part. It's just so eerie. And the first part of the song, there's a minimalism to it that I love, that you then hear later in something like the soundtrack to *Halloween*, John Carpenter. And so "Cygnus X-1" starts with that eerie, distant bass, which to me is Rush having the musical and compositional confidence to be so minimalistic in how they construct their songs.

POPOFF: But once we're into the track, we find out that Rush can still rock pretty hard, which again, is another link back to the very first song on the album, the title track.

CHAPMAN: Yes, which brings up a point. One of the reasons why that album is my favorite album is they never sounded like that again. On *A Farewell to Kings*, they were the perfect blend of old and what would be called "new Rush." So their use of keyboards, and let's call it production, were comparatively quite minimal on this record. It was just synthesizer lines, effects, well-placed bells, double-necked guitars, but they were still a rock band. They still made you go, "Hell yeah!" But they were progressive enough to allow you to float off to these places. With *Hemispheres*, they started layering and becoming more ambitious, and they lost, to me, a lot of the rawness that ended with *A Farewell to Kings*.

I just want to say one last thing, and it's about the context of that record within the wider musical industry at the time. There was the illusion, in 1977, that the kind of music that Rush was doing was on the ropes, that it was marginalized by these aggressive punk kids. But when you think about '77, really, and the great records that came out of that—*Animals*, Pink Floyd; *Songs from the Wood*, Tull; *Even in the Quietest Moments*, Supertramp; *The Grand Illusion*, Styx—there was an enormous taste for records that allowed you to dream and that took you places. And to me, *A Farewell to Kings* belongs in that company. It's a fantasy record, one that introduces you to all these different characters and all these different places and all these different time periods, all in one record—even if, unfortunately, it eventually lands the listener in deep space.

Who says 1977 was all about punk? Rush was keeping good company with *Farewell*.

CHAPTER 6

Hemispheres

with Ian Grandy, Michel Langevin, Jason Popovich, and Mike Portnoy

(all music Lee and Lifeson; lyrics Peart, except where noted)

1 SIDE 1

Cygnus X-1 Book II: Hemispheres.....................18:04
   I. Prelude
   II. Apollo (Bringer of Wisdom)
   III. Dionysus (Bringer of Love)
   IV. Armageddon (The Battle of Heart and Mind)
   V. Cygnus (Bringer of Balance)
   VI. The Sphere (A Kind of Dream)

SIDE 2

2 Circumstances 3:40
3 The Trees 4:42
4 La Villa Strangiato (An Exercise in Self Indulgence)...9:34
   (Lee, Lifeson, and Peart)
   I. Buenos Noches, Mein Froinds
   II. To Sleep, Perchance to Dream . . .
   III. Strangiato Theme
   IV. A Lerxst in Wonderland
   V. Monsters!
   VI. The Ghost of Aragon
   VII. Danforth and Pape
   VIII. The Waltz of the Shreves
   IX. Never Turn Your Back on a Monster!
   X. Monsters! (Reprise)
   XI. Strangiato Theme (Reprise)
   XII. A Farewell to Things

Geddy Lee: *vocals, bass, Oberheim polyphonic, Minimoog, Moog Taurus pedals*
Alex Lifeson: *electric and acoustic guitars, classical guitar, guitar synthesizer, Moog Taurus pedals*
Neil Peart: *drums, orchestra bells, bell tree, timpani, gong, cowbells, temple blocks, wind chimes, crotales*

Released October 29, 1978
Recorded at Rockfield Studios, Wales, and Advision, London
Produced by Rush and Terry Brown

The height of prog lunacy—and therefore many a fan's gosh-darn favorite Rush album—*Hemispheres* gets sensibly paired with *A Farewell to Kings* as the second part of a two-pack, due to both records being made at Rockfield in Wales, and also to the continuation of the Cygnus story in a side-long song of confrontational pretension. Indeed, Rush construct a song so long that nobody can even figure out what it's called, the common parlance being "Hemispheres," although its real title is "Cygnus X-1 Book II: Hemispheres," about as ridiculously *Tales from Topographic* a song title as you'll ever squint.

To my mind, *Hemispheres* is the record where Rush let their belt out so their pants could sag, versus *A Farewell to Kings*, which sounds pants-hitched-up, one notch too far, thinner of recording, overcast like its imagery, and just somehow aspirational but not quite there, an echo of *Caress of Steel*. On *Hemispheres*, the band attempts the impossible and then achieves it, creating what will forever be the band's most egregiously escapist epic as well as its most complex instrumental (Neil has quipped that the band worked on "La Villa Strangiato" longer than the entire *Fly by Night* album).

That leaves only two tracks, and they are deep fan favorites: "The Trees" coming as close as

STAGE
J
WARNING
RED LIGHT
STEADY
COMPLETE SILENCE - SHOOTING
FLASHING
QUIET - REHEARSALS
NO
PARKING
IAN
ENGLAND
PFM
STAGE RIGHT

anything would to a single on the record, and "Circumstances," being an aggressive, belligerent, heavy, and yet still dauntingly progressive rocker (the author's favorite song from the catalog and, in a sleight-of-hand bend of the universe, somehow under four minutes long).

Hemispheres went gold immediately, but took fifteen years to achieve platinum status. But, as I say, fans are passionate about it, and as Geddy famously puts it, it's "the straw that almost broke the camel's back," an allusion to the near nervous breakdowns resulting from recording the damn thing, and then—bonus—having to play and sing it live.

POPOFF: Let's begin by placing this record in the context of the band's catalog.

PORTNOY: Sure, well, for me, *Hemispheres* was the perfect combination of the prior two albums, *2112* and *A Farewell to Kings*. It has the conceptual side-long piece like *2012* had, [and] it's got the even more technical progressive nature of where they were going with the songs in *A Farewell to Kings*. So it's the best of both worlds for me. And I think it's the quintessential and most progressive album Rush ever made. Basically just four songs: a huge side-long epic, with each of the others being mini-epics, and one an instrumental, which was, I guess, at that time, the first real full-blown instrumental that they had ever done, not counting *2112*'s "Overture" or the little drum solo on *Caress of Steel.* So really, to me, *Hemispheres* represented the ultimate prog rock presentation from Rush.

LANGEVIN: That is a very consistent period—*2112, A Farewell to Kings, Hemispheres*—plus they have the continuation of "Cygnus X-1", and so these are albums that are probably hard to distinguish one from the other, for many people.

It just happened that I heard "The Trees" on the radio, and I phoned and I asked who was singing that, and they said Rush. And I thought it was an environmental song. It's only after I bought the album I thought that it's more of a *Lord of the Rings*–type of song, with trees fighting. I mean, this was also a big influence on Voivod, the way the messages were put across, like folktales in a way. Magma did the same to me, but they had their own world, discussing the destruction of one planet somewhere that was very reminiscent of Earth. I really loved this concept. But I really took from these two bands, Magma and Rush, because of the themes and because both drummers are involved in the writing concept; that was a huge influence.

Anyway, so after hearing "The Trees" on this college radio station, I thought it was amazing, and I went and bought *Hemispheres*, and that was my first Rush album, which makes it very, very special to me.

POPOFF: Ian, you were actually there on the ground watching the band record this album. What did you think of "The Trees"?

GRANDY: "The Trees" is a good song. At Rockfield, there's kind of a three-quarters square, like a courtyard. And so Alex was out there doing the classical intro to "The Trees," and Skip and I were in our chalet, I don't know, forty yards away, just talking,

Height of prog. "Circumstances" is one of only two conventional tracks on *Hemispheres*, **much of the vinyl being taken up by the epic suites "Cygnus X-1 Book II: Hemispheres" and "La Villa Strangiato (An Exercise in Self Indulgence)."**

about as loud as you and I are right now. And I guess it picked up on the mics, and Geddy comes in, "Fucking shut up!" All right, take it easy. So we went out of the chalet and sat on the porch and watched them record that. And it was very nice. Alex would practice his classical guitar. He would be in some room backstage, and he would be doing that, and he worked hard at getting better and learning those things. And I think "The Trees" was a real good show of what he can do.

PORTNOY: I agree. At that time, Alex was experimenting with a lot of classical influences, a lot of acoustic guitars, reminding me very much of Steve Howe's application of guitars in Yes. The early Rush albums . . . the Jimmy Page influence is obvious. But I think this period of Rush's catalog, you can hear more of the classical influence, and like I said, Steve Howe, the way he would experiment with different guitars and different sounds. I think Alex was doing a lot of that at the time. *A Farewell to Kings*, I think was when he was starting to go down that road, and then *Hemispheres* was just a further expansion. *A Farewell to Kings* was, in a lot of ways, the album that was the bridge from *2112* to *Hemispheres*, which was full-blown prog and the most experimental album they would ever make. It's one of my favorites because it was just filled with such exploration. The instrumentation, the songwriting, the fact that everything was epic, is why it's one of my favorites.

But yes, "The Trees," as well as "Circumstances," represent a good balance to the two epics on the album, a good foreshadowing of what was to come with *Permanent Waves*. Both obviously shorter than the other two epics, "Circumstances" was the quote-unquote "radio song" on the album, although it didn't really get radio play. But it was certainly the one on the album that could've crossed over to radio play at that time. And "The Trees" was a great example of a shorter song that still had all of the incredible progressive elements, an idea they ended up mastering on *Permanent Waves* and *Moving Pictures*. It was the perfect example of what was to come.

POPOVICH: It was a funny little song, basically. You can read a lot into it, but essentially you have an oppression by the rich, which translates to today, with the rich getting richer, the poor getting poorer, no middle class. It's funny, you go thirty years back, was he writing about stuff that is happening *now*? Probably not, but it's funny how things happen. The oaks being greedy, taking up all the light and all the wealth. That's an interesting concept, and it reflects today's situation, just the way North America has gone.

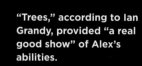

"Trees," according to Ian Grandy, provided "a real good show" of Alex's abilities.

Geddy and synth at the rehearsals for the tour to support *Hemispheres*—the height of prog lunacy. *Fin Costello/Redferns/ Getty Images*

POPOFF: And from a drummer's perspective, Jason, what is the magic of "Circumstances"?

POPOVICH: As a drummer, it's got a nice, in-your-face punch to it. And when I was a young musician listening to it, it was like something we'd never heard before, so original, the way the guitar chords and the bass worked with the timing. Everything is connected, and I guess that's the thing about the power trio philosophy.

I don't find drumming it difficult, but what can happen is when you're counting 7/8 time, it's very easy and natural to want to just play in 4/4. And when you're constantly thinking about counting it, you can get screwed up. You've just got to remember that 7/8ths as a musician, as a feel, it's a little bit shorter; every bar is a quarter note less . . . it drops off one quarter note, and so it's just the same as a lot of their other music. But a lot of it goes back into 4/4. With Rush, it's about, "Where's the extra eighth note?" or "Where's the one they took away?" [laughs] That's what you've got to remember.

LANGEVIN: Yes, and of course lyrically, *Plus ça change / Plus c'est la même chose* to people in Quebec, it really connected, it played a lot on the radio, and it's very catchy. I'm a big fan of Boston, Styx, and Journey, and Rush can write songs like that, that are super-catchy and fun singalongs to hear on the radio; if you are driving down the road, you'll automatically crank the volume up a bit. And so, yeah, that's a great song that got radio play here in Quebec, for sure. Sometimes Paul McCartney would do that also and add just a French sentence that becomes the chorus. And then all of a sudden it plays here, even on mainstream stations like CHOM-FM—they like to give Montrealers these types of songs. So it was a big hit in Quebec City, and probably here in Montreal, an even bigger hit.

"Canadian hard rock, the tree falls." German *Hemispheres* ad.

POPOFF: And "Circumstances" features a fierce Geddy Lee vocal performance, with Lee famously saying that so much of *Hemispheres* was written in keys he wasn't going to be able to sing live with any regularity.

GRANDY: I recall being in there and they'd ask, did you like the fourteenth take or the thirty-first take? And you're like, I don't know! It's all mushed together by now.

And Terry Brown would be famous for, "You will have done it tonight!" and "You will do it again!" So they worked hard in there. I think they wrote most of the songs on the spot. I know Neil would be given music and come back . . . with "Circumstances," he came back the next day with lyrics, and they're like, yeah, good. But, no, Geddy was at the peak of his singing there as far as I was concerned. He hit the notes, but they weren't easy. We put the vocals on at the mixing studio, and, yeah, he had to work hard. I guarantee he couldn't hit any of them today.

At Rockfield, there's a place called Mill House. It's an old house with, like, eight bedrooms and a studio, and they jammed in there for, I don't know, a week or ten days, working out songs. As a roadie, they're playing for eight hours straight, and you're trying to get away fishing or something, to get the hell away from that. And then we went to the studio part of Rockfield, and the funniest thing that happened there, we were at supper, and supper had just ended, and we're sitting around having a smoke and a glass of wine, and there's a knock on the door, okay? And this incredibly decrepit-looking guy is at the door, and like, oh my God, what is this about?

And Neil had answered the door, and the guy had mumbled something to him, which I didn't hear. And so Neil goes over to this thing, and pulls off about three grams of hash out of what he had, and gives it to this guy. And okay, mumbles, and he goes away, and it's like, who the fuck was that? It was Ozzy [laughs]. And that's the only time I saw him. I don't know what kind of shape he was in there, but he looked pretty bad. And so I always remember that, because Neil gave this guy some hash.

But they worked hard. There was the odd artificial stimulant, but nothing too crazy. They were all pretty good. I mean, if Alex is overdubbing or something like that, he's right there. He knows and works at it, and they were professionals in the studio. We would go out and get hammered sometimes, you know, after twelve hours, let's go do something, go have something to drink for fuck sakes. But I don't think that's unusual. But all I know is that in the rehearsals and at the studio they worked hard; they really did. We took the expression for the end of the day as "the interval," because you can't say it's nighttime, because it's five o'clock in the freaking morning. It's the interval now, until noon. What are you going to tell them? "Eleven o'clock, boys, time to check out." No, they worked hard—and it was one of their most successful albums creatively, that's for sure.

A classic period print ad goes to great pains to explain the concept behind *Hemispheres*— and in the process offers up frightening illustrations of Geddy, Alex, and Neil.

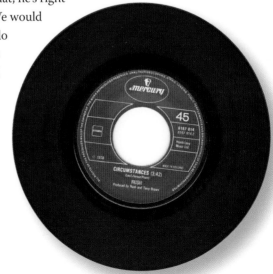

Fierce vocals, in-your-face drumming, guitar and bass working in concert— "Circumstances" exemplified the idea of a power trio and gave a shout-out to folks in Quebec.

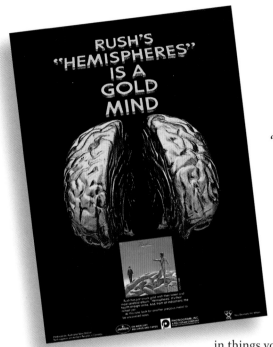

Puns and entendre galore.
It's, well, mind-boggling.

POPOFF: And probably the best expression of all this hard work is "La Villa Strangiato," correct?

GRANDY: Absolutely, and you know that one part? As soon as I heard it, I went, that's a Looney Tunes or Popeye cartoon. That came from Alex sitting around with his boys on Saturday morning goofing around. And they later settled with the estate or whoever wrote it. "Powerhouse," I think it was called. It was an old jazz standard, but it had kind of morphed into cartoon music by the time we heard it. So Alex came up with that riff, but as soon as I heard it, I went, "Cartoons!" But that song, at least they didn't have to sing it. But yes, they worked so hard at it, and it's an awesome song.

POPOVICH: It's something that happens with musicians. They hear things. Your subconscious picks up things and sometimes they come out in things you play, subconsciously.

PORTNOY: "La Villa Strangiato" was something like the most challenging instrumental ever written at the time. I don't know if any band had ever made a piece

Backstage at the Gaumont, Southampton, England, May 13, 1979. Interestingly, Geddy sports a Stiff Records T-shirt—a decidedly un-prog label. *Fin Costello/Redferns/Getty Images*

that technically challenging. I think they set the bar, and since then lots of bands, including what I was doing with Dream Theater for all those years, were following the blueprint that they laid down with this album and that kind of music. Nobody was making music that technical and musically challenging. All three of them were exploring their instruments beyond anything anybody was doing. And Neil Peart was working with all kinds of percussion. His kit was no longer just a drum kit; it was like a drum *village*, with everything from tubular bells, glockenspiels, and every kind of handheld percussion instrument. And Alex's solo on "La Villa" was, I think, the greatest thing he'd ever recorded up until that point and maybe even ever since. And Geddy's bass playing was complete virtuoso bass playing, taking what Chris Squire was doing and going well beyond. So all three of them were raising the bar.

POPOFF: I've had quite a few people say to me that this is Alex's greatest moment on record.

POPOVICH: Yes for sure, I think you get to see the personality of Mr. Alex Lifeson here. To me, that's the guitar song—"La Villa Strangiato" shows off Alex Lifeson as a guitar player. But when you get into that guitar solo, it starts out very quiet and mellow and the drums are quite in the background. Neil's doing straight 7/8, which lets the guitar solo explore and build. And it just keeps building tastefully toward just this shredding guitar. To me, that's a real exercise in self-indulgence, as they say, but also just a clinic by Alex Lifeson.

There are a lot of parts to "La Villa," and it was one of these things where, to record the song perfectly, they had to admit defeat. It was not a song that they were able to do in one take or all the way through. They actually had to record it in pieces and put the pieces together. Which was understandable, because it does go on a long time and there are so many different moods and changes to it. As a drummer, I can tell you it's tough to get through it. Is it the most difficult one to play? Probably not, but it's very much an exercise in endurance—you definitely have to be in good shape to finish it.

LANGEVIN: Again, there are tons of parts where you think oh, it's a 5/4 beat or 7/8 beat, but it's not. Because every three measures they'll add one time or one beat. So there are some very strange signatures. For a teenager, back then, I was fourteen or fifteen, and it really pushed me to learn more about counting while playing. Because before that, I had been playing straightforward material, although very difficult, like Led Zeppelin, Black Sabbath, and Deep Purple. But when I bought *Hemispheres*, it was another challenge, that's for sure.

So I was trying to figure the time signatures on "La Villa," which was hard. I would be listening to the song in my bedroom and running to the garage, trying to play it from memory until I finally memorized the whole thing. And playing on a smaller kit, I definitely was not able to imitate the style of Neil Peart. He was on a higher range of drummers in my head.

I believe the same year as *Hemispheres*, I went to see Jethro Tull and the band UK were opening, and that's where I saw Terry Bozzio. And he was in another category

Print advertisement for *Hemispheres*, Japan's *Music Life* magazine, December 1978.

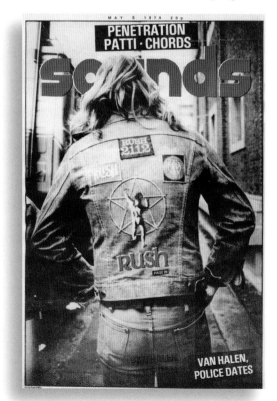

A poster for a May 25, 1979, show in Stockholm gave a nod out to the trio's homeland.

with Neil Peart, where I couldn't match their technique and their style and all that. It was just, for me, a way to improve my own style. Because before that, I was playing Ringo Starr, and then Peter Criss and AC/DC. But when I jumped into the Deep Purple material, and then Rush and other prog rock, I knew that I would have to spend like hours every day for the rest of my life to match certain drummers [laughs].

As far as Neil goes, the magical part is how controlled everything is. In the studio, live, every roll is so solid and he plays with such confidence. It's almost like, how do you say, transcendental meditation. There's something very sage-like about his playing, and that's a characteristic of his style. It's so well executed and controlled and considered, every little detail. It's very impressive. It's something that you have no choice but to look up to. It's very positive.

POPOFF: And then finally there's "Hemispheres," which, I gotta say, is pretty electric for something this long, as is the other side. So, really, pretty much a progressive "metal" album, start to finish.

Sounds magazine, May 5, 1979.

POPOVICH: That's true, no ballads, right? There were some amazing guitar chords put on by Alex Lifeson—just the opening chord in "Hemispheres" is very profound. I don't know what it is, some kind of G sharp or G minor chord or something. But it's got a sound that he kind of invented, or he patented, with that particular chord [laughs].

PORTNOY: I covered that with my Cygnus & the Seamonsters Rush tribute band, and that to me was one of the most challenging Rush pieces in their whole catalog. It was taking that technical prowess they had at the time in their career, but expanding it to a full-blown side-long epic. It was very creative, because they were making a sequel to "Cygnus X-1" from the previous album.

Drumming-wise, and actually everything on this entire album, it's Neil at his absolute height of technical prowess. He was just playing with such fire. Neil had the fire and reckless abandon of Keith Moon, but it was a very controlled version of Keith Moon. It was the energy of Keith Moon mixed with kind of the militant technical prowess of maybe Michael Giles from King Crimson—a great combination of the two. And for me, a big influence was not only the style but also the drum kit. He actually had one of the biggest drum kits in rock at that time. And to me, that was something that was very inspirational. I would sit down to just stare at pictures of his drum kit for hours. The way most kids my age were staring at a Playboy centerfold, I was looking at a *Modern Drummer* centerfold and salivating over the whole kit.

POPOFF: Funny. And just a final thought: there were only two people ever who sort of got across to me this concept that magic can happen when a band is right at the edge of their capabilities, and that was Ronnie Montrose talking about the first Montrose album and Geddy Lee talking about *Hemispheres*.

POPOVICH: Yeah, I know what you mean. It was almost like they were reaching beyond their abilities. It's like, you throw a rock drummer in to do a Buddy Rich tribute—and I'm not alluding to Neil Peart—but you throw a musician into something foreign, or your mind wants to create this song, but you as musician aren't there yet. They stretched a bit beyond what they felt comfortable playing; they were overreaching. As I've said before, Neil doesn't change the fills he does when he plays *Moving Pictures* songs. But

Neil, perhaps pondering 7/8 time signatures. *Fin Costello/Redferns/ Getty Images*

"La Villa Strangiato," live, he actually plays with quite a different feel, more direct, where it's a lot more follow-able [laughs], especially in the 7/8 section that can go a little wonky on the album. He now keeps it simpler and the song holds together better live. And I think that's very much a progression of maturity as a player, and not overplaying something that doesn't need to be overplayed. There are other examples of that as well.

And so you feel the personality of the band change with *Moving Pictures*. They become comfortable in their own skin. And you've got to remember, these are young players. Being together just six years is pretty normal to say, okay, now, the band is really starting to gel. It does take that long to really iron out what you're doing. But the beauty with Rush was they had the ability and they had the record label and the freedom, really, back in those days, to make albums and learn all along the way.

So you're progressing. Who has that kind of latitude this day and age? It doesn't happen any more. But they were lucky enough to have that freedom. The pressure was on after *Caress of Steel*, but they found themselves after so many years. They put out so many darn albums so fast, but like I say, that's just a normal amount of time to grow and connect and to really get the glue of the band . . . it's really just five years these three guys were together, and then *Moving Pictures* is out in year six—and they're still young guys on that album!

CHAPTER 7

Permanent Waves

with Kirk Hammett, Michel Langevin, and Mike Portnoy

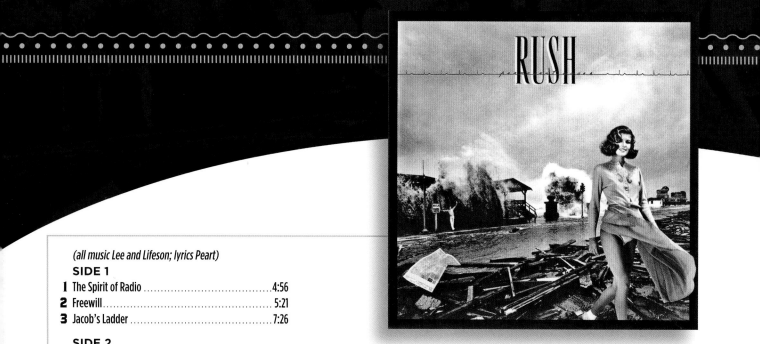

Geddy Lee: *lead vocals, bass, Oberheim polyphonic, Minimoog, Taurus pedal synthesizer, Oberheim OB-1*
Alex Lifeson: *electric and acoustic guitars, Taurus pedals*
Neil Peart: *drums, timpani, timbales, orchestra bells, tubular bells, wind chimes, bell tree, triangle, crotales*
Erwig Chuapchuaduah: *steel drums on "Spirit of the Radio"*
Hugh Syme: *piano on "Different Things"*
Released January 14, 1980
Recorded at Le Studio, Morin Heights, Quebec
Produced by Rush and Terry Brown

Representing a new wavey frame of mind/reset for the band, *Permanent Waves* would find Rush writing at a bucolic Canadian cottage retreat on Lake Huron, cutting demos at Sound Kitchen Studios in their native and comforting Toronto, and then transitioning to Morin Heights, Quebec, for their first of multiple happy recording experiences at Le Studio, that quintessentially Canadian rural studio paradise.

The songs would be more succinct than previous, but more importantly, any conceptual conceits would be further softened, even though Neil was givin' 'er at the beginning, trying to write another epic, this one ill-advised and grasping, based on Sir Gawain and the Green Knight. It was not to be, though parts were recycled for what would be "Natural Science," still a pretty long song at over nine minutes.

But the band was still defiantly fussy and progressive. Even though four of the songs were shorter, there were just six songs on the short album, meaning, of course, two long ones, and both—and arguably also "Freewill" and "The Spirit of Radio"—were filled to the brim with parts, even though "Spirit" was artisanally and cannily stuffed for maximum comprehension and radio consumption.

Perhaps what is most remarkable about *Permanent Waves*, however, is its energetic, bubbly quality—the work, it seems, of a Rush renewed, still in love with what it is they've been doing since halfway through *Fly by Night* and still searching for brief flashes of performance with the integrity of a King Crimson, who were always ahead of any other prog band in terms of arcane quality and fearlessness.

I mention this only because the band indeed succeeds, venturing into downright eccentricity all over "Jacob's Ladder" and "Natural Science" and even "Freewill," Neil, arguably turning this record into a drummer's album, aided by Terry Brown's liveliest and punchy recording thus far at the percussion end of things (and in fact ever, given the plush recline of both *Moving Pictures* and *Signals*). But testimony to the mindspace of all four makers, drummer's album or not: Alex and Geddy are also exacting and provoking and crisply turned out.

Funny, but I've never got it out of my head that this record looks like and feels like and sounds like Rush's first EP, my entrenching self unable to dispel the nagging thought that it's exactly one six-minute song too short. Don't get me wrong: always loved *Permanent Waves*—it's the punk rock version of *Moving Pictures*—but, yeah, when I see an album this short, I think of Van Halen, and I also think of a band that was, sort of unfortunately, including everything they had, rather than one that picked from twenty recorded songs to make their album. Rush just was never like that, and I always wonder what it would've been like if they had been. After all, it's healthy to be suspect of a band that has to use everything.

Recording *Permanent Waves* at Le Studio, Morin Heights, Quebec, 1979. *Fin Costello/ Redferns/Getty Images*

POPOFF: To start with, what was your initial reaction to *Permanent Waves*?

HAMMETT: Well, that they thanked Michael Schenker in the credits! Yeah [laughs], when I first got the album, took it out, and was reading it on the BART train on the way back home, I thought, "Oh my God, they thank Michael Schenker in the credits." And I showed it to a couple of my friends, and for like the next hour, that was the topic of discussion. Why were they thanking Michael Schenker?

Other than that, I think it's a perfect album. You know, I think it's probably my most favorite Rush album. And don't get me wrong, I love most of their albums—ninety percent of their albums—but there's something about *Permanent Waves*, where it has the epic-ness, it has the progressiveness, but it also has the catchiness, the melodies—they weren't demanding as much at times from the listener as they did on previous albums, which was also a product of the tracks being shorter.

PORTNOY: The most significant thing about *Permanent Waves* is its release date. It was one of the very first albums released in the '80s. . . . So it was really like the flagship of a new dawn or new era for Rush and for music in general. And right out of the gate with "The Spirit of Radio," they were establishing a new vision and a new direction for the band, with the songs being shorter in general. Obviously "Jacob's Ladder" and

Behind the board at Le Studio. *Fin Costello/Redferns/Getty Images*

"Natural Science" were longer, but coming off of *Hemispheres*, *A Farewell to Kings*, *2112*, they were streamlining the songs a bit more—but they didn't lose any of the technical elements.

So, to me, *Permanent Waves* is the perfect balance. A lot of people would say that *Moving Pictures* strikes the perfect balance—and that was the one that really broke them—but for me, *Permanent Waves* is the perfect balance. Because it still had all of those tremendously progressive elements and the technical prowess that they had on *Hemispheres*, but in a more streamlined sound. And they were starting to incorporate more hooks. "The Spirit of Radio" and "Freewill," those two back to back were basically showing how they could write shorter songs that could be played on the radio, but they didn't sacrifice anything with their musicality or integrity to do so.

POPOFF: Of course, "The Spirit of Radio" really dominates the narrative here, not only because it was such a big hit but because it was just so beautifully written and so anthemic, perfect for arena rocking.

HAMMETT: I love that song, bro. The minute we put it on, me and my friend John Marshall, we grabbed our guitars and had to figure out that intro [sings it]. And in fact, for like the next week or so, we were just walking around playing that little bit on our guitars. It was great. And, you know, I was blown away to find out years later that the part at the end of the song where they go back to the main riff, I was blown away that they were trying to reenact someone spinning the tuner dial, down the radio. Have you ever heard that? It was intentional, the way they wrote that [sings it]. And you're supposed to think when you spin a radio tuner to the left and right, you get all these different stations for like half a second—that's what that's supposed to be. That just makes me love the song that much more. And I love the reggae bit breakdown, because at that point, reggae was pretty big. Bob Marley's *Exodus* had just come out and reggae was everywhere. Me and my friends were catching the odd reggae show, here or there—yes, it's true [laughs].

LANGEVIN: When I heard "The Spirit of Radio" on the radio, it was just so catchy. I could tell it was made to be big and make the band a lot more popular. So to me, it was going to be a big break for them, and it made me buy the album. And then I was really happy. The reggae part to me was a bit of a twist on The Police, which became more apparent on the album after. But it was their first sort of reggae part in the middle of a song. So it was like a new twist for Rush.

On *Hemispheres* there were some attempts at radio with songs, like, "Circumstances." Here, there was that too, but there were still some prog songs like "Jacob's Ladder" and "Natural Science." But "The Spirit of Radio" is the big break in

Gig poster for 1980 show. *Permanent Waves* found the band still defiantly fussy and progressive, but at the same time energetic and renewed.

terms of being just commercial enough so it would really play on the radio, and it did in fact play a lot here in Quebec, all of a sudden.

PORTNOY: Sure, and I agree that it was such an anthem for them at the time. It's one of those songs . . . and they would get it right again on the album that would follow, with "Tom Sawyer." If you look at "Tom Sawyer" or "Limelight" or "The Spirit of Radio," those are songs that everybody can tap their foot to, you can hear on the radio, and they're catchy, memorable, and concise. It's under five minutes, but it still has all of those incredible musical elements that made Rush so appealing to us musicians.

So "The Spirit of Radio" is basically taking this incredible technical instrumental prowess and putting it in a catchy five-minute song. They nailed it—it was absolutely the perfect blend—and they nailed it with "Tom Sawyer" and with "Limelight." Those are the three songs that absolutely combined the best of both worlds: musicality and a kind of catchy, memorable, commercial approach. And that's why those are, probably to this day, the three songs that are still in their set list each and every show. But "The Spirit of Radio" was the first time they nailed it.

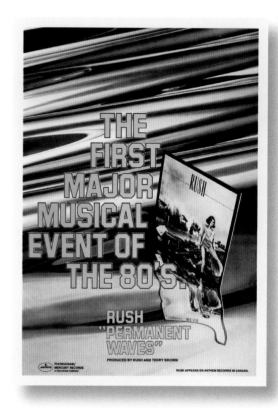

Permanent Waves was one of the first releases of the new decade.

POPOFF: There's a visceral, bubbly urgent sound to that song and everything on the record, which comes from, I don't know, Geddy's tight bass, Alex's crunchy guitar, and even his picking through chords. And I thought the album cover, probably my favorite, captured that as well.

LANGEVIN: Well, it had like a turbulent vibe to it, that's for sure. And I like the collage material from the '70s and early '80s. I always loved the old school collage, in both the prog rock movement and also the anarchist punk movement. And *Permanent Waves* is a good one for that. I like *Hemispheres* as well. These are great covers.

PORTNOY: I guess it's showing this kind of post-apocalyptic new world. I guess being that it was the first album of the '80s, they were entering a new decade, and really, it was their first time entering a new decade together as a band. So it was a kind of cool imagery to show them taking that next step, you know, into the future.

HAMMETT: I tell you, I still can't figure it out [laughs]. I know it's Hugh Syme, but it looks like a Hipgnosis cover, right? I'm still only now figuring out the Hipgnosis covers thirty years after the fact. What a testament to their work.

Yeah, I thought the album cover was pretty interesting. But what was more interesting was the fact that Alex Lifeson had cut his hair. That was the first picture of him with his hair cut. So that's how much of a geek, I was. I noticed a lot of these little things.

The visuals that went along with *Permanent Waves* reflected the record's urgent, bubbling sound.

"The Spirit of Radio" displayed incredible technical instrumental prowess" (with a reggae twist) in the framework of a catchy five-minute song.

POPOFF: And of course the most progressive songs on this album are probably some of their most explosive and complex ever. We didn't know this at the time, but they would be some of the last great examples of these instrumental showcases we'd hear.

HAMMETT: Oh, for sure. There's a riff in "Jacob's Ladder" that influenced a riff in "The Thing That Should Not Be." So, yeah [sings it]. And I love that guitar solo. That's one of the most dynamic solos, drawing on the melodic model, and it's orchestrated in a way that builds in so much drama and tension. It's orchestrated in a way that any time I hear it, I feel it so deeply. All of Alex's playing on that album was so influential to me—his choice of scales, his sense of melody, his dynamics while he was playing the solos.

Just in general, Alex as a soloist. I love the fact that he used the wah-wah pedal, for one, because I was already a disciple. And I thought that he had a real, real original kind of sound. I could tell that he listened to all the same guitarists we all listened to, but he had a way of following what was going on underneath him really tightly and really succinctly. It's the same with all Rush songs: when Alex goes into his solo, Neil and Geddy, that's when they start to work and provide a solid base for Alex to go wherever he needs to go.

So my favorite thing, other than checking out Alex's great guitar solos is that he had a great melodic sense, like with lead lines, melody lines, harmonized lines—it was great. Great sense of melody, great knowledge of chords, great knowledge of what notes to hit. When there's, like, you know, a suspended seventh chord, Alex knew that sweet note to hit over that suspended seventh chord, which is something I respect a lot. But whenever Alex soloed, I always dug in and listened a little deeper to which shifts in timing and rhythm Geddy and Neil would always go into—that was always a cool thing for me. Everything's happening on multiple layers, and if you listen deeply enough, you just keep on finding stuff.

PORTNOY: To me, the two drumming benchmarks on this album were "Jacob's Ladder" and "Natural Science." I've covered "Jacob's Ladder" a couple of times. I did it once on the *Working Man* tribute album in the mid-'90s, and then many years with Dream Theater. I had a tradition where every time we played Toronto, I would put a Rush cover in our set list. And through the years, we would play "The Camera Eye" and "A Passage to Bangkok" and various Rush covers every time we came to Toronto. And I believe it was 2004 when we did "Jacob's Ladder" live.

Anyway, the point is, "Jacob's Ladder"—[I covered it] once in the studio, once on stage—is probably the most challenging drum song from the Rush catalog that I would play. The whole tricky middle section, that is in [counts] one, two, three, four, five . . . it's actually in 6/8 and 7/8 alternating. I'm doing that off the top of my head. I could be wrong, but there are the two alternating time signatures. And the whole climax of the song, the drumming on that is absolutely insane and probably the hardest thing I've ever had to nail, covering Rush. Yeah, "Jacob's Ladder" is one of my all-time favorites.

And then "Natural Science," as well, with the whole 7/8 groove and everything, that to me was one of the coolest grooves and riffs in the entire Rush catalog. The whole [sings it], and then the drum fill that transitions from the 7/8 section to the 4/4 section . . . here's that one little drum break that, to this day, I still have never nailed perfectly. It's so quirky and just so perfectly random.

And, you know, with Neil, nothing's ever random. It's completely mentally charted out and thought out. But that's why he and I are very different drummers. With him, everything is so methodically planned out, whereas I'm a very spontaneous drummer. So a lot of times when I have to learn some of those drum parts of Neil's, it has to be perfect, because you know that every single rim was completely premeditated. And you have to execute it perfectly every single time.

LANGEVIN: "Natural Science" is exactly my favorite Rush song. There's all kinds of stuff in that song to the point where it's a concise version of everything Rush represents in one song. There's a killer 7/8 part, in the vein of King Crimson, and then there's a part where Geddy talks about a mechanized world, out of hand, you know, and there's the allusion to short-lived societies in the grand picture of space and time. And only Rush and, like, Magma would bring me to such territories. So in that one song, they've got everything that I found interesting and scary in the modern times we were living in, in the early '80s or 1980 specifically. Which definitely inspired Voivod. It was the spark that led to *Dimension Hatröss*—like microscopic worlds, compared to galaxies and all that.

But drumming-wise, in "Jacob's Ladder" and "Natural Science," there are some really good rolls. The thing with Rush is sometimes you think it's like a 7/8 beat, but it's not really. There's a lot of stuff in "Jacob's Ladder" and "Natural Science" that takes years to figure out and understand.

Dutch ad for *Permanent Waves*.

Neil dials in his drums during the recording of *Permanent Waves*. Fin Costello/Redferns/Getty Images

POPOFF: Back to the other end of the spectrum, there's "Freewill," which might be even more easily digestible than "The Spirit of Radio." Plus, with "Different Strings," we actually get a fairly focused Rush ballad.

HAMMETT: I love "Freewill," especially the main riff which, you know, it cuts off right before it's supposed to resolve. I love that, and it helped me launch ideas for my own writing of riffs— riffs that work on the upbeat, riffs that don't resolve, in 5/8 time

or 7/4, time or whatever. There was a band that really opened up that kind of diverse rhythmic and harmonic tension and dynamic, and *Permanent Waves* is an excellent example of how they did that, in a great guitar-centric sort of fashion.

LANGEVIN: In "Freewill" there is like a bass part and then a guitar solo on a jazz rock fusion beat that I really like in the song. When I heard that, I was like, alright, here we are, here we go, it's Rush, full prog again—and kind of speedy and nervous when it gets really into the middle part. I really love that song. And "Different Strings," that one really brought me back to a *Caress of Steel*–type vibe.

PORTNOY: In the middle of "Freewill," when I was in junior high school, that was the benchmark for all drummers and bass players—to play that entire middle breakdown of "Freewill." That was the big challenge. Because that whole middle breakdown was just so insane, between Geddy and Neil, and then Alex comes in with this amazing solo on top.

"Different Strings" is another one that I covered with Dream Theater, and that's . . . I guess, on their albums they had to have something that was more on the acoustic side, you know, or experimental side. *2112* had "Tears" and "Different Strings" was the song for *Permanent Waves*. It was just a nice breather in the midst of all the intensity of the other songs.

Everything about *Permanent Waves*, to me, is the ultimate quintessential Rush, melting pot. It's got everything. It's got all of the technical prowess of *2112*, *A Farewell to Kings*, and *Hemispheres* thrown into a melting pot with the more accessible, song-oriented arrangements that were to come with *Moving Pictures*. It still is my favorite Rush album of all time.

POPOFF: And, it's rarely talked about this way, but "Entre Nous" is almost like a progressive pop song, foreshadowing Rush of the '80s.

LANGEVIN: For sure, I really like that song because at this point there were some bands like Journey doing radio-type songs, and "Entre Nous" reminded me of that. I really like that type of radio music myself. I still listen to Boston, Journey, Styx, and Kansas, and so all of a sudden Rush had a song that reminded me of that, and I liked it.

PORTNOY: "Entre Nous" was kind of like the "Circumstances" of *Permanent Waves*. It would look like on paper that that would be the most obvious radio track before "The Spirit of Radio" and "Freewill," but it turns out that "The Spirit of Radio" and "Freewill" were the ones that American radio really took to. But "Entre Nous" sounds like it was designed to be the single, even though it ended up being more of a deep cut.

POPOFF: In the final analysis, would you buy the idea that Rush was the band that invented progressive metal?

HAMMETT: You know, I think progressive metal had already been around for a while. It's just if anything, they just widened up the scope of it all. They blew it open and showed what could be done. They definitely went down avenues that had not been gone down before. And the whole use of the synthesizer,

"Entre Nous"—progressive pop song foreshadowing the Rush of the 1980s?

I really thought that was cool, especially on *Hemispheres*, where I thought it worked really, really effectively. But when the synthesizers were starting to get too heavy, as a guitar player, I want to hear more guitar. But I understand that's the direction they wanted to go in. I'm certainly not going to knock them for that. But I liked their more guitar-centric sort of stuff, honestly.

POPOFF: So why do you think metalheads back then accepted Rush with open arms?

HAMMETT: That's because it's heavy; it was heavy stuff, plus great songs. They delivered on all the things hard rock and heavy metal people had come to expect. They weren't like crushingly heavy, but they were heavy enough. And I think . . . I take that back—there were times when they were crushingly heavy! There were times when they were just like the heaviest fucking thing, with those fucking licks that they would do, like, say, "Something for Nothing." But there was a level of musicianship that appealed to hard rock and heavy metal guys, obviously. And the energy. And the subject matter. There was just a lot of the same stuff we all like. So, yeah, they're a hard rock/progressive band with heavy metal tendencies.

POPOFF: I always wonder what it would've been like if, when the New Wave of British Heavy Metal came along, Rush was one of the bands that embraced it, like Budgie or Uriah Heep or even Ozzy and Black Sabbath with Ronnie James Dio, rather than running completely in the other direction. Like, what if Rush strapped on the bullet belts and leather jackets and went that way instead of the keyboard direction?

HAMMETT: That's a really interesting concept. But, you know what? It's just like . . . the New Wave of British Heavy Metal was probably too underground. And by the time it became overground, the New Romantics got to them instead. I think they started wearing suits, right?

Paula Turnbull models for the cover shot of *Permanent Waves* in Quebec, October 1979. *Fin Costello/Redferns/Getty Images*

CHAPTER 8

Moving Pictures

with Sean Kelly
and Jason Popovich

Geddy Lee: lead vocals, bass, bass pedals, Minimoog,
Oberheim polyphonic, Oberheim OB-X, Moog Taurus
Alex Lifeson: electric and acoustic guitars, Moog Taurus
Neil Peart: drums, timbales, gong, bells, glockenspiel,
wind chimes, bell tree, crotales, cowbell, plywood
Hugh Syme: synthesizer on "Witch Hunt"
Released February 12, 1981
Recorded at Le Studio, Morin Heights, Quebec
Produced by Rush and Terry Brown

With Rush finally riding high upon a (permanent) wave, time soon came for a follow-up, and the state of well-being within the band was such that this was not the time for a Keith Richards–style change of blood, as it were. But all that was to be worked out at Ronnie Hawkins's farm up at Stoney Lake, Ontario, where the band flew model airplanes and pieced together most of the songs that would comprise their biggest record, the now quadruple-platinum *Moving Pictures* wrapped in rich reds and blacks.

Putting aside the triple entendre of the cover art, it is instructive to know that Geddy looked at all of these finally tuned songs with storylines as mini moving pictures in themselves. Not all of them had plot, per se. "Tom Sawyer," with its spirited word-fight between the sensible Neil Peart and the sensitive Pye Dubois, was not exactly a yarn, and "YYZ" had no words at all. But much of the rest, particularly "Red Barchetta," "The Camera Eye," and "Witch Hunt," could play out cinematically in the mind, as the band percolated through their pristine and progressive rock soundtracks behind the pictures formed.

But fact is, Rush had found their way to nibble-sized pieces of guitar-charged prog on *Permanent Waves*, and were viewed by fans and critics and themselves as focusing their attentions with

Maple Leaf Gardens, Toronto, March 23, 1981. "Last night's 18,000 rockers came to listen to the hometown band, not to fool around," noted the *Toronto Star*. *Michael Stuparyk/Toronto Star via Getty Images*

still greater skill this time around. Only "The Camera Eye," elegant passage upon strident performance, would unfurl, serving as the last ten-minuter of the band's career. The fans certainly didn't mind Rush's newfound brevity, turning the entirety of side one into one smash single after another, even "YYZ" becoming one of the most famous instrumentals of all time across any musical genre. Truth be told, only "Limelight" and "Tom Sawyer" (along with "Vital Signs" from side two) would be launched officially as singles, but all four songs on side one are perennial classic rock radio favorites, challenged in frequency of rotation, really, only by "The Spirit of Radio."

Side two of *Moving Pictures*—the dark side—not so much.

In any event, why *Moving Pictures* is such a perfect album is up for debate, but the pastoral surroundings of the group writing sessions couldn't have hurt, with most of the songs ready to go by the time the band hit the equally pastoral surroundings of Le Studio. Only the final track, "Vital Signs," was essentially put together in the studio, and as would become par for the course, that interesting and obscure track steps out a bit: reggae-meets-Kraftwerk on the way from "The Spirit of Radio" to "New World Man."

St. Peter's Anglican "Church on the Rock"

Steamer Stoney Lake leaving Thurstonia, Ontario. — 35.

Greetings from Stoney Lake. The band worked out the arrangements that would comprise *Moving Pictures* while sequestered at the rural Canadian estate of rockabilly legend Ronnie Hawkins.

Moving Pictures would become the only contribution by Rush to the overplayed concept of classic rock bands performing one of their albums in its entirety, with Rush even commemorating the occasion with the release of *Time Machine 2011: Live in Cleveland* and a breakaway chunk of dedicated vinyl called *Moving Pictures Live: 2011.* And so renewed for that run, but really, never old, *Moving Pictures* represents Rush at its finest, arguably the last of a golden era, certainly the last on which the band would create eye-to-eye and shoulder-to-shoulder under the fully approving auspices of the band's ersatz fourth member, producer Terry Brown.

POPOFF: What was going on in the music industry that might have made this an ideal time for Rush to break through to another level?

POPOVICH: Well, I think you have, basically, the last prog rock album that was commercially acceptable. Rush somehow managed to bridge the gap between what prog listeners liked and what the radio listener, the average pop listener, liked, and that made for a super album. The fan base went from, whatever, twenty percent to one hundred percent overnight. And to me, the biggest thing is that Rush is not a metal band, they're not prog, and they're not classic rock. What they were, to me, was a hard-rocking progressive band. And there's a lot of difference, because you can't compare them to Yes. They rock out heavier, Neil hits the drums harder, and they have more aggressive solos. But they're progressive rock with a hard edge, but not so hard that they're heavy metal, and there's so much thought behind it.

So they had a niche, drawing in hard rockers and those who liked the flowery progressive style of Genesis and Yes. So you know what? You now had two groups of people that liked Rush. So it pumps up their popularity, through having a hard rock edge to their progressive rock-ness. There simply were not a lot of hard-rocking and edgy progressive rock bands.

Rush lifts rock 'n' roll to new heights, with "Moving Pictures."

See Rush in concert bringing "Moving Pictures" to life with their new show.

Rush created a niche, drawing in the hard rockers as well as fans of more flowery prog styles.

KELLY: Also you're kind of in a post-arena rock phase, where the idea of massive amounts of people going to see a concert is now well entrenched in society. You also have the emergence of bands like The Police beginning a new wave, but pre-MTV. It's the perfect time for a band to be experimental in terms of technology and still have the remnants of the progressive rock that came before. It's the perfect place for a band like Rush to exist, where classic rocking arena performance is still appreciated, but it's also time to add some new technology to the palette. So *Moving Pictures* is the perfect storm record, right?

Moving Pictures tour, Oakland-Alameda County Coliseum, Oakland, California, June 6, 1981. *Larry Hulst/Michael Ochs Archive/Getty Images*

POPOFF: But I'd have to say, being there at the time, Rush really were appreciated squarely as a metal band, or at least loved by pretty much any metalhead. Especially in the UK, during what they called the New Wave of British Heavy Metal.

KELLY: It's funny you mention that New Wave of British Heavy Metal thing. Because to me, my introduction to Rush was usually on compilations that had hair bands. So to my young self, sure, they were like a hard rock or a metal band— I felt they were inside the wheelhouse of those bands I liked, with heavy guitars and progressive playing. Even though now, when I listen back, it's got far more layers than typical metal. But they made perfect sense along with my Iron Maiden records.

POPOFF: And part of that perfect storm, as you call it, Sean, is that the band was considerably inspired as well.

KELLY: So this is it. They had just broken through, having just had a platinum album. I think *Permanent Waves* was a platinum record in the States. So they're at that point where they're an arena act, yet still new; it's still fresh. And this is the sweet spot, right? They've got the audience, and now we can break through to wider acceptance. So it's a pretty happy time, because there was so much time in the station wagons for those early arena opening slots, too, really slugging it out. They had the moral victory of *2112*. They had proven to the record company that they could stick to their guns and be successful. I remember reading an interview with Alex and he was saying, "We were so happy, we were arena headliners now.

Rush was in the enviable position of still being a relatively new platinum act at the time of *Moving Pictures*.

"Limelight" was just one of Alex's magical moments on the album.

People are coming to the shows and we've got a little bit of money." You're in that sweet spot where you're feeling good and certain types of pressure are taken off. And now I think they're also kind of reveling in their own editing process too, figuring, "Hey man, what happens if we shorten these songs? Make them more digestible chunks of music?"

POPOVICH: And they were prepared. They sequestered themselves to Ronnie Hawkins's farm. And as Geddy mentioned, when they did that for their later album, *Snakes & Arrows*, it actually made for greater concentration. It's more of a concentrated effort when they can actually just sequester themselves and work on songs and keep the flow going with the guy next door, down the hallway. While they're jamming out stuff, Neil is writing the lyrics in the other room, and they're passing stuff back and forth. There's that instant energy—and synergy—that becomes much more kind of who they are. That synergy between the three of them, when they're working together, makes for a nicer finished product.

And *Moving Pictures* is really finished to perfection. That is Neil in full flight. There was so much preproduction to those songs before they put them on the album. The parts are so well-crafted and stitched together, that there's really nothing to improve on them. Even thirty years later, you play it, and you don't go, "He could have done something a bit better here." Neil himself doesn't change anything when he plays those songs. Note for note, fill for fill, he very rarely changes them. Other stuff, you'll see him do a kind of different feel to the song or a bit different bass drum pattern, bass drum feel. But with that album, it's pretty much note for note from the studio. I think that's a testament to the writing of those parts. Neil's the kind of player that is always trying to push himself and trying to improve a song, even when he does it live. But he doesn't touch the stuff on *Moving Pictures*. There's no manipulation to the songs. So that's why I think it stands the test of time.

POPOFF: Alex is known for his own magic moments on this record, most notably his solo on "Limelight."

KELLY: To me, it's one of the most gorgeous solos of all time. And what he did for the guitar vocabulary on that record was, I notice from talking to other players, bringing in this Allan Holdsworth–type fluidity in terms of the legato playing, the smoothness of the scale ideas. But also the bending. Because there's so much going on rhythmically with Neil and Geddy, really, he couldn't . . . I mean, if he started just chopping away playing with like with a crazy pick attack, trying to play a million notes, it would just get cloudy. But he floats in between. And that solo is just so beautiful, so melodic, so fluid, and it's a combination of his finger vibrato, of the way he bends into chord tones and whammy bar work too, his vibrato bar work. Very Jeff Beck. Quite beautiful.

Plus, this album was a pretty big step, because I think this is the first record where . . . I think that technology has caught up. Before, he was using analog delays. Now we're getting to digital delays where you had more processing time, allowing him to be more expansive in the guitar palette. You see this in the concert video, where he could now have his lines overlapping. For example, the solo in "Limelight," he could finish off the phrase of that gorgeous, floating solo and have that note sustaining as he goes back now into another patch. Whereas before, with just an analog echo, he would've had less repeats and less decay and just less time to overhang, basically. So to me he's using the technology, thinking, "Oh man, I can do this as part of the band's kinda mission statement."

Exit . . . *Stage Left* tour, Wembley Arena, London, November 5, 1981. *Fin Costello/Redferns/Getty Images*

And I think his choice of parts . . . he's crystallizing suspended chords. He's using a Strat now with PAF humbuckers, so he's cleaning up the tone. The thing is, any guitar player with identity, he's got a sonic identity no matter what guitar he plays. But by moving over to the Strat, the whole thing just got cleaner and wider. To me the sound got wider, because he cleaned up his sound a little bit. He's now using those Marshall amps. The Club & Country combo? Marshall combos, anyway. So technology is catching up to where he's an arranger of guitar parts.

POPOVICH: "Limelight" is just a beautiful song. Technically the guitar solo is one of the most beautiful mood guitar solos Alex does. It's a strange guitar solo; it kind of ebbs and flows. It's almost not even going to the time of the music, when you first start learning it and hear it, it's actually outside of time. It's one of those where he just likes to flow. But overall it's just a very catchy tune, and to me, the most radio-friendly song on that album.

Lyrically, well, Neil doesn't like to pretend. Don't pretend like we're buddies. Although I think he's a bit misunderstood. He's a bit of an introvert, and he doesn't like to be accosted. He likes his privacy. You could go up to the guy and say, "Hey, I respect you," but don't go crazy.

KELLY: I just admire the conviction so much. As I get older as a working guitarist, I think, wow, that band had a courage and conviction that I don't think I could ever profess to coming close to. Like my own ambitions . . . you do learn as a musician to play the game. To work, right? At least some of us do. But he did not! Neil did not play the game [laughs]. He couldn't! He was actually a pure soul. And that, to me, is fascinating and admirable. When I hear that, I actually feel guilty. Most of the time [laughs]. Like, I can pretend a stranger is a long-awaited friend.

And *All the World's a Stage* . . . the Shakespeare quotes. Like, come on. Who else can get away with that and make it resonate? I would think that would be laughable with most people, using that kind of language. But that song is very powerful. I wish my

Exit . . . *Stage Left* tour, Wembley Arena, London, November 5, 1981. *Fin Costello/Redferns/ Getty Images*

younger self could spend a little time talking to Neil, because I remember him talking about not wanting to meet Keith Moon. He would say, "I didn't want to meet my heroes. I just wanted to enjoy their music and that's enough." And how he is so reticent about meeting people, this idea of idol worship? It's like, was my own love of music as pure as his? I don't think so!

POPOFF: Pretty funny, but Neil's most famous "solo" of the catalog is on this record too—his repeated fills in the climactic section of "Tom Sawyer." Jason, as a Rush tribute band drummer, what is interesting about that song?

POPOVICH: That solo is the one that pushed him to show off the most. I can't say it's the hardest to do. But there are four bars, four pieces to that one drum solo section, and I don't think that when they wrote that, that was really his intention. I think he was pushed more by the producer, Terry Brown, do this, do that. He's a great player, but I think someone pushed him a little bit further to do more than he wanted to do there. Just a theory.

But as a drummer, the song as a whole . . . well, first, there's a kickass vibe to the lyrics, attitude—I'm gonna do whatever I wanna do. There's that opening blast of keyboards, that iconic synthesizer sound, an immediate hook.

But as a drummer, musically, that's a very challenging song to play with the level of intensity that he plays it. Neil says it's the most difficult for him, too, and he's right. It takes everything you've got, playing that song. You can get into the style of his drumming, but if you're playing each song accurately, and then with the power he uses, you're superhuman. Any proficient drummer can play them correctly, but it's the added element of strength and power to what you're doing to them that takes it to a different level of playing. Are you going to play the song like a guy who is playing it with toothpicks in his hands or are you going to play with both finesse and aggression? And when you pump it up a notch, it becomes difficult.

KELLY: On this one I gravitate to the lyric. There's this sense of rebellion and this sense of being an individual, which is something that I think they'd progressed through, past that Ayn Rand kind of rugged individualist thing. I think [Neil] was really good at delving into the layers of what that meant. I know as a kid, when you're first yearning to be an individual in a world where you feel maybe your voice could be lost, Neil's message was really appealing. And Mark Twain, *Huckleberry Finn*, the river . . . that staple reading for all of us anyway, right? A clear reference point. And then you add the Pye Dubois weirdness, which made you feel you were listening to something artistic. I always said that Pye Dubois and Kim Mitchell brought hard rock to northern Ontario [laughs]. I felt like I was listening to something special and yet that I could understand. Whereas maybe something like Yes would've been lost on me. His lyrics felt important, but I could still relate to it.

POPOFF: Quite a bit of keyboards on this record.

KELLY: Yes, and it's funny, because I didn't get into *Moving Pictures* until a few years later. And the sounds Geddy was getting, those sounds to me sounded dated in 1985. Because they're so distinct. When you start dealing with Oberheims and Taurus pedals and Korgs, there is so much bloom in the sound. They're so identifiable, it sounded almost a little too organic to post-1985 ears [laughs]. They were so present and so big, and they kind of competed in the square wave space of the guitars.

POPOVICH: On *Moving Pictures* it was a nice mixture, the perfect blend, I thought, of having keyboards—really, a background instrument—and playing as a strings sound. If you listen to the background of even "Limelight" or "Tom Sawyer," there's a string ensemble sort of sound going on, which is sampled. But that's a synthesizer, that sound. And that's used to fill out the sound of the band, because, being a trio, you don't have an actual keyboard player per se, so having that extra element fattened their sound. Funny little thing, if you listen to the notes, the main riff of "The Spirit of Radio," it's actually the same notes as the keyboard solo in "Tom Sawyer." So there's some overlap sometimes [laughs].

POPOFF: Interesting how all the hugely popular songs are on side one, but *Moving Pictures* indeed has a side two, and the opening track is a major epic—and the last one for a long, long time.

POPOVICH: Yes, "The Camera Eye." Lyrically very cool. For one thing, it's another treatise on, or expression of, freedom, I think, like "Tom Sawyer." You listen to the city and the life of things in the big city, in this case two cities, New

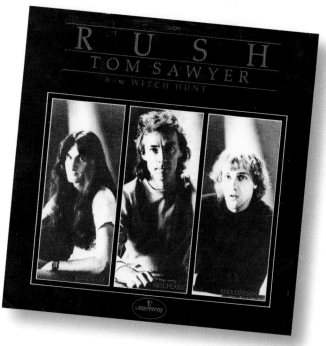

With "Tom Sawyer," Neil revisited Rand's theory of the individualist *and* offered one of his most famous drum "solos."

York and London. He's talking about a yearning for the other side of the world. A young person might dream about the glamor and the things that you don't normally have in your own small town, and so there are these cities you go and experience. You realize that there's a lot more to the rest of the world. Neil was becoming more international, and he started appreciating and writing more about his own experiences, and the influence the world was having on the band as opposed to just the science-fiction thing he was writing about before. So that was sort of the start of getting into his own experiences, and he started putting it into words, pen to paper. That's a song that is a lot of hard-core Rush fans' favorite. It has such nice movements and passages, and as you say, it's one of their last long songs. There really wasn't a song they did [after that] that was ten or eleven minutes long. They were leaving that chapter behind.

POPOFF: Rush certainly had enough singles, but they also have these huge FM radio hits that were never released as singles, "Red Barchetta" being one of the biggest.

KELLY: Yes, catchy song for a few reasons. Right at the beginning, Alex took those beginning guitar harmonics and made a hook out of it. Also, the way he implements a lot of the classic '60s rock guitar ideology into the piece is fascinating to me. I can hear that coming out of Led Zeppelin, coming out of The Who, the use of the suspended chords and the inversions he uses. And it's so clean and harmonically rich too. He carves out space with the right chordal choices—that's the best way I can describe it.

POPOVICH: And it strikes a chord lyrically too! You think back to when you first got your driver's license, what was that like. That freedom to drive a car and maybe go see your girlfriend or go downtown and visit some spots. That's about discovering that first independence of your own mobility and freedom. And it's a charming song. As Sean says, it starts off with the harmonic guitar, and then tells a story, about his uncle, going back in time, reminiscing.

POPOFF: And if it was possible to have an instrumental tell a story, it would be "YYZ." Or even if it's not a story, this one is perhaps the Rush instrumental closest to a "song."

KELLY: Yes, well, there's a bit of a narrative. You felt like you broke into a secret when you knew that that was Morse code. I actually remember this clearly. Oh yeah, man, like the sixteenth notes are the dots, and the eighth notes are the dashes. Whoa, cool. And it's the airport code for Toronto and they're from Toronto. It was like a secret welcome into virtuosity. And there's the tritone. I mean, the tritone is the heavy metal interval, right? The *diabolus in musica*. And that's always exciting to people, that taboo interval. Also there's this cool kind of Phrygian mode, flamenco-type

The 1981 EP "Vital Signs" featuring the backlist tracks "A Passage to Bangkok," "Circumstances," and "In the Mood."

thing, and Alex explores all these different variations in the rhythm, going between the two chords, which was fun to learn and actually manageable. And the solo itself, that to me is his most Holdsworth-ian moment. At the time, I didn't rate him technically the same way I would rate someone like Yngwie Malmsteen. But when I go back and listen, what he was doing was very advanced and next level. What he did with that mode, that Spanish Phrygian mode, or that fifth mode of harmonic minor in that solo, is crazy musical.

POPOFF: And it's a testimony to music fans that they could and would get out there and buy this record in droves. One supposes it's an appreciation for a level of creativity with which they aren't usually served.

KELLY: When I think about Rush, I think you've got two overt virtuosos and one covert virtuoso. You've got Geddy Lee and Neil Peart who were physically doing all these incredibly difficult things, and Alex . . . I don't know if it's by default or by choice— and he's got chops to burn, don't get me wrong—but he's certainly not doing as much physically compared to the other two. But then having to cover all that space, I think his style is forged out of that. And really, he's more of an arranging virtuoso than a technical virtuoso to me.

POPOVICH: Well, the "Vital Signs" lyric says it all: "Everybody got to deviate from the norm." That speaks to people. The whole approach of Rush is to keep moving forward, not sit back and just do it again. *Moving Pictures* was a classic album, and they didn't want to do a second *Moving Pictures*, so they made *Signals*, a completely different thing, a new direction. The mentality is that they're constantly pushing in a different direction, and that keeps the fans interested and engaged in where they're going next. And when you have good musicianship and good songwriting, you're willing to take the twists and turns as a fan.

CHAPTER 9

Signals

with Chris Nelson
and Ray Wawrzyniak

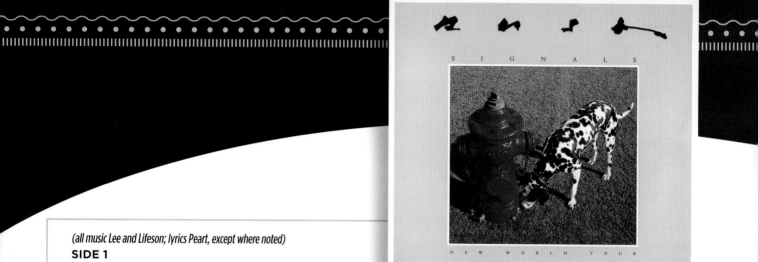

(all music Lee and Lifeson; lyrics Peart, except where noted)

SIDE 1
1 Subdivisions..5:34
2 The Analog Kid..4:47
3 Chemistry...4:56
(music Lee and Lifeson; lyrics Lee, Lifeson, and Peart)
4 Digital Man...6:23

SIDE 2
5 The Weapon...6:27
6 New World Man...3:44
7 Losing It..4:53
8 Countdown...5:48

Geddy Lee: *vocals, bass, bass pedals, Minimoog, Oberheim OB-X and OB-Xa, Roland Jupiter 8, Moog Taurus pedals, Oberheim DSX, Roland TR-808*
Alex Lifeson: *electric guitars, Moog Taurus pedals, vocals*
Neil Peart: *drums, percussion*
Ben Mink: *violin on "Losing It"*
Released September 9, 1982
Recorded at Le Studio, Morin Heights, Quebec
Produced by Rush and Terry Brown

(opposite)
**New-look Geddy on the *Signals*
tour, Wembley Arena, London,
May 20, 1983.** *Peter Still/Redferns/
Getty Images*

R ush emerged from the *Moving Pictures* album cycle energized with the possibilities of the future, most notably Neil, with his post–new wave frame of high hat–centric percussive mind, and Geddy, who would find himself constructing with his mates sturdy, sober songs in which synthesizers would usurp guitars for the main riffs, or at least participate boldly in keyboard and guitar weaves throughout many verses and choruses.

Fans would be shocked at the preponderance of new sounds on *Signals,* but unlike their reactions later in the '80s, they would be intellectually seduced, won over without incident, sending *Signals* platinum in the United States just two months after the record's September release date.

Also gone completely, for the first time, is a notably long song. The album consists of eight sensible tracks stuffed with rich lyrical themes. Neil expands on the intricacies of character (explored so splendidly on "Tom Sawyer"), celebrates various forms of nostalgia, and looks toward the future, the least abstract of these being "Countdown," about the launch of the Space Shuttle *Columbia.*

It's a bitter irony indeed that *Signals* would mark the departure, by mutual agreement, of the band's stabilizing George Martin presence, Terry Brown, who was with the band from the start. And the irony? Well, as he had already established on fully four

"Countdown" picture disc. Neil's *Signals* lyrics delve into nostalgia, but also look to the future, most notably in this track about the launch of the Space Shuttle *Columbia*.

records previous (whether he knew it or not), Brown had been really good at massaging keyboards into the burbly and bubbly power trio hive of activity. And here he was at it again, he and his technology-tinkering charges coming up with the richest, most organic, and competently blended marriage of guitars and synthesizers they would ever concoct.

And then Terry was gone—glad to be gone, but somewhat dismissed, essentially over the fact that his enthusiasm for the amount of synthesizers that Rush wanted to use (and really, we're talking about Geddy here) was lacking and thus reflected in what he could be bothered to offer using the palette now preferred by the band.

But it is somewhat surprising that, given the passage of years—years over which certain Rush albums have become pretty much agreed upon as dated—that *Signals*, with all its use of synthesizers, does not sound dated but emerges from the deep past withstanding the sands of time to become a favourite of many a deep-considering Rush fan. Neither of the *Moving Pictures* ilk nor that of *Grace Under Pressure*, *Signals* is so well regarded, in fact, that it is the rare Rush album that rejects a stylistic pairing with another Rush record—and for all the best reasons that a work of art could and should stand alone.

POPOFF: First off, how would you contrast what Rush was doing on *Signals* versus *Moving Pictures*? I mean, there's a good year-and-a half between the two, with the assembly of the band's second double live album, *Exit . . . Stage Left*. But things have changed, have they not?

NELSON: Yeah, obviously, it was a game-changer for the keyboards, which were no longer used as just part of the recipe. You could sit down at a piano and perform a version of "Subdivisions" and not much would be missed. So they really brought the keyboards to the forefront. I don't know if I should jump ahead to tracks, like "Subdivisions." And vocally, for my ears, this is the first pretty much full album where Geddy has really got away from that, I don't want to say screechy, but that kind of scream-y approach, in his vocals. It seemed like he really fell into a pocket of just singing more open, at a high range, without that screechy kind of grit.

WAWRZYNIAK: With respect to the keyboards, I definitely agree with that, and this was part of Geddy's love of electronic music at that point. He was falling in love with bands like Ultravox and Devo; all the music he was listening to was keyboard-laden. And Alex and Neil also showed a willingness to take elements of what they heard in other music and to bring it to Rush—that also ended up being represented on *Signals*. But the keyboards in *Moving Pictures* were pushed even more to the fore—to the chagrin of some fans, to the love of other fans, such as myself. To the disdain of Alex himself? He's said that he had great difficulty accepting the role that

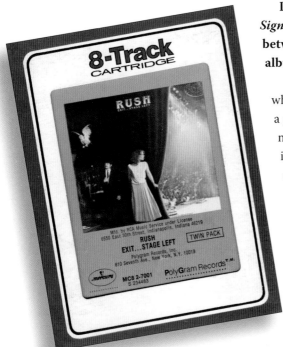

The gap between *Moving Pictures* and *Signals* was bridged by the double live LP *Exit . . . Stage Left*.

he was now almost just part of the rhythm section in the band, while the keyboards took a more vital instrumental role. Alex did some interview, and I love his line, in which he responded or referenced keyboards as just saying, "Hey, they're not even a real instrument"—I loved that.

There were other elements of *Moving Pictures* that were pushed to the fore as well. The reggae element in "Vital Signs" was pushed a little further with "Digital Man." And reaching back, the beginning of "The Analog Kid" has a similar kind of thread or progression to that at the beginning of "The Spirit of Radio," refined a bit. It kind of feels like they had some unfinished business.

POPOFF: Oddly, the most keyboard-centric song was also the album's biggest hit. What are the various charms of "Subdivisions"?

WAWRZYNIAK: "Subdivisions" is Neil exploring the background that the three of them came from, and where he thought most of Rush's fans had come from. And maybe it was that link that drew even more fans to the band. They really hit with *Moving Pictures*, with this incredibly slickly produced record, but you put a song like "Subdivisions" on there, that's going to draw in a whole new fan base, just from pure relate-ability. I'm not sure what kind of relate-ability there is to "Witch Hunt" or "Limelight" or "Red Barchetta," but is there relate-ability on "Subdivisions?" Yes. And I believe there are a lot of people who came onboard right at that era.

NELSON: Another cool element of the song is that it starts off in like a 7/4 time, and yet I think it's tangible to anybody, even the nonmusician. I've seen people happily tap along to that 7/4 groove without realizing it's in odd time. Plus I love some of the production in there. I don't know if its Terry Brown's doing, or Geddy, but I like the use of the slapback delay on parts of this album and which happens in the chorus of "Subdivisions," at which point, to my ears, the vocals just explode.

POPOFF: One song previously relegated to the status of deep album track was "Losing It," but through its inaugural play on the R40 tour, it suddenly became quite famed.

WAWRZYNIAK: Oh, my God, it's funny. Here we are in 2016 talking about something that Neil wrote lyrically in the early '80s, and I just think it resonates now. *Sadder still to watch it die / Than never to have known it.* There's just something about Neil's incredibly strong conviction of him wanting to uphold the standards that he had set for himself, the standard that Rush had set for themselves, that I think is affecting his

Moving Pictures' most enduring single explored the notion of the 'burbs. In other words, the band's background—and the backgrounds of many of their fans.

"New World Man" came about when the band realized they needed one more track to complete *Signals*.

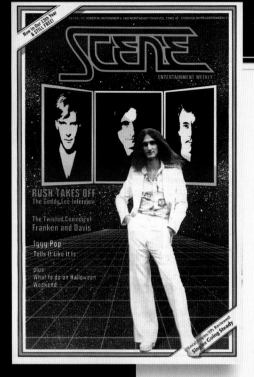

indecisiveness about continuing on with Rush. Just because of the physical labor that drumming presents. And it is sadder still to watch it die. His drum solo on this most recent tour consisted of two short aborted drum solos. Granted, we don't go to a Rush concert anymore and need to hear Neil Peart do a twelve-minute drum solo. And if you do want to hear it, pop in any DVD from the last X number of tours.

So "Losing it," that seminal line there, *Sadder still to watch it die / Than never to have known it*, has been a source of conversation for me with multiple people in recent years. I think that is so thought-provoking. You and I can sit here and have a separate conversation about, what do you think? Is it really sad to watch a baseball player lose his ability, or is it sadder to have never known it? It's so poignant. And the emotion that they ended up representing in that song . . . how they represented emotion melodically there is just a perfect marriage of music and lyrics. I was convinced that the first time I saw Rush in Toronto, March 6 of 1986, the *Power Windows* tour, and FM were opening, and I just convinced myself that violinist Ben Mink was going to come onstage and Rush was going to do "Losing It" for their hometown fans. So to be there last year when he came out and did it for the very first time was just chilling. That song is beautiful. And again, that is a song that could've polarized some people. "Losing It" doesn't sound like "Limelight," it doesn't sound like "Freewill," it doesn't sound like anything off *Hemispheres*—you're right, it doesn't.

NELSON: "Losing It" has something tangible for everybody, right? It's a perfectly written tune and there's still Rush in it. A good deal of it is in odd time. It's written in 5/8, and sneakily so, because again, I don't think people hear it like King Crimson, hard to follow. Rush make it seamless. And it's in a minor key, which lends to the melancholy theme, which is just an amazing almost in-your-face message and not much really to analyze. It's tragic that the inevitability is that everybody's gifts will start to fade eventually. And I was thinking, as a musician, they're out there, and they're playing that solo section in that tune in that odd time. It goes from like 6/8 to 5/8, and that whole thing repeats, and they're just burning, especially Neil. And it kind of speaks to the message itself, showing gifted people doing what they do.

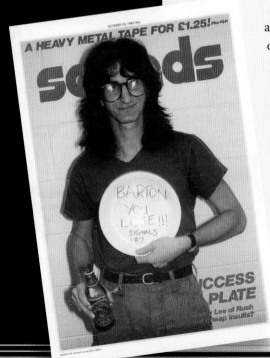

POPOFF: Besides "Subdivisions," there was another hit song on the record. "New World Man" subtly represents what I figure is one of the band's first "intentional" singles, or at least a song pushed by the record company. And yet it was an afterthought.

WAWRZYNIAK: I know that the recording sessions had finished, and they had seven songs done. They realized, okay, we've got seven songs done, we can put out an album now, but we have enough space to fit another song. So toward the end of the recording, as had become a little bit of their habit for three or four records prior, they pushed themselves to write one more song at the end. They said, "Hey, look at it. We have three fifty-seven worth of available space to use; to balance out the sides, let's see if we can come up with another song." Which they unofficially dubbed, in the studio, "Project 3:57," which ended up becoming "New World Man," with, you know, a little bit more reggae in there.

And it was a single but no video. Funnily enough, they did not play that song live for a long time. They played it on the *Signals* tour, the *Grace Under Pressure* tour, and the *Power Windows* tour, but after that *Power Windows* tour ended in April 1986, they did not play "New World Man," their biggest charting single, until the *Vapor Trails* tour began in May 2002. For sixteen years, they put this song on the shelf. And I've often wondered why. I've never heard them say anything about the song that would lead you to believe they ended up growing to not like it.

NELSON: "New World Man" features a sequenced kind of bass line on the keyboard, similar

Signals tour, Joe Louis Arena, Detroit, November 7–8, 1982.
© *Robert Alford*

to what was used on "The Weapon," but it was more of an arpeggio. The chords are pretty basic in that tune, for them. It's pretty straight-ahead, a no-frills rock tune, but they add that beautiful reggae part. And what is amazing is that they play reggae, but they play it really well. It doesn't sound like rock guys just trying to play reggae for the sake of it. Geddy's bass line is beautiful, and obviously Neil is great, and Alex is doing his thing with his super-lush chorus, and it still sounds like Alex. That's another example of that slapback delay I mentioned in "Subdivisions"—really effective.

POPOFF: How about a couple of deep album tracks each that you really cotton to and why?

WAWRZYNIAK: "Countdown" is interesting, because there was an interview that Geddy did in which he drew a parallel between "Countdown" and "Cygnus X-1" from *A Farewell to Kings*. Just in the science fiction–related nature of the song, although

"Cygnus X-1" is based on a little more fantasy than "Countdown." But it's the musical retelling of this event, of the three guys going back and forth to Cape Canaveral in Florida to watch the launching of the *Columbia* Space Shuttle. Now, they were on tour at the time of going to Cape Canaveral to watch the launching of the Space Shuttle, and they were going back and forth watching the launch, which was scrubbed, hopping on a plane, flying from Florida over to Dallas, coming back the next day to Florida, hopping back on a plane and going to San Antonio to play a show, back to Florida, back on a plane to go to Austin for a show, that sort of thing.

But it was almost like something that they had to do. Neil wrote in the bio that followed up *Signals*, "We just had to write a song about this." And funnily enough, when they went to watch the launch, the particular area at Cape Canaveral that they were seated in to watch the launch was an area called Red Sector A. And Neil liked that enough that he just jotted it down in his trusty notebook and ended up using that title on the next record, *Grace Under Pressure*, for a song called "Red Sector A." They did a video for that song that incorporated some of the footage that the staff had given them, and they incorporated it into the live performance as well. They would perform that song live, although something tells me that they ended up holding that song in a little bit of disdain, that it didn't end up being something that they ultimately liked.

But a favorite, really, of the whole catalog for me is "The Analog Kid." There's something about the majestic middle part, going from this definitive Rush rock riff to the majestic keyboards, to *You move me / You move me*. I just find that to be such a majestic part, a calling-out to where things may be better. You know, the grass may be greener. You move me, this big city that is calling out to me. You call me, this big city that is calling out to me. You may be happy with where you are, but you're wondering about where things might be even better.

POPOFF: And Chris, what are a couple you really appreciate on *Signals* among the deep tracks?

NELSON: Well, from a bass player's standpoint, we do "Chemistry," and what really sets it up for me is trying to work that part out, because the bass line is really syncopated under that vocal line. And what I mean by that is that it has pauses and stops that kind of complement the vocal. The vocal sings over these parts where the bass just stops, and that's a lot harder than it sounds [laughs]. Something like "Vital Signs," where the bass is constant, people say to me, how can you sing and play "Vital Signs" at the same time? Well, that one's a lot easier than you think, because the vocals are on the downbeat, and the bass doesn't stop, it plays right through. But "Chemistry," take a listen to that bass line [sings it]. It's really hard, man, to do the stops. So I'm always in awe of Geddy's ability for that kind of thing.

And, gosh, "Digital Man," to keep it bass-themed. That bass line is so busy, and as a musician, I'm in awe of how clean he plays those passages. They're just so beautiful. Again, in the same way "Subdivisions" could be played on a piano, "Digital Man" could be played on a bass and you would grasp the song, more so than you would just hearing the guitar chords. I think the bass really carries and acknowledges the chords at hand, under those vocal melodies he is doing.

And speaking of vocals, "The Analog Kid" has some great vocal parts. I love how that explodes at the end, without the vocal, because they go into that jam, with Alex with the octave effect on his guitar and playing that burning solo. Of course to my ears, I gravitated toward what Geddy is doing, and that's a solo in and of itself. They just burn out of that solo, and they play those big block chords, and then Geddy comes in with that higher, you know, *When I leave I don't know / What I'm hoping to find,* and it just really opens up. That's a climactic part that I think we all look forward to hearing. It's just beautifully saved—the song builds up to that part.

One last thing about "The Analog Kid." The song starts with a fast, old-school Rush guitar riff, plus Geddy is matching the guitar note-for-note with that fast riff there. And even before the vocals come in, the bass comes in to carry the tune, at about the fifteen-second mark, and it's all bass, and it's almost like a vocal line. It's the instrument carrying the tune, which keeps it interesting. So after the guitar riff, the guitar goes away and the bass becomes about the melody, and then the actual vocal melody comes in. And the keyboard sounds on that song, I think it's an Oberheim. I'm not sure, but that's what I read. And it's just got such a lush pad about it. Like the choral sound on the bridge of "The Analog Kid," I'd never heard Rush do that sound up until that point. The most keyboard-oriented tune up to that point was "The Camera Eye," from the album before. Okay, he's going somewhere with this for sure. But just the soft pad on "The Analog Kid," and that's of course in "Subdivisions" as well—just gorgeous.

Rush's insistence on focusing on new material during the *Signals* tour represented a real turning point for the band.

So yeah, I was into *Signals*, right away. I don't know if that's the album where a lot of people say they jumped ship because of the keyboards, but again, against my ears and my tastes, I just loved it. I loved the warmth of it. And you know, how many albums did they do leading up to this? I don't want to say there's only so many rock riffs, because Rush always find a way to be different, but it was just a treat as a fan to hear them in this new dimension.

POPOFF: Ray, I'm intrigued about this theory you have that it's not so much *Signals* itself but the tour for *Signals* that really catapulted the band into the '80s.

WAWRZYNIAK: Yes, it was a humongous turning point for them. Here's *Moving Pictures*, a record that thirty-five years later everybody still holds in high regard, as well they should. *Moving Pictures* is a flawless record. They had reached this new state of popularity, and so it would've been easy for them to go into the recording for *Signals* and just do *Moving Pictures Part II*. But just like Fleetwood Mac did when they said, "Look, we're not going to do *Rumours Part II*," and they went in and did this crazy follow-up record called *Tusk*, which polarized a lot of people—the same way Rush did with *Signals*. It was a polarizing record because they were pushing the boundaries in so many ways. But yes, what I really think took it to even the next level, if I may, is the supporting tour. And that's where I'm ready to go out on my rant. May I?

Signals tour, Ahoy Sportpaleis, Rotterdam, May 3, 1983. *Rob Verhorst/Redferns/Getty Images*

Geddy rehearses with blues great Buddy Guy and drummer Bobby Chouinard for the S.I.R. Studios benefit, New York City, July 15, 1983. *Ebet Roberts/Redferns/ Getty Images*

POPOFF: Yes you may!

WAWRZYNIAK: Okay, well, on the new world tour, they played, officially, seven out of eight songs on the record, except for "Losing It." The set list on the *Signals* tour was just so different, where for so many tours before that, from *2112* up to and including *Moving Pictures*, they were playing large banks of *2112*, large banks of *Hemispheres*, large banks of, you know, "Cygnus X-1" from *A Farewell to Kings*.

The *Signals* tour, they completely revamped their set list in such a way that it was, to me, a real dividing point, of them saying, "Look, this new record that we just put out is admittedly a brand-new and different Rush record. And we want to continue that thematically with a brand-new show." I mean, right from the beginning, they came out on stage to the opening strains of the *Three Stooges* theme that they ended up using many multiple times on subsequent tours. But even that little comedic element was different. Their presentation of "2112" on the *Signals* tour included their bastardized version of the lyrics where the priests of the temples of Syrinx became, in the chorus the second time around, *We are the plumbers who fix your sinks*. Which I just think was them saying, "I know we still gotta play this song, but good God, we've moved on."

And it was only six years between *2112* and *Signals*, but somehow they just couldn't play that with the same conviction. And so here they are in the previous tour, *Moving Pictures*, opening up with "2112" and playing a large part of side one of *2112* to open up the show. Now "2112" is toward the end, still in the regular set proper, but just "Overture" and "The Temples of Syrinx" with these comedic lyrics.

There was no sign of . . . no "Working Man," nothing from *Fly by Night*. *Caress of Steel*'s long hiatus was now beginning . . . I mean, nothing from the opening side one suite of *Hemispheres*. No "Cygnus" from *A Farewell to Kings*. Here are seven songs from *Signals*. You've still got four or five songs from *Moving Pictures*. There are two or three songs from *Permanent Waves*. It was a very newly laden material set list and so different from what they had done. Yeah, I really have a strong conviction about the tour itself being a real turning point for them at that point in their career, where, you're right, usually we focus on the record.

CHAPTER 10

Grace Under Pressure

with Douglas Maher, Jim Matheos, and Chris Nelson

(all music Lee and Lifeson; lyrics Peart)

SIDE 1

1	Distant Early Warning	4:45
2	Afterimage	5:00
3	Red Sector A	5:08
4	The Enemy Within	4:33

SIDE 2

5	The Body Electric	4:58
6	Kid Gloves	4:16
7	Red Lenses	4:39
8	Between the Wheels	5:36

Geddy Lee: *lead vocals, bass, synthesizers*
Alex Lifeson: *guitars*
Neil Peart: *drums, electric drums, percussion*
Released April 12, 1984
Recorded at Le Studio, Morin Heights, Quebec
Produced by Rush and Peter Henderson

With the departure of Terry Brown, Rush essentially left the analog warmth of the '70s behind. Even if *Signals* is defined forevermore by its keyboards, there was a charming, homespun antique-y quality to the record. On *Grace Under Pressure*, conversely, the band emerges squinting and snowblind onto the dystopian expanse depicted on Hugh Syme's harsh album cover, steeled for engagement within and sometimes against a new world.

And they traipsed into this unforgiving landscape essentially on their own, decrying the lack of direction given to them by last-minute production choice Peter Henderson, the guys feeling that most aspects of constructing this album constituted a grind they had to live through alone.

The end result is a record that the band—at least after they had shook the memories of its tortuous making—find fiercely artistically satisfying. From a musical point of view, what was a struggle between Alex and Geddy's new electronic toys on *Signals* is now a heroic battle between two bold adversaries. Alex has gamely embraced the '80s and has found a way to cut through in tandem with Geddy, surging ahead with keyboards that do the same. So both have vigorously modernized, as has Neil, who has integrated electronic drums into his repertoire, the most impactful visual of that being the percussionist and his Simmons kit (albeit behind him and not used!) as depicted in the memorable "Distant Early Warning" video.

And speaking of that apocalyptic opening track, "Distant Early Warning" would be the closest thing to a hit single on this album. Testimony to Rush and its legions, *Grace Under Pressure* immediately went platinum, with the maturing fan base tacitly telling the music industry that there still is a place for the album-length experience.

That is not to say, of course, that Rush had gone back to epic-of-girth tracks, but that *Grace Under Pressure* arguably constitutes the first of the band's conceptually compact record of otherwise quite individual songs. A considerably consensus world built from Neil's eight visions (four on the original vinyl's side one, and four on side two) is one of man versus machine, or the very real life-and-death struggles we go through within various machine-like constructs. In fact, one might call *Grace Under Pressure* the afterimage of The Police's *Ghost in the Machine*.

Again, to reiterate, from the album cover art inside and out, through the austere photography of the guys by the esteemed Yousuf Karsh, through the flashy and action-packed song titles themselves, the environment suggested is cold, mechanical, and futuristic. But also transcendable, with Neil declaring a war of words on the obscuring

Filming "The Enemy Within" video, Battersea, London, April 1984. *Fin Costello/Redferns/ Getty Images*

complexity of modern life, accompanied by a soundtrack of battle music that just might result in victories at the hands of our story's heroes, however merely "moral" and fleeting those victories might be.

POPOFF: *Grace Under Pressure* didn't get off on the right foot, with producer Steve Lillywhite backing out of the project.

MAHER: Yes, well they were absolutely dead set for Lillywhite to come in and take on *Grace*, the duties for production. And really, it was a last-minute cancelation, a back-out, that left Rush kind of hanging, more or less. I mean, in the studio itself, literally waiting for Lillywhite to arrive, within days. And he just decided to back out of the project and wound up, of course, dedicating more time to U2, Simple Minds, and Big Country.

So that was a real catastrophe on their hands. Essentially, this was their big leap that they were trying to make, to break away from Terry Brown, and prove that they were this massive world popular band, selling out multiple arenas in every country and whatnot. And this was them kind of putting on their own pants and saying, hey, you know, we can do this, and I'm ninety-nine percent positive that we can get a list of producers who will be breaking down the door to work with us.

It just wasn't the case at the time. A lot of people just didn't want to work with them. They didn't understand them, and they were confused in interviews by the direction that Rush wanted to go in. And it wasn't necessarily a sense that Rush wanted to become this big keyboard band, or an overly synth-pop '80s band. They really wanted to have a fresh perspective, other than Terry Brown. So the search for a producer really wound up more or less Rush doing *Grace Under Pressure* themselves, and then kind of having Peter Henderson come in, really halfway through.

They had no problem feeding their influences, their sound, with anything that inspired them, whether it was synths, whether it was a new wave style of guitar or an Andy Summers reggae-esque guitar that you can hear in "The Enemy Within," which you are hearing, actually, all over *Signals*, and had started more or less back on "Vital Signs."

So it became a very daunting task for them that they felt, essentially, that they were a band that could not get somebody to work with them. A lot of people were intimidated. They just didn't know what to do with them. So Peter Henderson basically came in to put the cherry on top, turned some knobs, cleaned up some areas here and there, but really offered very, very little in the way of difference from what Rush had already recorded and written themselves. So if anything, if there was a first Rush self-produced project, it would be *Grace Under Pressure*.

Rush left behind analog warmth, emerging into a harsh, dystopian world.

POPOFF: Jim, being a guitarist, you say that Alex is well accounted for on this album, even though we are famously in Rush's keyboard phase.

MATHEOS: Yes, I guess this falls right in the middle of the keyboard era, but still the guitars are very present. It's actually a really guitar-heavy record if you look at it in the right way. He's just not playing as blatantly and obvious as he does on some of the more rock records. He's not playing full bar chords; he's being a lot more inventive in his open chords and his high treble chords, which was something that was totally new again, to me.

Take a song like "Bastille Day," where he's just playing these three-string chords, D, B, E. He's playing fifths, basically, playing power chords all the way through it. There are some open chords in the chorus where he's kind of strumming, but on *Grace Under Pressure*, there's a lot of chords where he's just playing the top three strings or the top four strings, these high kind of more rhythm and blues–type things with full distortion. And for a lot of his soloing, he's doing a lot of chord soloing, which is very interesting. So yeah, I think they really reinvented themselves on this record, but Alex most of all.

POPOFF: And how would you characterize the production of *Grace Under Pressure*?

MATHEOS: I love the production on it. The guitar sounded amazing to me. In fact, I started getting into this record around '87, when I first went back to it and fell in love with it. And I loved the guitar sound so much that we [Fates Warning] found out that he was using these Gallien-Krueger amps, a pretty new brand on the scene at that time, and we went out and bought a whole backline of Gallien-Krueger amps for bass, guitar, and cabinets, before we went out on the *No Exit* tour, because I loved that sound so much. Still didn't sound close, but they looked the same [laughs].

MAHER: I would honestly say that the production captures 1984, that year in music, perfectly. You really saw it in Geddy, when he broke out his Steinberger bass, for instance, which made an appearance on the *Signals* tour. And then as far as the album was concerned, for *Grace Under Pressure*, that was really its first true appearance. On there you saw Geddy playing nearly as free and as flawlessly as he had ever played.

The Rickenbacker is a very heavy bass. And most certainly a double-neck is like carrying an elephant on your back, when you're playing live. So when you have a bass that, like the Steinberger, it's something that you could literally swing around, you know, if you wanted to do like a Juan Croucier from Ratt [laughs]. If he wanted to do that, he could have, although that's not Geddy-esque. But the sound that Geddy was achieving at that point brought us more into where he was taking us for the rest of the '80s and early '90s, which was this jazzier tonal sound, with the funk slap into it, which you hear in "Red Lenses" and "Body Electric" and whatnot.

"Distant Early Warning" Japanese picture disc.

Battersea, London, April 1984.
Fin Costello/Redferns/Getty Images

As far as the keyboard sounds, you would have to go back and listen to the British music sound, the UK sound, of that time. I absolutely can hear keyboard sounds in a Spandau Ballet song that I now hear in a Rush song. And yet Alex Lifeson's guitar work is absolutely blistering on this record.

Neil's high-hat work became more identifiable. You started hearing that really taking off in songs like "The Weapon" on *Signals*, where you really started hearing the nuances. They were no longer being multi-tracked over and over and over with a million different sounds going on, as you are hearing on, say, *Hemispheres* or *Permanent Waves* and *Farewell to Kings*. Neil's sound became more simplified, with the Simmons electronics. He was really recognizing at that point, that carrying around and lugging around an enormous drum kit, as far as the multi-percussion instruments are concerned, behind him, was something that he was growing out of, that he was maturing from. Live, he still carried some percussion like glockenspiel, chimes, temple blocks, and crotales.

POPOFF: So where are we hearing electronic drums on here?
MAHER: Well, you had "Red Sector A," of course, which is completely electronic, all the way around. And you have that also being a song that Geddy does not bring his bass out at all on. And as far as pure electronic drums, you're hearing those on "Red Lenses" as well—no acoustic drums, other than bass and snare. But he only used the rear kit on those two songs exclusively. And you saw Neil being influenced by Africa and African drumming. You hear it inside of the middle solo section of "Red Lenses."

POPOFF: Does the record feel thematically cohesive to you?
MATHEOS: Yes, it seems to be a very dark record. There are references to the Cold War and also some environmental things, which I think is what "Distant Early Warning" is partially about. "Red Sector A," there seemed to be some Holocaust references in there. Honestly, I don't know what it's about, but I love the way the lyrics sound. Sometimes to me that's more important in the end, what it sounds like rather than what they're trying to get across, how the lyrics fit the melody. That song stands out for me the most in that regard.

Japanese print ad for
Grace Under Pressure.

NELSON: "Red Sector A" is extremely moving. You know, these rock stars you listen to your whole life, that provided the soundtrack for your life—you know how near and dear that whole thing is to Geddy, as a son of Holocaust survivors. So you connect in that sense. It's like, as a friend you've never met. It's very moving, and this is what you want in a song.

POPOFF: But I suppose the song that has stood the biggest test of time is "Distant Early Warning."

NELSON: Yes, which has just amazing bass. And I'm not talking so much under the verses, but under the chorus. You see a pattern that I like with Rush. They come out of that burning section, at the end of "Distant," especially live, back into that chorus, and you just hear how hyped they are and excited to play that. That's a great live song because the vocal goes up at the end. It's definitely a pattern of like, okay, verse, bridge, verse, bridge, chorus, you know, guitar solo, everybody is burning, and then exit with those big Who-like chords, and then a climactic vocal part—that makes an amazing Rush tune.

But also "Kid Gloves" sticks out for me, because I just love that guitar solo and it's in an odd time. "Body Electric," that's like one of the funnest tunes we [Lotus Land] do as a band. Kind of sign of the times—Geddy's experimenting with an '80s kind of bass popping up front. But he never loses his identity—he's still Geddy Lee, and he does his traditional finger-style stuff for the rest of the tune.

MAHER: Well, to me the most important song on the record is "Afterimage," which was written about Robbie Whalen, an engineer of theirs, who had died in a car accident leaving Le Studio. And when you're a child or a teenager, your concept of death really hasn't been fully developed. You're still naïve. When you hear that song at a much younger age, you're not as appreciative of the lyrical context as you are as an adult. Me, personally, that song and this album was released in 1984, and my father died in 1985, and I was only eleven years old. And so the song itself, to hear the words, *Suddenly— / You were gone / From all the lives / You left your mark upon / I remember,* was special.

You really get the feeling that Neil is starting to come out of his shell in allowing not so much this clinical state of lyric writing. You saw that start to develop in "Circumstances," plus "Entre Nous" and "Limelight." Little by little, he would give you little pieces, his personal feelings, regarding whether it was your mental state or emotional state or, in this sense, your grieving state. And that took a tremendous amount of pain, and it definitely affected him tremendously. Hence the title of the record, *Grace Under Pressure*.

German print advertising for *Grace Under Pressure* **and contemporary releases.**

POPOFF: Could you expound on that a little more, the concept behind the title?

MAHER: The idea is how fragile life is, being very graceful. And that's where the symbolism of the egg in the vise comes from, to represent how fragile life is, and how heightened the pressures are of the world around it. It's a chaotic scene, that gorgeous album cover that you see, done by Hugh Syme. You see this graceful being, and it's kind of up for debate whether it's . . . the android that is represented in "The Body Electric" looking out onto this almost serene, placid ocean. And you see this drop of water, almost, that is there, and you see a chaotic storm that is brewing up on top, and this guy that is peeking out at you. It's a very evil eye, if you will. And again, you get this real sense of how quick everything can change, just how fragile we all are and the circumstances in which we all are living in.

And the lyrical context of the record reflects that in nearly every song. I would probably say every single song, whether you have Neil saying, in "Distant Early Warning," *I see the tip of the iceberg— / And I worry about you*. If you see the video of "Afterimage," it's the child mourning over the sudden death of his mother, and he's patting his mother's hand as her body is laid out, and he doesn't understand it. He's completely naïve to . . . he thinks that she is still asleep. And the theme of the song is this just can't be understood. Death can't be understood. And the fact that things can be just moving along so normally, and all of a sudden, it's just gone.

"Red Sector A" is another one that's extremely important, which is about the fight for survival in a concentration camp. And again, Neil opens certain doors on records, and without people really recognizing it, he never really fully shuts that door. He keeps that conversation open in later songs, on other albums. Like "Heresy" on *Roll the Bones*, where he asks, *All those precious wasted years—Who will pay?* It was about communism and the wall coming down and Berlin, and all these millions of lives had been lost and changed, and who will pay?

And then you have "The Enemy Within," which deals with fear. And that was the original ending of "Fear," as Neil had executed it to be part of the "Fear Trilogy," with "The Weapon" and "Witch Hunt." And it's really about getting into one's own psyche and dealing with your nerves and your suspicions. Essentially, you can be your own worst enemy in life.

Battersea, London, April 1984. *Fin Costello/Redferns/Getty Images*

POPOFF: Speaking of communism, a curious one on here is "Red Lenses"—really, to mix metaphors, the red-headed stepchild of the album, like "I Think I'm Going Bald."

MAHER: Right [laughs]. Again, you're dealing with the Soviet Union, the red scare, and you're dealing with a lot of seeing life through rose-colored lenses. I don't really think that anybody who listened to "Red Lenses" who was a fan of Rush in 1977, went, "Oh yeah, yeah, this is where I'm at." No, "Red Lenses" is an absolute acquired taste and nothing more than an acquired taste. You have to be able to be open-minded enough to hear Geddy Lee doing scat, you know, a jazz scat with jazz and fusion and funk bass going on.

You have to be able to appreciate Neil doing what would be considered almost silly-like fusion—on electronic drums that he is just becoming familiar with. But he mastered it. That was the amazing thing about Neil's playing at that point. And to this day, oddly enough, even though they don't hold the song "Red Lenses" high as far as popularity or favorites, drummers love that song. What you see and what you get about "Red Lenses" is nothing but pure musicianship and how they play with each other—it's a jam session. And nobody really takes anything lyrically from that song to heart, or to mind. It's more or less beat poetry about Soviet nuclear ambitions and the fear that is portrayed in North America about that. It's not a song that goes into any other philosophical quarters or anything like that. If you're using it in context with anything else, you think of "Tai Shan" from *Hold Your Fire*, and you lump them together as Rush's experimental songs that they gave us.

POPOFF: Chris, as the keyboardist/bassist/singer in a Rush tribute band, you've had an interesting time grappling with the keyboard sounds on this record.

NELSON: Yes, I suppose in comparison to *Signals*, I'd say there was a lot more pulsating. For example, the way "The Weapon" had the arpeggiated pulses for the center, they use that more and more on *Grace*. "The Body Electric" especially has a lot of that stuff, and obviously "Distant Early Warning" with that big '80s sound. I think it's a Yamaha DX-7 he played on that; something like that, but yeah, beautiful tune.

I've got to say, my buddies were into that sound; at least they said they were. I wasn't super-excited about it at the time. I liked *Signals*, keyboard-oriented as it was, and beautifully so. Whereas *Grace Under Pressure*, it might have been the sounds themselves, of those keyboards at the time. Sounds have come so far, and you would think when the sounds were

Hotshot producer Steve Lillywhite backed out of *Grace Under Pressure* at the last minute. *Ebet Roberts/Redferns/Getty Images*

Rush point-of-purchase display.

new, at the time people would be excited about them. And they were for the most part. But I wasn't excited about those kinds of keyboards. And this is sacrilegious to say, they sounded like they could be in a Madonna song or something—they didn't resonate with me as well.

So I would say those smooth keyboards on *Signals* have dated better. That said, I have come to really appreciate *Grace Under Pressure*, and I can be nostalgic about these tones. I've leaned on those songs for so long now, I've had time to grow into them. In fact, I would be almost offended to hear those keyboards replaced, with like a newer, hipper sound [laughs].

POPOFF: Again, the record's lyrics evoke futurism as well, and maybe none more so than "The Body Electric," with its "1-0-0-1-0-0-1" chorus.

MAHER: Neil was absolutely enthralled with, at that point, computers and the theme of *1984* itself. Where were we going with this? In the video, by the same director that was used for "The Enemy Within," you have this android, robot-controlled culture and society that was very futuristic and spacelike, and yet it wasn't that far off, as far as where they were coming from. It was about computers and technology coming into your life and taking control of it. You can't release an album in 1984 and not address the George Orwell book, *1984*.

And as this is going on, you've got other dystopian themes, as in the "Distant Early Warning" video where there's a kid that is replaying out *Dr. Strangelove* on this rocket. And again, it's a symbol of future generations. Everybody was concerned about outspending the Russians, making them broke by outspending them militarily, and building more nuclear weapons than they could. You saw a lot of people concerned about this, especially Neil, and that's why he puts it in his writing: *Who can face the knowledge / That the truth is not the truth? / Obsolete / Absolute.* You have a whole panic feeling that is going on there.

And the album ends up with "Between the Wheels," where you have this boy figure, this generational figure, that Neil seems to carry on and talk about. And Neil has never *not* had a character in his albums, in his writings. In "Kid Gloves" he's talking about peer pressure and what you're facing, and how we don't live under the Golden Rule anymore. I mean, what is the Golden Rule?

And to wind it up with "Between the Wheels" and talking about lost generations. . . . All of these things that Neil is trying to express to us—like in "Distant Early Warning," he's saying "Red alert, red alert." Neil saw a lot of things to be afraid of and that we should appreciate what we have around us. Or that we should appreciate each other and that we should appreciate the planet.

Neil was doing a lot of the stuff that a lot of people did ten or twenty years later—except he's not a public guy. He's not going to be Bono. He's not going to go up there and make political statements on stage. Or he's not going to be Peter Gabriel. He's not going

Pretty tough to release an album in 1984 and not address George Orwell. Dystopian themes abound in *Grace Under Pressure.*

to go do the Amnesty International stuff. Neil is the type of guy who's going to put that in his lyrics and is going to write a check. That's how he does things. He sends checks out. He's a big philanthropist as far as how he feels and as far as his passionate beliefs go.

POPOFF: Jim, in closing, even though it took you a while to come around, *Grace Under Pressure* is now one of your favorite Rush albums, correct?

MATHEOS: Yes, and I have to be honest with you, I didn't really get into this record until, probably '86 or '87. I'd lost touch with what was going on in the broader sense. I was really immersed in metal at that time and what our band was doing. I was the heavy metal kid in 1984, and Rush seemed to have lost *that* plot, for sure.

That's why when I did go back to *Grace Under Pressure*, to me it was so fresh. Like I said, it took me a while to understand what was going on. And now, going back to LPs, the first side of that record is probably one of my favorite Rush sides. All four songs on that side are amazing. For my taste, there's probably a little dip in quality on side two. But it's made up by the last two songs, especially "Between the Wheels," which is maybe—although not as blatantly—one of the heaviest Rush songs that I can think of.

But I appreciate that Rush went on to new areas, which at first, I didn't do. They should be congratulated for that, for pushing the boundaries and not doing the same prog records over and over again. And once I opened my mind, it led me into all kinds of directions that I never thought I would be led into, and for that I'm deeply appreciative.

Grace Under Pressure **tour, Great Western Forum, Los Angeles, May 29, 1984.** *Marc S Canter/Michael Ochs Archive/Getty Images*

CHAPTER 11

Power Windows

with Mike Portnoy and Robert Telleria

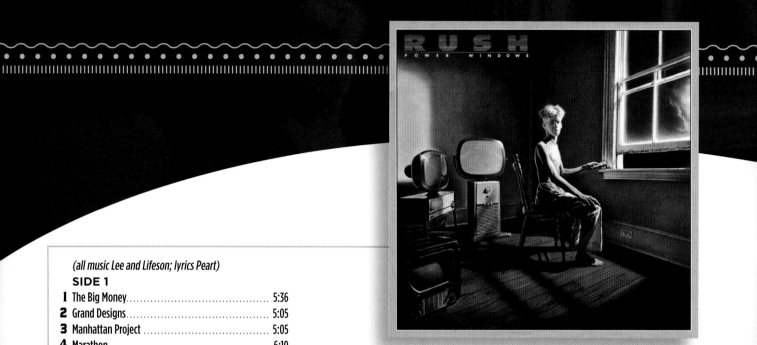

(all music Lee and Lifeson; lyrics Peart)

SIDE 1

1	The Big Money	5:36
2	Grand Designs	5:05
3	Manhattan Project	5:05
4	Marathon	6:10

SIDE 2

5	Territories	6:19
6	Middletown Dreams	5:17
7	Emotion Detector	5:10
8	Mystic Rhythms	5:46

Geddy Lee: *lead vocals, bass, bass pedals, synthesizers*
Alex Lifeson: *guitars*
Neil Peart: *drums, percussion*
Andy Richards: *additional keyboards*
Jim Burgess: *additional synthesizers*
Anne Dudley: *string arrangement*
Andrew Jackman: *conductor, choir arrangements*
The Choir: *additional vocals*
Released October 15, 1985
**Recorded at The Manor Studio, Oxfordshire, England;
Sarm East Studios, London; Angel Studios, London; Abbey
Road Studios, London; and Air Montserrat, Montserrat
Produced by Peter Collins and Rush**

(opposite)
**Alex's wiry guitar served the jagged
geometric angles and airless spaces
of *Power Windows*. Fin Costello/
Redferns/Getty Images**

For all the furrowed brows upon the fan base's faces whilst listening to *Grace Under Pressure*, the record still felt, in its architecture, the work of a power trio, with keyboards up top. That all changed with *Power Windows*, which shocked the public with geometric and jagged angles; confined, airless spaces; and wiry guitar bent to be no more than equal with all manner of keyboard sound as Geddy and surprise guest newcomer Andy Richards gang up on a pliable Alex until his axe could only squawk.

Written somewhat the same way as in the past, in a Canadian country retreat, songs were further worked on as the band left Elora Sound to conduct a warmup tour starting in Florida. Neil worked in his Miami hotel room on some lyrics while Geddy mused about new toys, and by the time the band arrived at The Manor in Oxfordshire, England, they were well rehearsed enough to come up with the most high-tech album of their career—that is to say, high-tech for the mid-'80s, but twenty years later, just dated (there's a lesson in here somewhere).

The band was now working with Peter Collins, along with engineer Jim Barton, who together delivered a hard, precise, futuristic sound for this eyes-forward band of possibility-seekers. Burning through the money, Rush also worked at Air Studios in Montserrat and Sarm East in London, then commandeering a

With *Power Windows*, Rush forsook power in favor of ear candy—a certain type of songwriting without ego.

thirty-piece orchestra in Studio One at Abbey Road along with a twenty-five-piece choir at Angel Studios, as always with this sort of thing, because they could.

The end result sounded as expensive as all that sounds, but greatly lacked in power, which was the intention all along, Rush deciding that their priorities were more about ear candy, a certain type of songwriting without ego, while still being progressive, just more subtly. Also subtle was Neil's approach to the idea of concept, which he liked, and concept albums, which one assumes he didn't, because Rush hadn't done one yet. Ergo, *Power Windows* was conceptual like *Moving Pictures* and *Grace Under Pressure* were, and not so much *Permanent Waves* or *Signals*—that is to say loosely but still deliberately, with Neil looking at different forms of power.

Power Windows reached number ten on the Billboard charts and achieved platinum status, the last (at least officially—long story) until Rush would have somewhat of a late-career surprise hit with *Roll the Bones*, which in turn would be the last platinum album Rush would notch.

POPOFF: I guess to start with, Mike, you guys were forming Dream Theater right when *Power Windows* is coming out. What did you think of that record at the time?

PORTNOY: To be honest, they started to lose me around that period. I do love the *Power Windows* album today—it's actually a great album—but, '85, '86, my musical tastes were going more in the metal direction, toward bands like Metallica and Slayer and Megadeth, and the whole thrash movement that was coming around. But of course, once a Rush fan, always a Rush fan. I always kept tabs on what they were doing, and always checked out the albums, and always saw them on the tours. But I wasn't, at that stage of my life, an obsessive Rush freak like I was during the *Hemispheres*, *Permanent Waves*, *Moving Pictures*, and *Signals* time. It was the late '70s, early '80s, where I was completely obsessive. But come the mid-'80s, once their sound got a little more streamlined with keyboards, I still followed them and kept tabs on them, but my musical taste was changing as well.

I don't know, I think it's just the next logical album. *Grace Under Pressure* was the first one there, where they were really experimenting with keyboards, and the guitar was taking a back seat to the keyboards. Which, to be honest, was something that didn't appeal to me. But I like *Power Windows* better than *Grace Under Pressure*. For some reason, I think they got the balance a little bit better there than they did on *Grace Under Pressure* or really *Signals*, for that matter. Yeah, for some reason, of all the post–*Moving Pictures* albums, *Power Windows* is one of my favorites.

But you're right about Dream Theater. We were at Berklee College of Music in Boston, and that was the album that came out when we formed Dream Theater. Myself, John Petrucci, and John Myung were all Rush fanatics, and that was the album that came out when the three of us were together and had already formed the embryo of Dream Theater. And we went and saw them on that tour at the Worcester Centrum.

Alex and Geddy on the *Power Windows* tour, 1986. *Chris Walter/ WireImage/Getty Images*

And, you know, back then, to get concert tickets, it wasn't like it is now, where you can just wake up at ten in the morning on Saturday and go to your computer and punch in a number and have your tickets. In the '80s, you would have to sleep in line the night before at your local Ticketmaster or Ticketron to get tickets, so we were sleeping out for tickets to go see Rush on the *Power Windows* tour. And that was when we came up with the name Majesty, which we used briefly before Dream Theater. We were listening to Rush on the boom box, and came up with the name Majesty. We were listening to "Bastille Day," and at the end of that, we were saying, "Oh, that's really majestic." And that's when we came up with the name Majesty. . . . And I believe Marillion was the opening band; they were touring off the *Misplaced Childhood* album. And seeing that tour at the Worcester Centrum . . . it was just amazing.

POPOFF: I guess the lack of crunch at the guitar end shocked a lot of people, but the light production didn't help either, did it?

TELLERIA: Yes, it was a brighter album, a poppier album, but it was an overproduced album. Honestly, it's not the best-produced album. A lot of people have said it's such a perfect balance. I don't think so. I think it's lacking a bottom to it. It's lacking in a lot of meat, and for lack of a better term, balls. Which is a problem we had on the Rupert Hine–produced *Roll the Bones*. It sometimes happens. But it's Peter Collins who became a better producer a couple albums later with Queensrÿche's *Empire* and Suicidal Tendencies and other bands—including Rush, including *Counterparts*. He was a way better producer by then.

I think his arrangements, knowledge, expertise . . . he had been working with artists that had very little in common with Rush before then. Like Jermaine Stewart. Do you

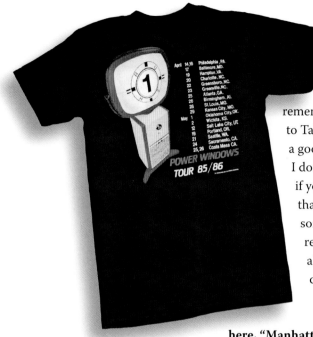

remember who Jermaine Stewart was? He had a song called "We Don't Have to Take Our Clothes Off." Kind of a funk, urban single. But Peter Collins was a good orchestrator. So the parts of the songs sound very well orchestrated. I don't mean in an orchestra sense—I mean it in a composition sense. So if you listen to the demo for "Manhattan Project," they presented it as . . . that was one of the few demos that leaked out, due to Justin Lifeson, Alex's son. But basically, the song was a reggae song. It was just an out-and-out reggae. And if you listen to the final "Manhattan Project," it sounds a little, almost Air Supply in the beginning there. And, well, here comes—by no coincidence—Peter Collins, who worked with Air Supply just before that.

POPOFF: Yes, let's talk about a couple of the marquee songs on here, "Manhattan Project" and "Marathon" fitting that description, I suppose.

PORTNOY: Yes, I love "Manhattan Project" and "Marathon." Those had some really cool progressive elements. Although, first, here's a subtle thing about the ending of "Grand Designs." I absolutely love the accents that were going on with the drums and bass through that whole phrase at the end of "Grand Designs." I thought that was really creative. I don't think Geddy and Neil repeated a rhythmic pattern once. They're doing these different rhythmic patterns every bar, and each one of them is completely different from the last, and that was always a big challenge, to air-drum the ending of that song.

But "Manhattan Project" and "Marathon" . . . I think that was the first time they'd worked with an orchestra, and strings, if I remember correctly, and I thought that was a really cool element and a really cool addition to their arsenal. The real strings made everything sound that much more majestic. Those two songs were a little progressive, with their odd time signatures. I guess those were the two epics off of *Power Windows*, which was a more commercial album, in general.

But I still really love the production on that album. First album produced by Peter Collins. The production, although it was very clean and pristine, was very deep as well; there was a lot of sound and texture in there. More so than on any other Rush album up until that point. Albums like *Permanent Waves* and *Moving Pictures*, as much as I love those albums and they're my favorites in their catalog, they are pretty basic productions. You know, Terry Brown is a big part of their sound for all those years, but the albums basically sounded like a live band. You're just hearing guitar, bass, and drums, with an occasional keyboard on top, and Geddy's vocals. Pretty straightforward production. For

Neill Cunningham, owner of Toronto's Pandemonium Records and the model who appeared on the cover of *Power Windows*, poses with a Rush record-store display on the occasion of the album's thirtieth anniversary. *Carlos Osorio/Toronto Star via Getty Images*

Power Windows, to me, that was the deepest, lushest production they ever had, at that point. It was the sort of album that you would listen to with headphones and hear lots of different things going on. A big part of that was the keyboards, but Peter Collins's production I thought was really top-notch.

POPOFF: So who is inspiring Neil at this point as a drummer?

TELLERIA: Well that's a great question. You know, if you listen to a song like "Grand Designs," or even "Manhattan Project," it sounds like he would be influenced by Omar Hakim, who was the drummer for Sting at the time, and Sting had a big solo year in 1985. And I'm kind of hearing, possibly, some Terry Bozzio, from Missing Persons. Because, I'm hearing quarter-note patterns and attempts at ostinato patterns, and they're just brief. I mean, I say attempts, but they're executed well. I'm hearing polyrhythmic things that he probably picked up from Peter Gabriel's drummer, Manu Katché. So again, parasitic, and Neil would be the first to admit. I remember those old *Modern Drummer* interviews where he lists his influences, and, boy, he liked everybody on the scene back then in the '80s. So he's definitely influenced by the contemporary modern rock/alternative rock kind of guys. And as far as his kit, you know, he wasn't doing the roundhouse fills much, on that, or double bass.

PORTNOY: I wasn't on board with the electronic drums. The first time I saw him incorporate the electronic drums was the end of the *Signals* tour. It wasn't even the *Signals* tour. It was these one-off shows that they played at Radio City Music Hall in New York City. It was actually after *Signals* and before *Grace Under Pressure*. And at the shows, they premiered three songs that were to be on the *Grace Under Pressure* album. And for "Red Sector A" and "Red Lenses," Neil was playing on this electronic kit behind him. But he didn't have the spinning drum riser. So he actually played those two songs with his back to the audience.

I remember, I'd snuck in a tape recorder to that show and bootlegged my own copy of the show, just so I could listen to those three songs over and over and over before the album was released. So I was familiar with those three songs when *Grace Under Pressure* was finally released. But to be honest, the electronic kit thing never really appealed to me. In my years of drumming, I've never incorporated any of that myself. But I know it's always been a great outlet for Neil, and he's always embraced it and utilized it in very creative ways. But for me, personally, it was never my cup of tea.

POPOFF: What about Neil's inspiration on you as a drummer/lyricist?

PORTNOY: Yeah, that as well. I can't think of many other drummers in the '70s who were writing the band's

Print ad heralds the "extraordinary tracks" "Marathon" and "Manhattan Project." The songs added an orchestra to Rush's arsenal.

ALL ACCESS

NEIL PEART SEMINAR
May 5, 1986
Presented By
THE **PERCUSSION CENTER**
Fort Wayne, Indiana
OTTO

Neil admittedly soaked up contemporary influences in the 1980s.

"The Big Money" continued a Rush tradition of leading off albums with big singles.

lyrics, and then after that, Phil Collins became one and Don Henley became one. But at the time I can't think of any other drummers who were writing all of the lyrics for their bands. So he was definitely the blueprint for that. As a part-time lyricist myself, he was a big inspiration, having such a big voice and being a big part of the songs beyond just the drumming.

POPOFF: And back to "Marathon," Robert, any comment on that one?

TELLERIA: "Marathon," that should've been the Olympics theme. It was a year too late. "Marathon" is just such a timeless song; thematically, that one has all the ingredients of a Rush blockbuster. You have the compelling bass line, and really, it's not the same all the way through. It's altered just enough in the second verse and stanza to make it interesting. And, boy, even just the last couple lines, *You could do a lot in a lifetime if you don't burn out too fast*. You could apply that to the band. They certainly did that. So it's very prophetic, even for them. It's really practicing what they preach on that. And, yeah, it's a very loud recording. You play something like those *Retrospective* CDs, where you have different samplings from different Rush albums, and you have like a *Grace Under Pressure* song and then you have a *Signals* song, then it's like, *bang*, you gotta turn your stereo down, it's recorded so loud and ferocious.

POPOFF: And why does "Middletown Dreams" seem to connect with so many people?

TELLERIA: Because of clever lines like *The middle-aged madonna / Calls her neighbour on the phone / Day by day the seasons pass / And leave her life alone.* And then we find that she is going to eventually leave where she is, but only in her imagination because she's just painting these scenes from a lonely attic room. She never has, you know, the wherewithal or the resources or the bravery to leave where she is. Middletown is anywhere; it's any small town. Even though there are real Middletowns in the US, many in fact. One of the most famous is in New York, and I'm sure Rush has passed through them and saw them on the signage. So it's sort of like Lakeside Park. Everybody's got a Lakeside Park, everybody knows a Middletown. And it's just the dreams of these people, these characters, these little character portraits. Occasionally Rush uses characters to get the point across. You know, music-wise, I don't think there's too much excitement going on. It's not a roller coaster like "The Big Money." It's more in the "Mystic Rhythms" kind of vein.

POPOFF: Mike had mentioned "Grand Designs." Any thoughts on that one?

TELLERIA: "Grand Designs" is a lovely, dynamic song, and it almost sounds like the group Icehouse. Because as I say, Rush are very—well, they used to be—very parasitic in their influences. I'm sure you've noticed. Because you've listened to so many heavy metal albums. But if you listen to some progressive albums from Genesis and ELP, many other groups, Kansas—Rush leeched off of so many little things. So when you listen to "Xanadu," you're hearing ELP, and when you hear the ending of "The Spirit of Radio," you're hearing a little Genesis. When you hear "Digital Man," you're hearing "Freeway Jam" from Jeff Beck—it's the same beat. Lyrically, "Grand Designs," to me, that song is about the music business, and charts and graphs and lines. It's basically the monetary end of things, and it plays into "The Big Money." It plays into the big money these corporations are looking to make.

POPOFF: And, of course, "The Big Money" is pretty much the album's most famed track.

PORTNOY: Yes, and Rush kind of got into the habit of the first track on the album being the radio song. They had that with "The Spirit of Radio," "Tom Sawyer," "Subdivisions," and, what else? *Grace Under Pressure*, with "Distant Early Warning." So "The Big Money" was the next in line with that tradition. And it was toe-tapping and memorable and had the hooks, but it still had that musicality and technical prowess. So it was the obvious album opener/radio song.

TELLERIA: I love the wordplay there. *Big money got no soul*—it just doesn't get any truer than that. It's just a real zinger at the end of that song. *Don't feed the people / But we feed the machines*—that one stands out from "Territories." *Sometimes our big splashes / Are just ripples in the pool*, from "Emotion Detector." The album was complex thematically, and I think Bill Banasiewicz was quite right in his book *Visions*, where he said the songs fit together like a puzzle. So you take a song like "Territories," which is about global power and also naïve globalism, that hasn't stood the test of time as far as open borders go. And "Manhattan Project"—well, these global powers don't build a bomb without big money. So these things go together, right?

POPOFF: And to close, let's jump off of the music. What did you think of the *Power Windows* album cover?

PORTNOY: Well, I've done six album covers with Hugh, so he and I have worked together extensively through the years, and I know how his brain works. And having gotten to know Neil very well through the years, as well, and even before getting to know him personally, knowing him as a fan, knowing how his brain works, Neil and Hugh Syme are together a really great combination of minds. Because, you know, you have Neil's lyrical sense and then you have Hugh Syme's artistic sense. And Hugh has a great sense of taking words and translating them to images, in many different ways. He can take one phrase and create, you know, ten different images off of that phrase. So he and Neil working together, through all these years, all these different album covers are a great combination of literal and artistic interpretation.

Geddy and his Steinberger headless bass on the *Power Windows* tour, Maple Leaf Gardens, Toronto, March 6, 1986. *Boris Spremo/*Toronto Star *via Getty Images*

CHAPTER 12

Hold Your Fire

**with Douglas Maher
and Jeff Wagner**

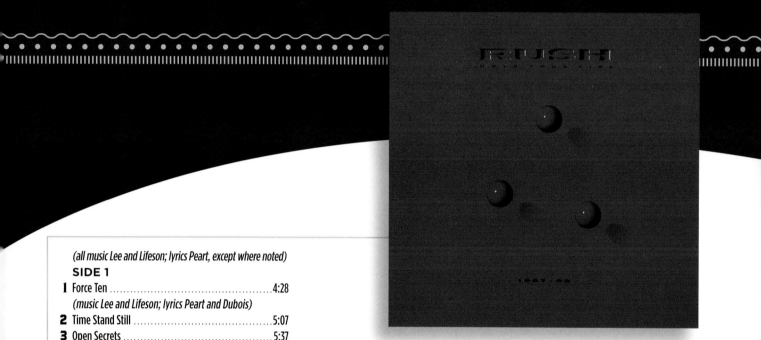

Geddy Lee: bass, synthesizers, vocals
Alex Lifeson: electric and acoustic guitars
Neil Peart: drums, percussion
Aimee Mann: additional vocals
*Andy Richards: additional keyboards, synthesizer
programming*
Steven Margoshes: string arrangement and conductor
*The William Faery Engineering Brass Band: arranged and
conducted by Andrew Jackman*
Released September 8, 1987
*Recorded at The Manor Studio, Oxfordshire, England;
Ridge Farm Studios, Surrey, England; AIR Montserrat,
Montserrat; McClear Place Studios, Toronto; and The Lerxt
Mobile, Toronto*
Produced by Peter Collins and Rush

ontinuing the trajectory initiated in earnest way back on *Signals*, Rush essentially re-created the vibes from their 1985 album, *Power Windows*, recalling Peter Collins, strongly opinionated producer of brittle Britpop, to take the band further from the old Alex and into even more refined and formal music for adults.

Geddy was headlong into writing with judicious use of computer, as was Neil. Even Alex was on board with his trusty Roland drum machine, putting together his "experimental tapes," which in the final analysis, were used for color commentary more than anything. Geddy's riffs, licks, and other ideas culled from soundcheck jams were summarily organized and cataloged to be plundered at will for bits and pieces here and there in the building of songs of mostly conventional construct. Given the growing shift to CDs, the band had it in mind that they would allow themselves a drift toward fifty minutes of music this time out, exploring themes around "instinct," although in the end *Hold Your Fire* might be one of the band's less thematic, even as it represented a Neil Peart passionately of this world and concerned for it.

Writing happened mostly alone all over Ontario, but recording occurred all over the world, including the band's Canadian home

(opposite) Geddy's soundcheck riffs and licks were plundered at will in the writing of *Hold Your Fire. Ebet Roberts/Redferns/Getty Images*

'Til Tuesday

'Til Tuesday's Aimee Mann turned up to provide poignant vocals on "Time Stand Still." *Epic Records photo/Laura Rossignol*

base, multiple rock starry locations in England, and even AIR Montserrat in the Caribbean for guitar overdubs, because why not? Keyboardist and programmer Andy Richards reprised his Collins-complementary role established on the previous album, but a second guest was introduced in the guise of 'Til Tuesday's Aimee Mann, who provided angelic and poignant vocals on "Time Stand Still," Neil's hooky treatise on the fleeting nature of life.

The song would be the second of five singles from the record, as Mercury worked in vain to recoup the enormous stacks of cash spent to build the band's sober and sanctimonious play for the mature listening segment of the music market. Due to the album's twee sounds and a video strategy that failed to recognize the transcendent power of MTV, nothing much from the record stuck with fans. Ergo, *Hold Your Fire* became the first of the band's albums since *Caress of Steel* a dozen years earlier to fail to reach platinum status. Touring pockmarked by bad attendance ensued, and after a synthetic and apathetic live album called *A Show of Hands*, the band shuffled off to Atlantic Records, leaving Mercury, home since the beginning thanks to Cliff Burnstein, once an enthusiastic metalhead fan but now a mysterious mogul with Q Prime.

POPOFF: Fans tend to think of *Power Windows* and *Hold Your Fire*—both produced by Peter Collins—as a pair. Are they?

MAHER: No, definitely not. *Power Windows* was by far an album that was presenting Rush as more of a rock band, whereas with *Hold Your Fire*, they were more of an adult contemporary rock band, with a jazzier tonal sound. As the album itself was taking shape, thematically it was really developing to be more about personal conversations and experiences with friends' lives and each other's lives, and what was going on in their families. That had never really been addressed before on previous Rush albums. This was more of a discussion, creating a personal album more than anything else. And you find that, really, from start to finish.

And I think what Geddy called Neil's more honest songwriting approach really wasn't ready yet, for the fans. The fans were still riding this high exploring where Rush was taking them with various concepts on each record. You started to see a little bit more in terms of character personalization on *Signals*, and these characters developed, always with Neil, whether it was "The Necromancer" or the character in "2112." "New World Man," "Digital Man," "The Analog Kid," "Body Electric" . . . you always had a running theme about a character. For at least half an album.

Hold Your Fire, you just didn't have that. You had more of an insight into their personal lives and his personal thinking, poetically and socially and emotionally, especially when you get to a song like "Open Secrets" where he's talking about a relationship. Neil talks about, I believe, in his book *Ghost Rider*, the occasional trial separations that him and Jackie had. You know, these things were starting to take shape, and this comes around the time where after the *Hold Your Fire* tour, the band basically wanted to end as an entity, as a touring act, because it was affecting their home lives so much.

Hold Your Fire offered fans more insight into the band members' personal lives and Neil's personal thinking.

WAGNER: When I listen to *Hold Your Fire*, I feel like the band's new technologies, electronic drums et cetera, are integrated a lot more seamlessly than on *Power Windows*. They don't seem as dated. It's like Rush is finally comfortable and made friends, really, with that technology. And that's why I think it's a better album. When I listen to *Power Windows*, I hear a very 1985 album. Whereas *Hold Your Fire* sounds more integrated, not as cold. I thought *Power Windows* was an alienating-sounding album.

And as a singer, Geddy, he was rounding off all the rough edges. Obviously, he wasn't up in the stratosphere with the highs any longer, becoming more of a vocalist in the vein of, like, a Crowded House or The Outfield or something. It was strange to hear him tempering himself so much. But then again, it fit the material.

But I hear a lot of passion. Like, "Turn the Page," I think that's a really galvanizing kind of vocal—he's really passionate, really putting forth. If you don't expect it to be *Hemispheres Part II*, then you kind of understand where he's coming from. I hear it as a kind of cool and confident reflection of the times. I like what he is doing on the album, and I think it fits the material that they were writing.

"Time Stand Still" was clearly one of the big songs on *Hold Your Fire*.

As a bass player he was doing some different things. I think he was still exploring the instrument. I don't know if you call it a chord, but that two-note plucked thing at the beginning of the album on "Force Ten," you weren't going to hear that from him in the '70s—he did nothing like that. With this snappier, poppier, slappier kind of playing—again, very '80s. It showed Geddy as still a really great bass player, just in the different mold.

POPOFF: But it's the same people, right? There's a validation that *Power Windows* was a valid direction to take the band.

MAHER: It was just a matter of having that comfort zone. Rush tends to stay with somebody for a few records and say, "Hey, this was kind of successful, we liked where this was going; let's see if we can go deeper with this again." They loved having long-lasting working relationships. Paul Northfield is another example of that. Peter Collins was more of a pop producer, and that was a lot of the music that the band members themselves were really into. They were into the British pop scene. And they really wanted to incorporate more of that sound into their records. And who better to do it than a Britpop producer?

So they traveled the world extensively recording the album. I think the label was banking on getting a real bang for their buck, and it fell really, really flat. They just didn't deliver a rock album. And that's what happens when you go with a 1980s producer who was feeling his way through the rock world at the time.

Because it was only about five short months later, that you see Peter Collins working with Queensrÿche . . . and Queensrÿche basically went in and raided all the people that Rush used to work with, like [engineer] James "Jimbo" Barton. When they started the whole *Operation: Mindcrime* thing, Rush fans gravitated more toward that than they did *Hold Your Fire*. So he had Queensrÿche and *Hold Your Fire* right in that time frame, and Queensrÿche is where you saw Rush fans going. At that point, they wanted a little bit more cerebral, a little bit more rock, and a little bit more thinking and a little bit less feeling. Because these were people that got into Rush [when they] were in junior high or just getting out of high school . . . at, say, *Moving Pictures*. And so there's that six-year span between those original fans and now they get this.

By this time the band that you're dealing with from the 1970s, you have a crowd that shows up and, they're lucky if they're going to get three songs from the '70s that night in the set list—"2112," "La Villa," "Closer to the Heart," and that's about it. "In the Mood" was the closer, but that was only about a minute and a half. No, *Hold Your Fire* was really the isolationist album of them all. They made a tremendous amount of errors with both that record and the tour.

Hold Your Fire **tour, RPI Fieldhouse, Troy, New York, November 12, 1987.** *Chris Walter/ Wirelmage/Getty Images*

POPOFF: So there are obviously the big songs on here— perhaps "Time Stand Still" and "Force Ten"—but in talking to deep fans, they seem to gravitate to the creases of *Hold Your Fire*. Do you have a similar experience with this album?

WAGNER: Oh, yeah, I think after "Time Stand Still," you get this clutch of like "Open Secrets" and "Second Nature" that gets a little deeper, laying out a wider dynamic for the album. "Open Secrets" is just total atmosphere. It has a melancholy darkness that stuff like "Afterimage" and "Red Sector A" had on *Grace Under Pressure*.

And then you continue on with "Second Nature", which is very New Age-y, almost world music, reminding me of what Mike Oldfield or Peter Gabriel or Tangerine Dream was doing in the '80s. It's a little bit dippy in the lyrics. *Folks have got to make choices / And choices got to have voices*—that's kind of dippy [laughs].

But I don't want to be too negative on Rush. And what happens is the bigger guns start happening with "Prime Mover" and "Lock and Key," which is probably my favorite. Geddy's bass playing is all over the place on that song, really tight and driving. He does a lot of doubling of his vocals too, under very lush '80s production.

And you get into the solo area, Lifeson in this whole era was really downplayed in terms of his role. But if you listen closely, he's a lot more stealth, is what he is. His solo on "Lock and Key" strikes me as alien and kind of nuts and unconventional and weird—and it's too short. I would've liked to hear him go off on a longer segment on this song. But he's testing the limits of unconventional for this pop era of Rush. You can't say it's like a "Cygnus X-1" or something, but it's still Rush at the top of their game, and in a really smart way. They are delivering some really amazing musicianship.

Then I think "Mission" is a real centerpiece to this album. It just got this all-inspiring chorus. It could border on sappy, but the delivery is so sincere that it wins you over that way. It's got a bright and upbeat verse, and then with the chorus, they sonically widen the landscape. You almost feel like the room you're listening in just got bigger. It's a really dramatic moment.

MAHER: "Lock and Key," I agree is important. It's basically 1987's version of "Limelight." You're talking about fanaticism. Neil always has this divide, this barrier that he puts between instinct and privacy. And again, remember him talking about in "Limelight," the gilded cage, and *I can't pretend a stranger / Is a long-awaited friend.* There are these messages of duality that Neil seems to put out there. And I think if you didn't know Neil or where he stood, and if you hadn't heard "Limelight" before, and you hadn't read any of his interviews, and you didn't know that this was an album that was written from a personal perspective rather than a conceptual, you wouldn't have a clue what he was talking about. He absolutely expands [on] how his privacy in the '80s was very invaded with Rush's increasing popularity. So that's where "Lock and Key" stems from.

POPOFF: But there is a moment of embarrassment as well. "Tai Shan" is considered, arguably, the most embarrassing song of the Rush oeuvre. I mean, there are other songs you can go to, but this has become the song that just emerges on any deep fan's list.

MAHER: "Tai Shan," the band themselves loathe it. I don't know if Neil loathes it as much. I think he just calls it an experiment that went in a direction it shouldn't have. Whereas Alex and Geddy are more like, "Just what the hell were we thinking?" It was more of like they were doing a favor for Neil than anything else. But then again, you have people who like the song.

Personally, in 1987, when that song came on, by the time you got to that point in the record, near the end, you've pretty much accepted that Rush has released probably their most subpar album in their career at this point—and you're in shock [laughs]. There was absolutely nothing

Rush's 12-inch maxi-single featuring live versions of "Distant Early Warning" and "New World Man" on side B. Side A offered "Prime Mover" and "Tai Shan," the latter arguably, the most embarrassing song of the Rush oeuvre.

Maple Leaf Gardens, Toronto, November 12, 1987. Critic Craig MacInnis wrote that the lads "made a whole-hearted effort to at least seem interested." *Colin McConnell/Toronto Star via Getty Images*

The synthetic and apathetic live album *A Show of Hands* was one result of the battle between Mercury and Rush, who wanted to put promotional money into touring.

that comes from the song "Tai Shan" that grabs a Rush fan introduced to the band from, say, *Permanent Waves* forward. If you had owned *A Farewell to Kings*, for instance, and you heard "Madrigal," or if you owned *2112*, and you heard "Tears," it's totally different. "Tears" is a ballad and "Madrigal," you're talking about dragons and mystical things.

Whereas "Tai Shan," you're talking about a mountain in China—and that's not really relatable. People who get lost in that Yes or King Crimson fantasy world, they could relate to what was going on in *A Farewell to Kings* or *2112* or *Hemispheres* because it was that cerebral style that was going on at the time. What's going on with "Tai Shan" is, again, this really nuanced adult contemporary, this music that was trying to be experimental but was unnecessary. It just did not fit anywhere. As far as true disasters on that record, that really is the only musical disaster.

WAGNER: "Tai Shan" was personal, because it's about a climb that Neil did up on a Chinese mountain, which for him had some kind of holy or spiritual significance. Him being a full-blown atheist, I still think he's a human being and he feels things spiritually no matter what. But "Tai Shan," personally, I think it's a cheesy song. Still I feel there's something there that he is expressing about feeling very small in this big world, at the top of that mountain. So it has that nice vibe.

POPOFF: Back on the positive side, opener "Force Ten" is quite respected.

MAHER: "Force Ten" is an extremely strong song. I think it borrows very heavily, bass-wise, from Chris Squire, especially from the *90125* sessions, a song called "Our Song." If you listen to the bass line from that, and you put it with "Force Ten," you'll hear a tremendous amount of borrowing that goes on there. Lyrically it's a very strong message, and it sucks you in, like a Rush song should.

WAGNER: Yeah, "Force Ten" is great, and what I think about is when I first heard it as a kid, I thought Rush was going in a direction I didn't want them to go. I didn't like it. But that was the case with the whole album. I've since come around to the whole album, and I hear the song in a totally different way now. Like I say, that plucked two-note chord from Geddy is really fun. And it's concise and precise; they cut out anything that doesn't really need to be there.

The writing is a lot more direct than I think they ever had on *Power Windows* or *Grace Under Pressure*; it's maybe "Kid Gloves"-ish in its directness. The rest of the album is a little more complex, but there's a lot of production and ear candy and subtle nuance on "Force Ten" as well. But because of the nature of the actual songwriting, you don't hear that right away. But I think if you have any kind of decent hi-fi or you're listening deeply, there's a lot of soundscaping and interesting production choices throughout these otherwise pretty simple songs.

POPOFF: Jeff, you like the way the album ends. Why is that?

WAGNER: Well, "Tai Shan" and "High Water," the last two songs, represent these big kind of overarching things. "High Water" boils everything down to everything beginning with water and this is where we come from. It's meditative on human nature and nature itself, addressing our bond and relationship with water. So once you get to the end of the album, some of the more personal themes that build up throughout the album are really addressed at the end. I'm not sure if that was intentional, but that's how I've always heard it.

MAHER: "High Water" was a song they never performed live. "High Water" is what I consider a sleeper on the album—great closer. Something that most people aren't aware of is that although the song itself hasn't been performed live, the drumming and the drum sounds and the samples and the triggers that Neil used in that were all used many, many times again, in all of his drum solos, and in "Scars" on *Presto.* So he wound up actually recycling that song many times over.

It's got an absolutely gorgeous guitar solo on it, and a beautiful message, basically that we're all from water and whatnot, and how the water takes us home. It's a song that is highly underrated. Hard-core fans have had that on their target list of songs, mainly because it's never been performed, like "Emotion Detector." People have this thing where they want to get songs off their list, more or less, in terms of what they want to hear. And that's really one of those songs that has been elevated over the years and has grown on people.

POPOFF: We really haven't talked about the biggest song on the record, "Time Stand Still."

MAHER: Yes, of course, very well-written, reflective song. I think it works much better as you get older. You appreciate it much more in your thirties, forties, fifties than as a teenager, as someone who has had a family, seeing time fly by, experiencing people growing older and friends leaving your lives. It's more reflective to where they're at in their age.

But to touch on a few others, in "Prime Mover," Neil tackles the concept of God, and the prime mover, and that figure in your life, and what that means to his life. If you

Hold Your Fire **tour, Ahoy Sportpaleis, Rotterdam, May 2, 1988.** *Rob Verhorst/Redferns/ Getty Images*

look, you will see that Neil uses lyrics in there that you will find in probably half the other Rush songs that have been written already. It's a very strong track on a very weak record—that and "Force Ten" are probably only two of maybe three real rockers. And the love affair people have with "Mission" . . . it's not that "Mission" is necessarily a monster song musically. I think people just like the fact that they have a jam session in the middle, where Rush really doesn't do anymore at that point. Later on, especially on *Clockwork Angels*, you got more jamming. But at that point, on *Hold Your Fire*, to hear an extended solo piece in the middle pop up, it's like, oh, there's that prog side of Rush that still exists. So they're kind of throwing fans a bone.

Lyrically, "Mission" is about failures and dreams and possibilities and experiences that people didn't live up to, and about keeping that inner spirit alive to achieve your mission. It's more of an appeal to people who have failed and failed and failed to keep that mission alive, that driving mission and ambition. It's a good song to be inspired by. But you really have to be older to appreciate that it was just not going to appeal to kids wearing a Judas Priest shirt or going to see Maiden at the same arena the next night. You're not going to get the crowd that you would've four years prior.

WAGNER: I agree that "Time Stand Still" was the album's biggest song, but it's my least favorite, probably, on the album. I just think that it's too far into that Crowded House/Outfield area, and I'm saying that from someone who likes Crowded House. But this is Rush, and I think they bit off a bit too much of the pop-sounding stuff from the time. Still, it's well-written for what it is, and I like Aimee Mann's vocal on it. It's subtle, she's not taking the lead part, and I think it works. A lot of people have called Geddy's voice somewhat feminine, so I think it works in tandem with his kind of tones.

POPOFF: Doug, earlier you spoke of errors. What were the main errors concerning *Hold Your Fire*?
MAHER: Well, they had a hit single on radio with "Force Ten," as their first single, and they had no video for that. This was a time when MTV was pretty much everything. I have every single MTV playlist chart. I want to say that they went the first seven weeks of release with no active video, after the release of their album. That is suicide. And "Force Ten" was extremely popular and remained popular in their set for a very long time.

"Time Stand Still" was the video that came out, much later in the fall. And the album had already been out six to seven weeks. And this was an introduction to people who really weren't listening to all that much radio. And you see Aimee Mann, with a spinning camera, Geddy looking radically different than he did the last time they saw him on *Power Windows*, the band sounding absolutely different.

So any rock audience that was looking for that "Big Money" heavy guitar Rush sound would've gotten that with "Force Ten," but they didn't get it with "Time Stand

Still." So "Time Stand Still" basically became the fate of the record. And while it's a very well-written song, became a fan favorite, other songs on the album like "Mission" and "Prime Mover" were never really . . . they didn't make videos for them. "Prime Mover" was released as a single, and they did nothing with that. They made a video for "Lock and Key," which was a complete failure. That was not commercially received well. And that lasted on MTV the shortest of any of their videos in history to that point.

They wound up doing a live video release for that when they did the *Show of Hands* live album a year later, along with the video that they didn't shoot for *Power Windows*, for "Marathon," which, again, this was Rush's and the label's war that was going on. Rush didn't want to be known as a video band at the time. This caused tension between Mercury/Polygram and Rush themselves. They wanted anywhere between four to five videos a record. Rush said that they would rather spend the money and the time out on the road as a live act. So that hurt the band.

You know, this was also the first time since *Permanent Waves* that a Rush album was not sitting in the Top 10. *Hold Your Fire* comes just outside of that. And that's starts to spell a case of, "Well, what now?" We're used to Rush sitting in the Top 10 for four or five weeks and selling a million albums. Where did all the fans go who bought *Power Windows*? So you're looking at a band that was not struggling so much as musicians, but they were taking a direction away from . . . where their base was.

Ahoy Sportpaleis, Rotterdam, May 2, 1988. *Rob Verhorst/ Redferns/Getty Images*

Presto

with Sean Kelly
and Robert Telleria

Geddy Lee: bass, synthesizers, vocals
Alex Lifeson: electric and acoustic guitars, backing vocals
Neil Peart: drums, percussion
Rupert Hine: additional keyboards, backing vocals
Jason Sniderman: additional keyboards
Released November 21, 1989
Recorded at Le Studio, Morin Heights, Quebec, and
McClear Place, Toronto, Ontario
Producer: Rupert Hine and Rush

The mere fact that Rush desired to work with Peter Collins a third time speaks volumes as to why *Presto*, the band's first album in their new deal with Atlantic Records, was of a similarly thin and reedy progressive Britpop style to *Power Windows* and *Hold Your Fire*. But Collins bowed out of the project, with Rush signing on with Rupert Hine, who had been on the band's wish list when they were scrambling to find somebody to help them with *Grace Under Pressure*.

What was subtly new this time was a reduced role for the keyboards, which, in the grand tradition of Rush confounding expectations, didn't make so much for a power trio record as a trio record. Also new is a further honing of and focus on the band's songwriting, along with some of Neil's sharpest lyrics and some of Geddy's most emotive and convincing deliveries of Neil's ideas, which this time around centred on the personal and experiential—essentially involvement and interaction with society.

The flagship songs from a popularity point of view were "Show Don't Tell" and "Superconductor," both modestly rocking—that is to say, guitarist, bass, and drummer flailing away in a matchbox. But in terms of artistic timelessness, deep fans look to *Presto*'s deep album tracks, along with the band's anti-single, "The Pass," which the band professes is one of their proudest moments of the catalog.

Also different is Rush's return to their quintessentially Canadian home base, Le Studio, that storied and idyllic (and now, shockingly, abandoned) rock star retreat in rural Quebec, with additional work taking place at McClear in Toronto. The end result was an album politely tolerated by the fans and almost grudgingly sent gold by these longtime loyalists (but not particularly clicking with the next generation of rock fans). Judging from the sonic origami enclosed (and the effete portraiture on the back cover), hair metal and grunge rockers weren't the band's preferred audience anyway. And yet Geddy, Alex, and Neil, along with their miniature pop sculptures, were perhaps viewed as yesterday's news by the younger generation of sophisticates Rush might have imagined were out there for the courting.

POPOFF: So clear the air for me. Do fans go too far when they frame *Presto* as a return to more of a guitar-based sound?

KELLY: I'd say they do, because it's funny, they make that move from Peter Collins to Rupert Hine, and it sounds like it. Hine's got the new wave thing—he's worked with Howard Jones—and there's this breathy, glassy, airy quality to the whole record. And it really sounds like that's a post-production decision. And when I say "post," it's in the effects, the application of effects. I hear a really compressed sound, lots of reverb, lots of delays, but I don't think that was the initial intention. And certainly not from an Alex Lifeson perspective. It's funny, because that was always in my head: the album where

Presto **brought a renewed focus on the songwriting and some of Neil's sharpest lyrics yet.** *Mick Hutson/ Redferns/Getty Images*

A pair of Brazilian 12-inch promos provides good context as to other acts the label was promoting at the time of *Presto*, including Tom Petty and the Pixies.

Alex was going to come back and reclaim the rock. And I remember reading about that and certainly even hoping it. I was in a band and we tackled "Show Don't Tell," and there are lots of classic-rock-isms in that tune, and those typical Alex Lifeson guitar devices—big, strumming sixteenth note chords—and there's some cool ensemble riffing going on. But when you listen to it, there's so much effect on it. But it's after the fact. So no, in the scheme of things, it's not a big guitar record.

POPOFF: Not much power, so no power trio.
TELLERIA: Yes, I'd agree with that, and in fact I think Neil and the boys would agree with you, by that definition. And by that sound—it's another bright album. It's got the twinkly synthesizers. By then, starting more with *Hold Your Fire*, Geddy was using the Sequential Circuits Prophet synthesizer, which was the first synthesizer they were using that emulated piano notes, piano chords. You hear pianos on "Different Strings," of course, but that's Hugh Syme on an actual piano. But the piano sound you hear on "Presto" and on "Red Tide," those piano notes, it's because of that Prophet synthesizer.

So that was a new kind of color to the Rush sound. Between that and the Fixx-like guitar . . . and they're still using Signature guitars. During the tour Alex switched to PRS, which are phenomenal guitars. No wonder he used them for so long, they're kind of like Gibsons and Fenders—best of both worlds. But Signature guitars, made in Canada by Russ Heinl, they were custom-made with Alex, and those guitars were very thin-sounding, single-coil [pickups], very passive-sounding. And that, to me, hurts the *Presto* sound. And *Presto* is actually one of the albums that Neil said that he would like to rerecord, if he had his druthers.

POPOFF: But enough about the sound. There are some very well-respected Rush songs on this record. Let's start with one or two folks don't necessarily talk about.
TELLERIA: Okay, "Hand Over Fist," hands down, to me is one of the standout tracks. And it's funny—it's second to last, and you would think that it's placed there because of its supposed inferiority as far as priority of the tracks, but that isn't always the case. That song's got a tasteful drumbeat.

There's also "Chain Lightning," which has got the backward recorded guitar solo. People are wondering, well, how come that was never played live? Well, they could simulate that, but it is recorded backward. "Chain Lightning" is just a great hard rocker song for Rush. That was a good change of pace. You can compare "Chain Lightning" to anything on *Hold Your Fire*, and you get my drift why, to me, it's a more exciting song.

Illusion was a key theme Neil weaved through the lyrics of *Presto*.

KELLY: A favorite of mine is "Anagram (for Mongo)," just for someone who is intrigued by wordplay. I mean, pretty cool, right? Something tickled Neil's fancy that he's going to use anagram throughout the whole thing, and yet there's still a narrative there. I'm kind of feeling it's a shot at organized religion or something.

What is also interesting is that it's yet another softened chorus. This record is like the anti-chorus record, or at least anti-rock chorus. It seems by the time you get to the chorus, they thin out all the textures. They kind of pull everything back to make it more dynamic. And this one has that too. The verse is pretty rocking and nasty. The intro, with the piano figure, and later on the guitar figure . . . it could be like a Coldplay tune. It's very sparse and arpeggiated.

I also like "Scars." It's like "Rise Up" by Parachute Club meets Megadeth "Peace Sells." And I wonder if this is a Toronto thing, because it also reminds me of some of the Rough Trade material that Terry Brown worked on. Even though Terry didn't do this record, the whole idea of this tribal, funky, riffy thing heavy on bass. Maybe I'm free-associating. There's also some really nice Santana-esque overtones in that, in the lead guitar fills, and they're panned back and forth. It's really subtle, but with headphones on, it's really cool. I'm hearing timbale-type things going on too, so yeah, a Latin vibe.

POPOFF: *Presto*'s considered by Neil to be at least in the bottom half in terms of being conceptual. But with a personality—in this case *his* personality—there's always going to be focus or at least preoccupation. What do you think he's preoccupied with in 1989?

TELLERIA: I'd say a key theme of the album is illusion, which you would definitely get from the song "Presto." You get that with the characters in "War Paint" and their illusion of who they are, their identity. And of course there's the illusion of onstage persona and celebrity in "Superconductor."

Presto **wasn't quite Alex's reclamation of the rock that some fans had hoped for.** *Steve Eichner/WireImage/ Getty Images*

"The Pass" offered some badly needed dark contrast.

Not so much power trio. Geddy employed a Sequential Circuits Prophet synthesizer to emulate piano. *Tony Mottram/ Getty Images*

Illusion is also hinted at in "Available Light," where it seems to be about living life in a non-mystical way. And there's the photography imagery, which reminds me of their photographer, Andrew MacNaughtan. But it's probably a comment, an observation, about life without the filters of mystical and supernatural contrivances and magic. There's a line in it that says *Chase the wind around the world*, and the chasing of the wind is an old biblical expression, of, you know, basically chasing nothing—it's not there.

POPOFF: Of those, "Superconductor" was *Presto*'s biggest song. Would you say this was a successful single artistically?

KELLY: With that riff, it's kind of "Son of Red Barchetta," right? To me it feels very much like Rush attempting a single, if they ever attempted such a thing. It has all those elements. It's still got the progressive thing, but there's that goofy pseudo-spoken "superconductor," which they kind of went for it in spades on "Roll the Bones." There's a goofiness there. But the changes are sophisticated, really, and like so many on here, it's really melodic, really vocalist-oriented. Great lyric, too—Neil is calling bullshit. I always thought, is it about politicians, evangelists, movie stars? But basically it's Neil railing against artifice.

TELLERIA: I'm glad you asked—no! [laughs] "Superconductor" was an awkward, clumsy little tune. It starts with that cowbell plunk, and then it goes into this riff that just isn't quite heavy enough to pass for what it needs to be. I feel like I can spank Rush every now and again—listen, I've paid my dues—and that's one of those songs you can spank them on. And I don't think the public related to it the same way they did with "Show Don't Tell," which was a number-one FM mainstream rock radio single; it was a "Welcome back, Rush. We'll give you Number One."

But by the time you get into April 1990, when "Superconductor" was making the rounds at radio, the tour was winding down, only had two months left, and you never saw this video on MTV. There was a video, by the way, shot, for "Superconductor," where notably Geddy and Alex switched sides of the stage, for the video. It was directed by Gerry Casale of Devo, who had done "Mystic Rhythms," I might add. So they were already familiar with him; they were fans of Devo. But people are hearing "Superconductor," and most don't know what a superconductor is. So they're thinking, is it a train conductor? And of course superconductor turns out to be Neil's cute term for a celebrity with pull, with influence, with almost the power to sway and fool, deceive, like magicians, *Designing to deceive. / That's entertainment.* Hoping you'll believe. That's basically the purpose of that song. But I just think it was an awkward single, not a strong one. You never heard it in concert since the *Roll the Bones* tour.

POPOFF: Almost diametrically opposed is "The Pass."

TELLERIA: Yes, "The Pass" was a stark contrast to some of the other bright songs. They definitely needed some darkness in there—and they got it in there for a block of songs on that section of the album. "The Pass" is deceivingly simple. Note selection is what makes that song work. The feel and the emotion there was surprising for Rush.

Paul Stanley from Kiss introduced that song on MTV for the very first time, on a show called *Hard 30*, a show of hard rock songs, thirty minutes of hard rock videos, and "The Pass" was a great song, I think, for your ears but not for your eyes. The video is a stark, black-and-white video—the first black-and-white video that they did—and it looks like the prototype for Matt Muhurin's "The Unforgiven" video [for Metallica]. And that's not a coincidence, because Matt Mahurin directed "The Pass."

But "The Pass" is such a personal song for them, especially Neil, and what he had been reading about and talking to his daughter about, as far as teen suicides. Even though it sounds dark and depressing and melancholy, it's one of the most positive anti-suicide songs ever written. Which is ballsy for a rock group to do.

KELLY: For me, that album's all about "The Pass." And yeah, it spoke to me because I'm sixteen when this record came out. And the whole idea of, you know, you're coming into manhood, the sense of bravado, but you're also flooded with all these emotions too, emotions that, most of the time, society was telling us to suppress, right? So that really spoke to me.

And even though I wasn't going through some of the things that I think the person he is talking about in the song was going through, I could certainly see it in some of my

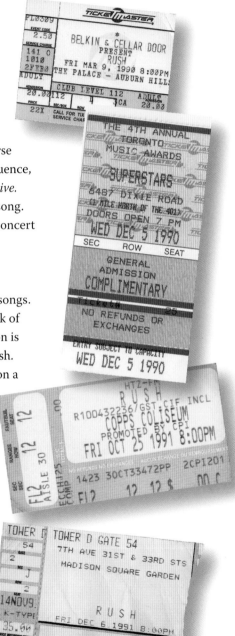

peers at the time. You know, the *Proud swagger out of the schoolyard / Waiting for the world's applause.* I get all that stuff. You're testing your mettle against the world when you're at that age.

But what I like about this, he takes on the notion that there's nothing great about killing yourself, you know? But he gets it. Those lyrics are at the heart of why so many people do drastic things, right? You get tired of living. And I think it's a classic lyric, because here's a guy who refuses to compromise. Compromise is just not in his lexicon. So it's kind of admitting other people might have this, but at the same time, he said no, you fight, you stand your ground, and you deal with it.

And then the musical soundtrack is perfectly sympathetic, which I think is why "The Pass," out of all the songs from this record, lasted. Geddy, the way he sings, the range he is singing in, it's not strained, it's not acrobatic, it's very conversational—but heartfelt conversation. And it's a very melancholic, emotional, hopeful chord progression, too, as we get into the *trembling on a rocky ledge* section. When you hear that, it's actually a melodic and harmonic lift. There's an elevation there, even though this is the most precarious part of the lyric [laughs]. You could fall off. Like, what's going to happen here? So there's hope. And to me, great melancholic songs always walk the line between hopefulness and hopelessness, and this one does it beautifully.

POPOFF: Sean described "Scars" earlier." Robert, what are your thoughts on that one? Very strange song for Rush.

TELLERIA: "Scars" is a strong song. It's got an African vibe, and you can close your eyes and maybe think, depending on your imagination, that you're out in the Serengeti or you're doing all those things that Neil did by bike. But even if your mind doesn't take you to those places, the song is about the feelings and the stinging memories of things that have scarred you, and not just physical scars.

Neil's approach is that worldview, observational kind of thing, at the same time tying in feelings that everybody has, no matter where you come from, or how bad your life, or how good your life has been. Because there are good scars and bad scars. It's the human condition, really. "Scars" is a testament to all the things we sense; we're sensory animals, and that song's a great showcase for that.

POPOFF: Intelligent and important lyrics aside, there really wasn't a place for Rush with this kind of music in 1989.

TELLERIA: No, and that's a great point. Atlantic wasn't even quite sure, because they would stick the song "Available Light" on heavy metal samplers, along with Ratt and Great White, and all the other great Atlantic label groups that were heavy metal hair bands. And here's little Rush with "Available Light." And, you know, there's heavier than that on *Presto*, if you're gonna go there. So where do they fit in?

I think they really did have an identity crisis, because in a way they sounded passé. Even at the time, I thought that. I thought, is *Roll the Bones* really the current

Next one . . . I promise. *Tony Mottram/Getty Images*

thing? Is this what bands sound like today? And someone might stop me and say, "Ah, but maybe you shouldn't have them sound like bands today. They should just do their own thing." But, come on, they always sound like the contemporary thing that's going on. That's a characteristic of theirs. Yet *Presto* is one of their most mature albums. But, like *Hold Your Fire*, that maturity is often hard to sell to the youth. Whereas before, the youth definitely got into *Grace Under Pressure*, they got into *Signals*. When you're that mature, it's almost like you've grown up too fast.

CHAPTER 14

Roll the Bones

with Jillian Maryonovich, Eddy Maxwell, and Ray Wawrzyniak

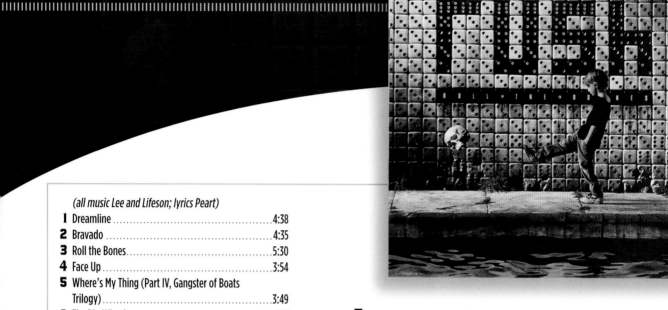

(all music Lee and Lifeson; lyrics Peart)

1 Dreamline 4:38
2 Bravado 4:35
3 Roll the Bones 5:30
4 Face Up 3:54
5 Where's My Thing (Part IV, Gangster of Boats
  Trilogy) 3:49
6 The Big Wheel 5:13
7 Heresy 5:26
8 Ghost of a Chance 5:19
9 Neurotica 4:40
10 You Bet Your Life 5:00

Geddy Lee: *synthesizers, bass, lead vocals*
Alex Lifeson: *electric and acoustic guitars, backing vocals*
Neil Peart: *drums*
Joe Berndt: *digital effects*
Rupert Hine: *additional keyboards, vocals*
Released September 3, 1991
Recorded at Le Studio, Morin Heights, Quebec, and
McClear Place, Toronto
Produced by Rupert Hine and Rush

(opposite)
Despite similarities to its fizzled predecessor, *Roll the Bones* returned Rush to platinum status. *Mick Hutson/Redferns/Getty Images*

t's amusing that *Roll the Bones* shares with *2112* the idea of a career rejuvenation for Rush. *Caress of Steel* and *Presto* were the respective preceding (relatively) hitless stumbles. And so in the fall of 1991, Rush returned with a record that on a material plane was not so much different from its predecessor, *Presto*—an unsure happenstance underscored by the fact that the uptight Rupert Hine had returned as a producer.

But lo and behold, *Presto* stalls gold and *Roll the Bones* returns the band to platinum status on the across-the-board strength of the songwriting, most pertinently the classic spirited Rush opener "Dreamline" and the title track, which attracts too much attention for its fairly inconsequential rap, and not the fact that it's a completely catchy, well-appointed song construct, handsomely housing some of Alex's most incisive acoustic guitar.

What's more, Neil came up with a sharper pan-album concept, so brilliantly exemplified by Hugh Syme's Juno Award–winning cover art. Dice for miles, and we're off to the casino where Neil is waxing eloquently on the fact that if there appears to be a chance at a good outcome, roll them bones, take that chance, and with a little luck and a little hard work (i.e., the loading of the dice), we can achieve our goals.

The amusing spot of irony here is that Rush was perhaps taking a chance with their career by not taking a chance at all, delivering

what is on paper a pretty similar album to its fizzled predecessor. Or were they taking a chance on ignoring what was going on in the music industry, a resurgence of heavy sounds with the Seattle scene, and continuing to deliver obsessive-compulsive Swiss watch music for a fifth straight year?

As rock 'n' roll invariably and ruthlessly proves time and again to be a young man's game, in terms of record sales and coolness factor, Rush would become also-rans as the '90s ground on. And so *Roll the Bones* represents one (more) little victory for the Canrock elders in that it was bought by a million Americans, even if it would be the last (officially certified) platinum record of their career.

But, hey, weep not for Rush—they forevermore remained a concert juggernaut of a relentless and show-spectacular nature.

POPOFF: So where is Rush in their career, circa *Roll the Bones*?

MARYONOVICH: Kind of in the middle. I mean literally, mathematically, it's in the middle. But it also sits in the middle creatively—*Roll the Bones* is like a redheaded stepchild to the fans. Just like it was on the tail end of the keyboard era, it was pretty well right on the verge of getting back into the rock sound. It was a transitional record, how *Permanent Waves* was, how *Grace Under Pressure* was; it transitioned them from where they were to the next phase.

But people make fun of the rapping skeleton and that kind of stuff. It was definitely a weird, dark album for them. The record before, *Presto*, was thinner-sounding, kind of like a diet Rush album [laughs]. I love *Presto*; it's one of my favorite albums in terms of songwriting, but it didn't have the kick in the stomach like most Rush albums do. "Superconductor" just doesn't rock the way "Dreamline" does.

WAWRZYNIAK: *Roll the Bones* was a ridiculously successful album that I think they envisioned wanting to make when they made *Presto*. They did *Hold Your Fire* in '87, and the tour supporting that was really taxing. That was the first time they ever really thought about, not necessarily breaking up, but, "We really need to rethink things." They were also up to here with all the keyboards.

So they decided, come *Presto*, all right, we really need to scale back in these keyboards, and they did so successfully. They also really scaled back on the tour, but the *Presto* tour only went from the middle of February until the end of June. That was their shortest tour since *Caress of Steel*. But they missed the mark on a few songs on *Presto*. And I think what they originally envisioned coming out of *Hold Your Fire*, needing a break, wanting to push the keyboards to the back, I think what they envisioned was *Roll the Bones*. They needed *Presto* to get to *Roll the Bones*.

And they hit the mark with *Roll the Bones* in so many areas. That is a fantastic record. They did push the keyboards to the back. You get a song like on *Presto*, "The

Pass," which was a great seminal Rush song, but what they really wanted with that, is they wanted to write a Rush song like "Bravado" on *Roll the Bones*, a song that Geddy openly cites in many multiple interviews as his favorite song for the band to play live. You ask him what he wants to play live, and he either says, "Bravado" or "Natural Science"—he loves to play that one as well. But "Bravado" hit the mark. It's the perfect marriage of music and lyrics, and the solo builds so emotionally; that is a perfectly crafted Rush song.

MARYONOVICH: "Bravado" is really good. This album is interesting, because it had these really thick rock tracks, and then it had these lighter, more romantic tracks, which Rush is kind of famous for as well. "Bravado" is one of these more romantic songs. It's slower, it's got a heavy message, it's somewhat war themed too. Neil always likes to write about humanity that's been destroyed, and how it recovers from that.

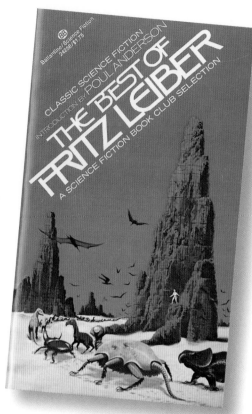

POPOFF: How do you interpret the overall theme to the record?

MAXWELL: I remember a bunch of us fans discussed this back when it came out. I think it's about the chance and the risk and dangers of just being alive. We're all very comfortable. So many of us here in the western part of the world, we have jobs and some sense of health and security. We forget that life is harsh and desperate. And it doesn't take much, like a disaster, for society and all those comforts to fall apart. That's what I get from *Roll the Bones*. Everything is fine, but a lot of it is just chance, luck to where we are born, luck to who are parents are, luck to our health. We can do a lot to take care of ourselves, but there's only so much we can do, and the rest is just nature.

Rock 'N' Roll Comics breaks down the genesis of *Roll the Bones*. © Rock 'N' Roll Comics/ Revolutionary Comics. Courtesy Jay Allen Sanford

So, yeah, if you think about "The Big Wheel," "Heresy," "Neurotica," "You Bet Your Life," there's a lot of gambling themes. It's not gambling like, "I'm going to go place a bet and win twenty bucks." It's "I'm taking a risk, I'm here, just living, just getting up, leaving my house every day, I'm taking a risk." But it's not to be scared. It's not, you only live once, therefore live in fear. It's go out there and do it.

POPOFF: How does "You Bet Your Life" feed Neil's theme for the album?

MARYONOVICH: I don't know that TV show, because I'm not ninety. But this is another one. *The odds get even—you name the game / The odds get even—the stakes are the same.* It's talking about, there's losers in life, there's winners in life, there's, there's "another gypsy with

a plastic guitar." All these people are trying to be successful and find happiness and are struggling in life, but you just take risks and keep going. The song is awesome. The whole ending, when they're doing the "Hindu Muslim Catholic creation/evolutionist," it's smart and cleverly written, like a rhythmic ostinato in the end, where Geddy's singing it. It's like a chorus, and he sings the melody on top of it. It's just so clever and rhymes so well; he uses fancy words, but it's funny—I love that song.

"Roll the Bones" feeds the theme as well. To me, that song's about people having faith and having faith kick you in the teeth. Like, faith is cold and why are we born only to suffer? It's rejecting the traditional thought of religion and belief, and not putting any stock in a predetermined fate. Why are these things happening? Do we blame religion? Do we blame God? No, they're just happening. You deal with the cards you are dealt. There's no use contemplating why all these terrible things are happening—they're just happening. So play on, keep going forward.

When I was eighteen and in high school, these were very new concepts to me, questioning religion. Being a proud atheist, all these things were really important to me. Discovering this sort of writing at that age in my life was very important. It sort of awoke a much more critical thinker. And that just fits so perfectly into my development as a human being. But yeah, Neil's good writing—when he was being so Neil—was when he was really questioning religion and writing about the human experience, the fact that we are all in this struggle, we all go through it.

So yeah, the whole thematic thing about this album is a lot of card playing, gambling, odds, betting, which "The Big Wheel" points to as well. It's another gambling

Bones (of all kinds) for miles. *Roll the Bones* featured another brilliantly executed Hugh Symes art concept.

Roll the Bones tour, Ahoy Sportpaleis, Rotterdam, May 3, 1992. *Rob Verhorst/Redferns/ Getty Images*

metaphor from Neil, but it's also a life metaphor. It's like, oh Neil, you're so clever. The big wheel is our life, spinning, there's the planet spinning, but you also gamble on this, and sometimes the odd numbers win.

POPOFF: And, Ray, same question, what is the theme of the record?

WAWRZYNIAK: The whole record is about chance. If there's a chance, take it. Sure, you might get burned: *If we burn our wings / Flying too close to the sun*, as the line in "Bravado" says. But still, just because you could get hurt taking a chance, don't deny yourself the opportunity of those chances.

"Ghost of the Chance," that song is all about, look, I believe there's a ghost of a chance there's someone to love. You're going to find someone to love. But do you have the will to make it last? I always liked the addendum to that lyric: "and make it last." Finding someone to love is pure chemistry, but making it last is a matter of will. I always loved the addendum of that. But again, the theme is reflected right in the title.

MARYONOVICH: Rush has never, ever been, like, "Let's write a love song to get the ladies to come to the concert," like Journey. Journey made a significant change— "Hey, if we write these ballads, chicks will come." That was never Rush's intention. But this was as close to a pop ballad as you can get for Rush. And it came out as a single, so you could buy it as a CD single, and it had different artwork than the album cover. So it was really fun to collect that stuff. So it's not a crunchy, driving down the highway song, but it's really nice, it's really well written, it's sonically a very solid song, but again, not one of those kickass jump-up-and-down songs.

POPOFF: And we should address the rap in "Roll the Bones," although it's almost over-discussed.

WAWRZYNIAK: Yes, well, them toying with that rap part, or the chat, however you want to refer to it, I know John Cleese was considered as someone they were going to use for that. But they decided that the treatment of Geddy's voice worked better than the other candidates they were considering. That was a big song live, and it represented the theme of the record. The rap was polarizing; it caused a division in fan circles. But to me it's just representative of them being a definitive progressive rock band. We're going to progress and try anything we want. If that means trying to rap, go ahead.

POPOFF: And then there's a strong instrumental as well, "Where's My Thing."

MARYONOVICH: This was a great era for that, for writing these great instrumentals, like this one and "Leave That Thing Alone," and then three on *Snakes & Arrows*. They're really fun, and they stick together well, and they're great live.

WAWRZYNIAK: Their first instrumental in ten years, their first instrumental since "YYZ." There was a song slated to be on *Presto* that was to be an instrumental, but

Neil waxes eloquently on the chance at a good outcome—roll them bones, and with a little luck and a little hard work, we can achieve our goals.

"Where's My Thing" was Rush's first instrumental since "YYZ."

Shoreline Amphitheater, Mountain View, California, May 31, 1992. *Tim Mosenfelder/ImageDirect/ Getty Images*

they ended up finding lyrics that suited that song well, and it became "Hand Over Fist." So they were adamant going into *Roll the Bones*, saying, "We're going to have an instrumental on this record." And to subtitle it "Gangster of Boats Trilogy" . . . at this point in their career, you really started to see a lot of their humor coming to the forefront. Plus, to see this song called the fourth part of a trilogy is nothing other than just pure comedy. And there's so many things that happened on stage, on the tour in support of the record, that they really started to show a lot of their personalities. Where beforehand they were looked upon as these serious musicians on stage. They still were, but they really opened up on stage in support of *Roll the Bones*.

POPOFF: But, really, the centerpiece of the album is "Dreamline," correct?
MAXWELL: Yes, but it was so different. My husband and I were on our honeymoon when it was released, and we started hearing it. We were doing a driving trip in the western US, and so fond memories of that. "Dreamline" is seriously one of their best songs ever. It's strong, it's got an interesting story, it's just beautiful.

MARYONOVICH: Well, Rush has to start each album with their kickass "Here we are" song. That's one of their traditions. And as a welcome, opening song, "Dreamline" is just so good. And then it's seriously brought to life live. It's about traveling, it's about existing as a person, being curious, chasing your dreams, it's a positive anthem—just wonderful.

WAWRZYNIAK: Rush say so many times in interviews how they want their opening song on the album to be the most representative Rush song. "Dreamline" absolutely is. I mean, the album charted well. The album went to number three, if I remember correctly. It was the first top five album since *Moving Pictures*. And "Dreamline" charted at number one on the album rock chart; it was a number-one rock radio song. And as Jillian says, it translated so well live. They ended up opening up subsequent tours with that song. The presentation of that song is so great. Yeah, "Dreamline" is a seminal representative opening song.

POPOFF: But still, as "driving" as it is, this was not exactly heavy metal Rush during this era.

MARYONOVICH: No, definitely not. And they're writing in a comfortable register for Geddy's voice. So he's not really slamming his vocal cords to hit notes and having to be super aggressive. There was maybe some kind of struggle between guitar and keyboards, as there always is. They really embraced the guitar sound for *Counterparts*, so maybe this was the final straw [laughs]. *Roll the Bones* was the final straw for having this much keyboards and whatnot.

MAXWELL: There's a lot of the clean, late-'80s, early-'90s, I hesitate to say, digital versus an analog crunch. There's stripped, clean lines to Alex's guitars. And so you have these beautiful melodies that he is laying out, very crisp, very clean, where you can hear every note, which I love.

So sure, against the music of the day, it felt like they were behind the curve. I'm not really sure about where their headspace was. But I think that's why people were so surprised by it. They wanted *Counterparts*, but the band wasn't at the point of making *Counterparts*, as they weren't in that headspace yet. They were still maybe recovering from *Hold Your Fire* and *Presto,* two albums that I truly love but are very soft, the softer side of Rush. They are great albums, but I need you guys to start rocking, come back, come back to us. So I think they were kind of on the back side of the curve in that sense.

And so *Roll the Bones* is a very odd album, and an album where it was kind of make or break. After this, if they had done something similar, I don't know that I could've continued the journey with them. But I am so glad we have *Roll the Bones*. "Ghost of a Chance," "You Bet Your Life" . . . I'm looking at the list of the songs, and I love all of them—I really do.

"Dreamline" continued the Rush tradition of opening each album with a kickass song.

"Ghost of a Chance" was *Roll the Bones'* third single, released in April 1992.

Counterparts

with Chris Irwin, Douglas Maher, and Jillian Maryonovich

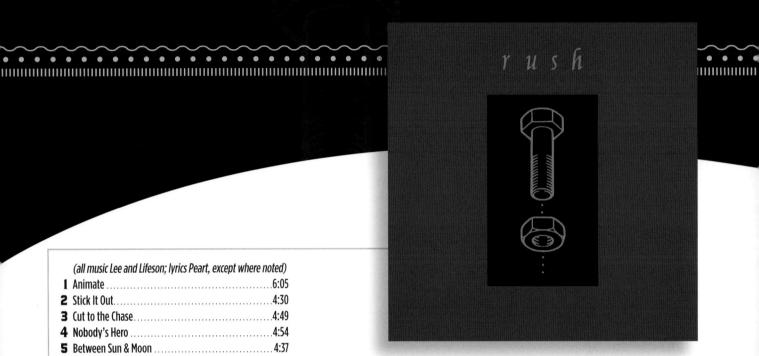

Geddy Lee: bass, vocals, synthesizers
Alex Lifeson: electric and acoustic guitars
Neil Peart: drums, percussion
Michael Kamen: string arrangements and conductor
John Webster: additional keyboards
Released October 19, 1993
Recorded at Le Studio, Morin Heights, Quebec, and McClear Place, Toronto
Produced by Peter Collins and Rush

(opposite)
Alex, feeling the guitar vibrate again. Engineer Kevin Shirley led the charge toward a more stripped-down approach. *Ebet Roberts/Redferns/ Getty Images*

The story of *Counterparts* is very much about the production of the album. Really, songs from the last two records, heavied-up, could've fit right here, and the sum total of *Counterparts*, strictly from a writing point of view, does not really back up the generalized storyline that it was such a heavy record. But it was a *heavier* record, and that had to do with the return of Peter Collins, who had now worked on some other heavy records, most notably Queensrÿche, and Collins tag-teaming with engineer Kevin Shirley, who was not scared to tell Rush what he didn't like about their recent music, along with telling Neil he could get him a better drum sound in twenty minutes.

Another storyline is that the band wanted to get back to more of a power trio sound, especially Alex, but also, fortunately for band relations, Geddy, who wanted more thump and less definition from his bass this time around. The guys were not ignorant of the return of the guitar, emblematic of the grunge scene, but one can apply too much importance to this, given that in the stirring of the pudding, only "Stick It Out" would really pound with doom. Peter, for his part, was still more into the construction of the songs, and noticing that Neil, as a lyricist, had really grown away from topical stories into an intense, and personal though poetic and abstract zone. Collins particularly loved "Nobody's Hero" from Neil.

A return to the rock trio concept meant simple and stripped-down recording—Alex playing in the big room rather than isolation, drums mic'd in almost a mono sense, and keyboards at a minimum.

Driving the sound, really, was Kevin Shirley, a proponent of stripped-down, simple recording values, and a big Zeppelin fan, bringing Alex to play in the big room and not the control room, drums recorded in an almost mono sense, and not, as Peter says, "spread throughout the stereo picture." As well, Kevin didn't mind bleed and basically worked quickly and vociferously, leaned on Geddy to keep keyboards to a minimum, furthermore quipping that he wanted him to chuck his Wal bass into the fire and just rock out.

Come time to mix, Kevin and his aversion to reverb was checked at the door, with mixing conducted by Michael Letho, he of the Jim "Jimbo" Barton school of thought. In the final analysis, *Counterparts* no doubt came out smoother-drinking and more befitting a band of wealth than if Shirley had had all of his druthers. But even with saner heads prevailing, *Counterparts* is still in possession of the band's most timeless production values since *Signals*. And by that I mean simply that the knob job stands the test of time and doesn't distract the way that the production does on fully the five previous albums (I repeat, five previous albums).

POPOFF: So what do we get with Rush circa 1993? Are we in a new phase or is it business as usual?

MARYONOVICH: No this is definitely a reset album. They were going back to older techniques of recording, where I believe Alex is quoted as saying, "I finally feel the wood vibrating against my body again" or something like that. And it was Kevin Shirley, rather than Peter Collins, who was saying let's get rid of all the fancy stuff—let's see Alex Lifeson again. I know that Alex was really talking about feeling the guitar in his gut again, and for sure, this album, sonically, is such a departure from *Roll the Bones* and *Presto*. It's a one-eighty; it's a "dust off your record and crank up the volume" album. But to answer your question, *Roll the Bones* was '91, and they toured and took a break and decided, oh, we're going to reinvent ourselves. Rush was already known for being like, "Okay, we've had this phase and this part of our life, and now that door is closed and we're onto the next thing."

MAHER: I think Kevin's the guy who more or less was the dictator [laughs], if he was anything. Peter Collins was there to make sure that Rush were still being Rush, that they weren't, you know, going to come out and release an album that was going to sound overly grungy, overly heavy, and that they were going to have that wall of sound or lose themselves in something that might come off as just too disjointed.

IRWIN: I remember one story where Rush tech Jimmy Johnson had found this old amp that was basically in a junk pile, and he managed to get it going again, and Geddy was saying, wow, this sounds pretty raw.

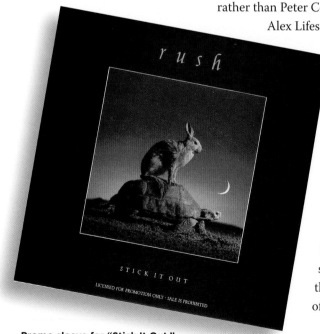

Promo sleeve for "Stick It Out," featuring a truly incredible guitar performance by Alex.

And they liked it so much they decided to go with it and use it. Also they'd maybe been getting flak for being a little synth-heavy in the mid-'80s, and although *Roll the Bones* isn't that synth-heavy, it has a little bit [of synthesizers], but not as bad as a *Hold Your Fire* or *Power Windows*. So I think it's a growth out of that, get a little tighter and toward using their main instruments. There's very little keyboard in there. But sure, Shirley was the one that was pushing for the heavier sound.

POPOFF: And what is the perception of *Counterparts* among the loyal fan base?

MARYONOVICH: When that came out, at that age, now I'm a fan, now I'm all the way in. So this album came out, and I'm waiting at the store. But fans like this album. There are no hard feelings about this album. There's not a single offensive blemish on this album that some people might feel there is on others. It's got a nice, refreshing, back-to-Rush sound. So I think this was received well. I know it charted on the Billboard 200 at number two, so that was a pretty big deal for them. And "Stick It Out" was a really strong single. But this was not one of their peak albums, although it's definitely solid.

POPOFF: Perhaps some of the lack of enthusiasm for the album was its short tour cycle, but we really can't ignore that this was the height of grunge mania, and Rush are pretty much the antithesis of that.

MARYONOVICH: That's true, that's true. Yes, you got a lot of that going on in modern music, with Soundgarden. And I know they were really inspired by Primus, who they toured with. So I would say on this one they're a little bit more susceptible to that than normally. Because again, this album does reflect a lot of current rock. Their songs were a little shorter, meaning they were trying to be on the radio a little bit. That's never been a trend, but I know that they do get some pressure from labels to have albums sell. Although, lyrically, they've never really caved to talking about stupid stuff that pop music talks about. Musically, I would say, though, they don't follow, but they lean [laughs].

POPOFF: And they were looking the part as well, right?

MARYONOVICH: Yes, in recent years, Geddy was wearing like leggings, and he was wearing long flannel shirts. And now he had jeans and a vest, and his hair, it wasn't '80s long, but it was '90s long, kind of at the shoulder. And he wore Converse All-Stars. And Alex was skinny back then—this was like skinny Alex, or Alex just beginning to gain some weight. And he just wore his normal stuff, which is like a blazer and jeans. And Neil . . . was he in a hat phase? Pretty sure he had his African tam hat and was in his goatee phase, along with the shorts and shirtless vests.

POPOFF: Okay, but the music is really good here, modern or not, and lyrically, it's top-shelf Neil Peart, and a brave one at that.

The lack of enthusiasm for *Counterparts* may have been a result of its short tour cycle.

Counterparts tour, Madison Square Garden, New York City, March 8, 1994. *Ebet Roberts/Redferns/ Getty Images*

MAHER: Yes, I'd agree with that. Without a doubt, where *Hold Your Fire* was Neil's first entrance into getting personal, *Counterparts* was the album that discussed everything to do with what was going on in his personal life. And that has been talked about from just about every source that I know. Lyrically, he's dealing with the demons and the struggles in his life. A lot of it is really controversial and personal, whether it's "Cold Fire" or "Double Agent," even "Everyday Glory."

There are areas where he addresses where there were separations in his marriage; there was trouble that was there. I mean, he was in a common-law marriage. He wasn't in a wedded church marriage. It was a really odd marriage and relationship, and he spent so much time away from home, on the road, and away from his family. His do-over that he is doing now is radically different than what his first go-around was. There's absolutely no question.

And when you listen to *Counterparts*, the rawness that Kevin Shirley brought out in it really fits the nerves of the lyrics in that record. And every single song on that record reflects something that is going on, of just how fast everything can change in a relationship and a marriage. "Everyday Glory" talks about Mom and Dad fighting, and the little girl hears the pounding on the wall. And he has a daughter, and she was younger, and so all of those things were there. "Cold Fire" is a huge thing. "Double Agent," there's no question Neil is looking into the two sides of himself. "Double Agent" is the darkest Rush song ever written, hands down—probably the most underrated as well.

POPOFF: "Cold Fire" is pretty dark as well, and it was an oft-played song.
IRWIN: Just the fact that in the lyrics he says, *This is not a love song*, that's actually in there, and the way Neil frames it, it's not a love song, but it's a song about love. And I really enjoyed that. Just the way that the woman is clearly smarter than the man.

And she's using that to kind of manipulate him. And the imagery he uses, like *phosphorescent wave on a tropical sea* and *The flame at the heart of a pawnbroker's diamond*, it's just the thought it evokes. And that's what I love about his lyrics. You're listening to a song, and you're always picking up different things.

MARYONOVICH: "Cold Fire" is another Neil relationship song. Lyrically, this is so in line with the theme of the self, the internal and the external, which are so different. *When we started on traditional roles.* You know, the man in the relationship and the woman in the relationship are different, and how those two reflect each other are as counterparts.

Which is the theme reflected in the artwork. The cover was very simple; that nut and bolt illustration was amazing, and I considered it for a tattoo about a thousand times. But the inner artwork is just stunning, with these pairs of things, the tortoise and hare, the salt and pepper shakers, these things that are counterparts to each other in real life. The metaphors were just so beautiful and so strong.

And then there were these little word arts inside the album that never made the light of day as major artworks, but I would go and dwell on them in my high school, put them on my locker. Yeah, there was so much thought put into this album artwork. I just absolutely devoured it when it came out. But again, these were counterparts, little phrases that kind of fit together, these series of things, and they also rhymed really well. Neil did that awesomely with the writing on those, and then I think Hugh Syme executed perfectly with his design concept.

And all the songs in this album really link up that theme of counterparts, how things are opposites and also complement each other. And no other band was putting together a theme of an album being this philosophical thing. . . . We do not appreciate enough how they did that, and how it was not so on-the-nose or hitting you over the head. It wasn't the same word in every song, but the themes were there, and it was like a riddle. It was like go through these things and find all the pieces that add up to this bigger concept.

POPOFF: Lyrics aside, what are some sonic highlights on the record? After all, as much as we speak of its rocking qualities, there's a lot of typical Rush detailing.

IRWIN: I like "Between Sun and Moon," which is a cowrite lyrically between Neil and Max Webster's Pye Dubois. It's a slow one, and it reminds me of when in your Max Webster book [*Live Magnetic Air*], they talked about the difficulty of playing slow songs like "Battle Scar," which of course is a

"Double Agent"—the darkest Rush song ever?

With "Nobody's Hero" Neil explored the idea of what constitutes real heroes. Spoiler alert: It's not film or sports stars.

massive band duel between Max and Rush. But I love Geddy's vocal inflections in it; it's just a really great listening tune.

I love Alex's guitar playing on "Stick It Out"—absolutely amazing. In fact, they were saying that if there was one song where maybe the guitars are a little too rough and too heavy, that would have to be it. Fantastic, especially the ending, where it really jams.

"Alien Shore," great song, and if you listen closely, you can hear the depth-sounding pings of a submarine. And I just love the vocals. Geddy is his best backup singer, when he layers his own vocals. *[T]hat's just us*—when he is singing that, that's always been a favorite part for me.

MARYONOVICH: "Double Agent" is awesome. They used an interesting technique with it. He wasn't singing, he was talking/singing, and they put a filter, a dark grumbly filter on his voice. It was like he was on the edge of sleep. It's more like scary storytelling. And then of course the chorus was really good too. "Double Agent" is the song that defined *Counterparts* for me.

IRWIN: Geddy and Alex were doing a radio interview for the album, and the DJ asked what they were doing with "Double Agent," and Geddy said, "We were losing our minds." And that's a great song, looking at the whole idea of the subconscious and conscious minds, dueling it out. "We were losing our minds." Geddy and Alex had a good laugh over that.

POPOFF: "Nobody's Hero" was a serious song, though, especially with the references to a real-life serial killer, striking too close to home.

IRWIN: Yes, there's the reference to the Paul Bernardo murders. Kristian French was one of Paul Bernardo's victims, and she was the stepsister of Brad French, who is Neil's lifelong best friend. And that's why *I didn't know the girl, but I knew her family.* And I think, in fact, Brad and Neil are second cousins. And it's a complicated point, but I think he's saying just because somebody is a victim, don't glorify that. You should basically think about the person that they were, rather than the fate that befell them. And then elsewhere, Neil's getting across the idea that a proper hero is somebody who does a great thing like lands a crippled airplane or solves a mystery or cures a disease, that sort of thing, rather than sports stars or movie stars.

POPOFF: But ultimately, again, we keep returning to the challenge of relationships.

MARYONOVICH: Yes, and "Alien Shore" is another one of these. This one is such a Rush song. It's a little less rocking, a couple steps back from the power of "Animate" or "Stick It Out." *Reaching for the alien shore.* This is about Neil in relationships. This is about, again, a man and a woman, him and a partner, sort of struggling to reach their balance. *We add to each other, like a coral reef.* Like, what other band writes about a coral reef? Yeah, so this was good. Not one of my favorites, musically, but it's got a lot of really good lyrics. *You and I, we are strangers by one chromosome.* Like, that's really brilliant.

POPOFF: And then a poignant end to the record with "Everyday Glory," a track often left out of the *Counterparts* discussion.

MARYONOVICH: Yes, Rush opens the album with a kickass, fist-in-the-air monster song like "Animate," and then they end with a thoughtful piece, like "Available Light," "You Bet Your Life," or "Everyday Glory." These are really like think-piece songs. This one is really sad. I mean, on the face of it, it's about a kid whose parents are fighting, and the kid is hiding. And she's really affected by the anger and the pain around her.

And it's sad. Neil writes a lot about very sad cities and the people who are lost in them, *In the city where nobody smiles / And nobody dreams.* Like he writes about bored people in bad cities. This is a theme [laughs]. "Middletown Dreams" is a classic example of that. And this is like some *Presto* stuff, like *one spark of decency / Against a starless night.*

So this is an anthem about the people that are suffering and kind of persevering. It gets better. *If the future's looking dark, / We're the ones who have to shine.* That could be the last paragraph to a presidential campaign speech, you know what I mean? . . . It's very motivational, almost in a kids' storybook type of way.

But, yeah, you look at *Counterparts* as a whole, and Neil was just on fire during this stage. Just the way he was rhyming and the strength of his messages and then the way that like Geddy could phrase his little rhymes . . . they nailed it every time. There wasn't a word or a syllable or a beat out of place. It was just magic.

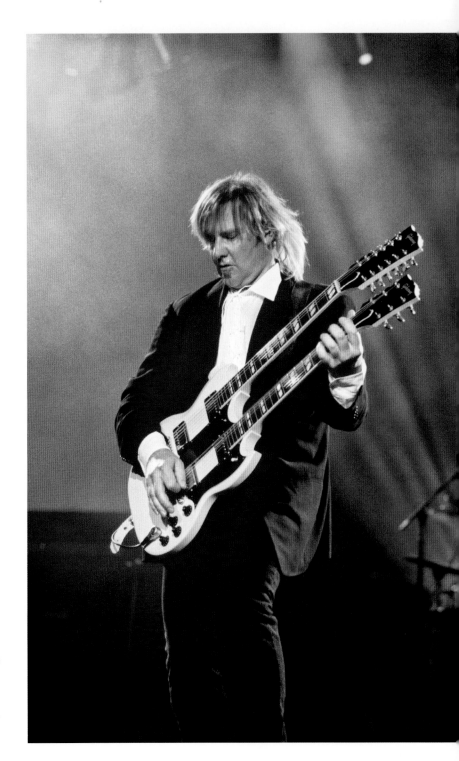

Counterparts tour, Madison Square Garden, New York City, March 8, 1994. *Ebet Roberts/Redferns/ Getty Images*

CHAPTER 16

Test for Echo

with Eddy Maxwell and Douglas Maher

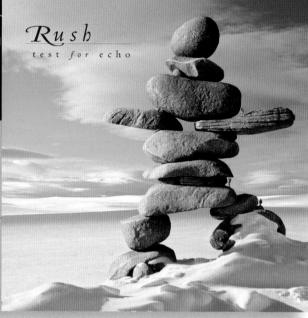

Geddy Lee: *bass, keyboards, vocals*
Alex Lifeson: *acoustic and electric guitars, mandola*
Neil Peart: *drums, percussion, hammered dulcimer*
Released September 10, 1996
Recorded at Bearsville Studios, Woodstock, New York,
and Reaction Studios, Toronto
Produced by Peter Collins and Rush

(opposite)
An eye toward semiretirement?
Test for Echo **tour, Nassau Coliseum,
Uniondale, New York, December 14,
1996.** *Patti Ouderkirk/WireImage/
Getty Images*

New blood constantly, the youth wheel of rock 'n' roll turns ever on, delivering new stars with new ideas, top to bottom, lyrics to drums. Into this environment— and what is essentially another nadir year for both progressive rock (long gone) and heavy metal (five years gone)—wades Rush.

And this is already a Rush with an eye toward semiretirement, voiced in interviews and through actions, longer periods between albums and not because of grinding, mammoth tours due to the success of said records (an older paradigm excuse that was always sensibly accepted). Nay, Rush arrives at *Test for Echo* as gentleman rock craftsmen, tacitly disdainful of the toil, even if Neil would explore a newfound enthusiasm for the art of the drum itself through his jazzy traditional-grip studies with old saw Freddie Gruber.

And so really, 1996 feels like nothing more than "time for another Rush album," lest people forget about us. Peter Collins is back for yet a fourth time as producer, but lacking a Kevin Shirley to bull-charge the sessions, resulting in a record weirdly heavy on paper but softly appointed to death. Not to say, really, what was in fashion or out—Rush clearly didn't know, either, positioned obscurely not through creative independence but through fence-sitting and (snow) drift in an old folks' approximation of the "hard

Test for Echo tour, San Jose Arena, San Jose, California, November 20, 1996. *Tim Mosenfelder/Getty Images*

Test for Echo felt emphatically like a leisurely album and tour cycle rather than a rip roarin' motorcycle ride.

alternative" music that came along after the fire in the belly known as grunge settled with antacid.

Up top, Neil calmly laid down, as if sorting through his office papers or conducting a spring cleaning there at Bearsville in nowheresville, New York, applying his latest musings to the tracks, again, as if a Rush album was on order, expected—ring the bell, table five.

Fully five singles were floated from the album, four doing well on the consolation "Mainstream Rock" chart, with, really, only "Test for Echo" and "Driven" temporarily catching on, due to, well, catchiness, but the way one catches a cold. Testimony to Rush's entrenchment in pop culture, the album would reach number five on Billboard and sell gold in the US, but this felt emphatically like a leisurely album and tour cycle rather than a rip roarin' motorcycle ride.

POPOFF: If we were to try to articulate a central theme to *Test for Echo*, what would it be?

MAHER: *Test for Echo* is another album where Neil opened his notebooks, with, you know, some concepts and some ideas that had interested him. And at the time, the big thing was the Internet coming into everybody's homes, and the oversaturation of cable TV going from the 1980s and having eighty-nine channels to now having three hundred–plus by 1996. The information overload was happening.

MAXWELL: Yes, a lot of it to me is about communication. The whole idea of "test for echo" is, "Is there anybody out there?" But communication is also there in "Dog Years," "The Color of Right," and "Half the World." The mid- to late '90s, we were all just starting to get on the Internet, starting to get email, starting to see the world as bigger and bigger, and making that connection. So what Neil did with "Virtuality" was kind of address the idea of it's not real, but it is real. It's real in my mind, but I'm actually not seeing or touching that person, and yet I'm still making that connection. And also there's a bit of fear about where it's taking us, with everything coming right at us, finding the need to be able to step away from that and find the color of right, find those people that are on the other half of the world. So yes, I think communication was a big theme on this album.

POPOFF: And how would you classify or describe the production job on the record?

MAHER: The album itself was terribly produced. Peter Collins just did not belong there, by that point. It just didn't make any sense—not at all. And again, we found ourselves in a position where we had a song like "Test for Echo" that comes out, enters in at number one on the album-oriented rock charts, and they make no music video for it. Now that's not to say that it would've been played on MTV if it had come out, but still.

MAXWELL: What Peter Collins brings is a bit of a jangle, a cleanness, so it's not crunchy, it's clean. I think *Test for Echo* is holding up well, in terms of the production. It's very crisp. I can hear all of the instruments. I can hear Geddy very well. It's very balanced. That's what I thought of *Power Windows* the first time I'd ever heard it, is that it's very balanced. Nothing is getting lost in both *Test for Echo* and *Power Windows*.

POPOFF: I take it you disagree on how much of a sense of mission there is with *Test for Echo*.

MAHER: Well, I'll just say that the time that they took with Geddy, obviously taking care of his new child at the time and whatnot in between [the] *Counterparts* tour—very short tour—and *Test for Echo* . . . *Test for Echo* seemed like an album where we're going to go in, we're going to make it with everybody who is kind of a familiar crew, keep it local, and we're just going to work off this basic ethos, acknowledging our lives.

And some of that doesn't translate when you have songs like "Driven" and "Totem" and "Carve Away the Stone" and "Limbo" and "Dog Years." "Dog Years" is about communication, I guess, and different signals that go on through dogs' brains and whatnot, and it's illustrative of a record that really goes off to various places—it really does seem like that. They were just ideas that were kind of lumped together that found themselves lyrically disjointed throughout the record. There wasn't this theme that seemed to connect.

You had "The Color of Right" in there, which, again is more of a relationship song, and so you think, are these just ideas that he's throwing everywhere? Is there a message that supposed to come out of this? I'm not getting the interconnection between the Marilyn Manson–type "Driven" video and "Half the World," which sounds like Hootie & the Blowfish. And it's Rush trying to figure out where they fit in the rock world. At this point, if you remember, six months prior to that album coming out, Hootie & the

With the dawn of the Internet Age, communication was a clear theme on *t4e*, especially with tracks like "Half the World."

Upon hearing the newly released *t4e*, some believed producer Peter Collins to be a poor fit—too much jangle, too little crunch.

Blowfish were the biggest band in the world. That *Cracked Rearview Mirror* album had sold something like twelve million copies at that point—it was obscene. And here we have Rush coming out, you know, using a mandola—what?! What is this going on here?

MAXWELL: Well, I thought that softer sound was more where they were going with *Roll the Bones*. I thought *Counterparts* was a reset for them. With *Test for Echo*, I didn't get the sense that they were lost. I got the sense that this was where they wanted to be. That they were going out and making an album because it was fun. And I just hear a lot of joy and little jokes in there, like "son of a bitch" and the stuff in "Limbo."

But I didn't get the sense of them being lost between grunge and Hootie. I got the sense of them going in a new direction. And if the tragedies that happened in Neil's life hadn't happened, I think [Rush] would've continued along this line, and maybe gotten a little harder as they got inspired. But no, I thought that they were pretty comfortable in what they were doing.

So I disagree. I think there is a freshness and there's a little more joy, certainly than *Counterparts*. *Counterparts* came in hard and heavy, and even the artwork is a little darker. Whereas on *Test for Echo*, they're letting their humor come out a little more, over music made by a band that seems to be in a very positive mood. When this came out, I was reading everything that was out there. Neil was definitely very comfortable with where he was at. Alex was reasserting himself as a guitarist and reminding people that this is a guitar band. You're hearing a lot of that with his performance. As for Geddy, he was in there, which you can really hear on "Driven," saying, "Look, I'm Geddy Lee, damn it" [laughs]—which is a *South Park* quote, by the way—"But yeah, I am one of the best bassists out there. So I just feel a lot of confidence."

POPOFF: Take me through a few specific tracks on the album that point to this idea of its liveliness.

MAXWELL: Definitely "Driven," because that song is such a kickstart. I don't know how else to say it. It's very moving, it grabs me and pulls me forward. It's one of those you don't want to be listening to in the car, because you'll be going eighty miles an hour down the road. There is humor in "Limbo," which caught a lot of us off guard. At first we were all like, "Oh my gosh, we're getting another instrumental." We were all so excited. But then Geddy layered some vocals on it, that moaning vocalizing. The idea of what happens if I put a little twist in there . . . there's a humor in that, and then calling it "Limbo," that really caught us off guard. Back then people weren't sure, but I listen to it now, and it's just beautiful.

And then "Dog Years" is a jam. I think that's the hardest-rocking song. Obviously it's a little sillier than most Rush songs are. And so it's going to be a little harder for some people to take. But I figured, hey, I'm just going to go with you guys. Let's go and have some fun. But it's the drum beat on it that makes the song.

POPOFF: But there are some serious lyrics on this album as well. What are some of Neil's most pointed messages on *Test for Echo*?

MAXWELL: "Carve Away the Stone" is a hidden gem that took me a while to warm up to it. The message in there is about getting everything out of the way and getting down to what you really need to be doing. And then get out of my way so that I can proceed on my own. Very strong final song for the album and really well laid-out.

"The Color of Right" I find musically pedestrian, but the lyrics really speak to me. And especially now, being in the social media business, I interact with people all over the world, with opinions all over the spectrum. And I have to remember that the concept in "The Color of Right," what's important to me, what matters to me, and what I'm close to, does not apply to everybody else.

"Totem" I like because it's exploring ideas of spirituality, and yet Neil says, *I believe in what I see / I believe in what I hear*. I actually named my company Totem Media. "Totem" is about perspective and it's about communication. I think it's poking a little fun. I'm not offended by it or anything. Neil's there talking about the holy cows—oh my gosh, he's putting down Hindus. Of course not. He's just talking about ritual and perspective, and what you believe can change the way you see things. It's just fun. *Angels and demons dancing in my head / Lunatics and monsters underneath my bed*. It sounds like Geddy is having fun singing it.

POPOFF: And I guess another plotline is Neil adjusting his game.

MAXWELL: I thought that was fascinating. As a fan of who I think is one of the greatest and most famous rock drummers ever, seeing him say that he could improve himself—very inspirational. And it did change his drumming; other people who are really into drumming could tell, but even I could see that he was more creative and dynamic. Working with Freddie inspired him to do more interesting, different, and more challenging drum parts on *Test for Echo*.

MAHER: This is changing the total setup for which we know Neil as a rock drummer. He's done his drum lessons for the last year and a half with Freddie Gruber. He comes out with traditional grip, and you can hear and see in his playing that the songs are different now. Neil is all of a sudden playing on a DW kit. The kit looks one hundred percent different. It's not the Neil that left us on the *Counterparts* tour. It's a completely different human being, a completely different drummer.

Test for Echo tour, Nassau Coliseum, Uniondale, New York, December 14, 1996. *Patti Ouderkirk/WireImage/ Getty Images*

Track two, the raw and in-your-face "Driven," served to kickstart the album.

POPOFF: And to reiterate our general point, *Test for Echo* emerges at an odd time for rock, definitely an odd time for any kind of rock Rush might make.

MAHER: Yes, I mean, for starters, Alex can't figure out whether he wants his guitar to sound like Korn or as I say, Hootie & the Blowfish. For instance, "Virtuality" features an unbelievably heavy riff. There's "Driven," which is real, raw, in-your-face stuff. But then there's "Half the World."

But Rush were always behind the times. They were always a year behind, as far as popularity was concerned, if they were trying to mimic a sound. When *Counterparts* came out, you heard a lot of grunge sound in it. When you hear the "Animate" riff, you can't help but think of "Evenflow" from Pearl Jam. And when you hear that, you're like, oh wow, imagine if they sounded like that two years ago. When *Roll the Bones* came out, you had songs like "Dreamline" and "Bravado" and "Ghost of a Chance," and that was going up against "Enter Sandman" and Nirvana, Pearl Jam, Soundgarden, and Alice in Chains. All those bands were lighting up rock radio.

But Rush made that last, and they won over everybody, and I'm going to tell you why. Bear with me, but this ties in with what happened for *Test for Echo*. What happened with *Roll the Bones*, basically that entire tour was with Primus. And Primus was just this burgeoning growing band out of the Bay Area that was just popping on MTV. Rush taking them out not only reignited them, but it brought in audiences that were in their younger teens or mid-teens, and they're hearing all of these Rush songs on the radio, and they're saying, "I love this. I love the fact that they're a trio, I love their old stuff"— they're discovering who Rush was. And the credit to Rush's longevity and popularity in the 1990s goes to Primus—it was nobody else. Primus opened the door.

And on the *Counterparts* tour, Rush had the Melvins opening for them, really alternative, just in California as a pickup thing, a couple of times. I think it was four shows the band brought them out for. But they also had I Mother Earth, the Doughboys, Candlebox. So that was the whole thing: Rush were tapped in with that scene, and that's when you saw guys from Soundgarden singing their praises. So they kind of had this ace that was there, where they'd go, "Hey, we'd like to bring you up for some shows."

And then the decision came about to go with a full "Evening with," meaning no support act. Which is fine in the context of the fans, okay, great. But in later years, Neil and Alex both admitted that they missed giving opportunities to bands that they loved, to play for bigger crowds and give them some exposure, but they just missed having that experience, being around younger musicians. And they had such a blast with Primus and became such good, close friends with them, that it really inspired what became *Counterparts*.

And to see what wound up happening with *Test for Echo* did not add up at all, in the context of the heavy sounds on *Counterparts*—it was confusing. When Geddy talked about it in *Beyond the Lighted Stage*, that with *Counterparts*, they really needed that, everything sounded meatier and heavier and it was straight through the amps . . . and

Test for Echo tour, San Jose Arena, San Jose, California, November 20, 1996. *Tim Mosenfelder/Getty Images*

all of a sudden you went to this really placid-sounding record with *Test for Echo* that sounded nothing like *Counterparts*. It sounded like a follow-up to *Roll the Bones* more than anything. You know, you'd swear it was produced by Rupert Hine, except I think Rupert would've added a bit more melody and friendlier hooks.

But *Test for Echo* just can't get out of its own way. And it was released at a time where bands from Rush's era were on that teetering edge. Even Van Halen were just getting out of that *Balance* era, and although they were still selling out arenas with Hagar, Van Halen couldn't get songs on the radio, or at least MTV, anymore.

So the question becomes, what can we do? And Rush had already established that they were not . . . Ray Danniels never made them an MTV band. He didn't put emphasis with the labels, and say, "Hey, look, this record's number one at radio, I need to get a video done for this, I need a video done for the next four releases that we're going to do or this album is just going to die off." And so, again, it went from where *Counterparts* sold a little over 850,000 copies, against *Test for Echo*, which sold about 525,000. That's a major drop-off from one album to the next, especially when you had *Roll the Bones* doing 1.5, 1.6 million.

Featuring a heavy riff evocative of grunge, "Virtuality" betrayed a band following trend and years late to the party.

CHAPTER 17

Vapor Trails

with Chris Irwin, Eddy Maxwell, and Mary Jo Plews

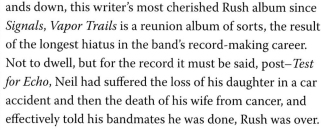

(all music Lee and Lifeson; lyrics Peart)

Geddy Lee: *bass, vocals*
Alex Lifeson: *electric and acoustic guitars, mandola*
Neil Peart: *drums, percussion*
Released May 14, 2002
Recorded at Reaction Studios, Toronto
Produced by Rush and Paul Northfield

Hands down, this writer's most cherished Rush album since *Signals*, *Vapor Trails* is a reunion album of sorts, the result of the longest hiatus in the band's record-making career. Not to dwell, but for the record it must be said, post–*Test for Echo*, Neil had suffered the loss of his daughter in a car accident and then the death of his wife from cancer, and effectively told his bandmates he was done, Rush was over.

Reversing the decision was a gradual and fragile process, and the artful result was a record that wasn't preordained or in any way scheduled, but one that emerged because it blossomed to its fierce light of life. In other words, unlike maybe a few Rush albums, and arguably very much so *Test for Echo*, *Vapor Trails* is a record with the power of purpose. Song after striving song, Rush is on a mission beyond being clever for five minutes and then five minutes again. Geddy and Alex are trying to heal Neil, and Neil is trying to heal himself, through sweat, muscle memory, identity, daily structure, and, most importantly, through the arrangement of words into philosophies that can take the pain from the heart to the page where it's imbued with some distance.

Bashed, mixed hot or not, textural and not so organized of riff . . . it is of no matter because the power is within the words, the performances, the surging melodic shifts, Geddy's passion-drenched vocals. The sum total of the band's arguably odd choices

against their vaulted emotion and creativity makes for a singularly strange Rush album, which, again, to try take another stab at this idea, feels very much like a record that simply had to be made, in the spirit of creativity, as a matter of life or death, far beyond the motivations for any other record by these otherwise sensible Canadian worker bees of prog metal craftsmanship.

POPOFF: Very difficult circumstances in terms of the making of *Vapor Trails*. How did the band navigate the waters of Neil's grief to bring that record to fruition?

PLEWS: Well, they waited until he was ready, and it took something like fourteen months to record this album. They went in knowing, take our time, and they knew it would be a real healing effort for them. So they were very patient. They weren't as driven, I don't think, and they didn't set deadlines. So it was a very different environment. And their producer, Paul Northfield, had been with them for a number of years, but first time producing. So I think there was some real level of comfort that they wanted to have with people around them. Because this was going to be a tenuous time and sensitive time. And they just had to take it as it came.

Healing through the miracle of sweat, muscle memory, daily structure, and writing. *Vapor Trails* **tour, MGM Grand Garden Arena, Las Vegas, September 21, 2002.** *Ethan Miller/Getty Images*

Vapor Trails' **power is found in the words, the performances, the surging melodic shifts, and Geddy's passion-drenched vocals.**

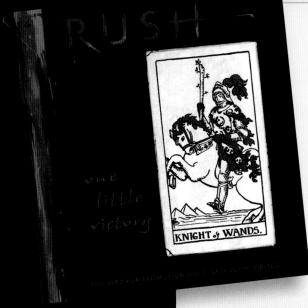

KNIGHT of WANDS.

RECEIVED FOR PROMOTION ONLY. SALE IS PROHIBITED.

Advance release, "One Little Victory" was *Vapor Trails*' anthem, and another kick-down-the-door opening track.

Criticism of the original release's noisy and hot mix begat *Vapor Trails Remixed* in 2013.

IRWIN: Well, we didn't even know if there was going to be another Rush album at that point—we have to remember that. There were all these tragedies, and there was probably a period of five years between *Test for Echo* and *Vapor Trails*. And I know as a fan, I was kind of worried, but if they were going to call it quits at that point, I totally understood. But sure enough, Neil got the urge, and I remember reading that Geddy had said they had gotten a phone call from him after so many years of not bothering him at all or pressuring him in any way to do an album. And I believe Neil said, "I think I'm in need of some employment," or something to that effect. And yeah, the spirit of that album, you can really feel it, with the rebirth, the need to live on and to push forward and to put the past behind you. It's really present and evident on that album.

POPOFF: And this spirit of rebirth is touchingly presented through Neil opening the record, thanking the base with a barrage of drums.

MAXWELL: Yes, "One Little Victory," that song was the anthem, not the "Anthem," but the anthem [laughs], small A, of the album. And having it as the advance release and the first song, it was a vote of confidence in themselves, but also where the fans could say, "Okay, you are back, we waited, we've been here, we were waiting for you. Oh my God, we're so glad you're back." And there's that sense of triumph. And even though our victories may be small, which is what all of us experience in everyday life—we're just average people—I think a lot of people could relate to it. And so the fans really grasped onto that song and took it personally.

PLEWS: Exactly, and you know, *Vapor Trails* was just a gift to us, as fans. To have somebody come back and come through what Neil had been through, obviously that affected Alex and Geddy as well. To me it was a celebration, right off the bat, right out the door, with that first song, and the drums opening up that song. "One Little Victory" is just right out of the box, kick down the door, here we are, just thrilling.

POPOFF: But there was controversy as well, with this idea that the mix was noisy and loud, that given this strange bank of texture-based songs, there was a flaw to the record, and hence the album *Vapor Trails Remixed* in 2013.

PLEWS: Yes, but for them to come back. I mean, really, I wasn't questioning whether it was overmixed. That wasn't my issue. So that remix to me was great. I liked it . . . but the original's fine with me. It was what it was at the time. And I can respect what they did at the time.

But they did say that it was overmixed, and you couldn't hear the nuances, and you couldn't hear the guitar solos or some of the bass lines. I don't know the technicalities of it all, but I like the original version just fine. I certainly hear the difference between the original *Vapor Trails* and the remixed *Vapor Trails*, and there's parts of it where I could clearly tell, oh yes, I didn't hear this guitar solo in the original version. I like both versions, but I can see why they did it.

MAXWELL: The mix was a little strange. It was overblown, too hot, which didn't bother me as much as it bothered people who worked in the music industry or worked with sound a lot. It's a very hot album and maybe a little muddy. I mean, when I put it on, I have to instantly turn my stereo down. And I can't wrap my ears around the remix album yet—it's a completely different album. I'm still trying to find what settings to use; I just don't know what I'm hearing. Of course on both versions there's definitely tons of guitar and some nice backing vocals, beautiful vocal lines, that Geddy does.

Vapor Trails tour, Shoreline Amphitheater, Mountain View, California, September 20, 2002. *Tim Mosenfelder/Getty Images*

POPOFF: But there's also the sense that it's a jammy, no-nonsense album.

PLEWS: No, there's not a lot of odd time signatures or many guitar solos. I remember people regretting that, saying, "Where are the drum solos?" I liked it because it was heavier and they got back to the roots. So it was new and old again at the same time. And it didn't have any synthesizers or keyboards, which was okay with me. I appreciated Rush wanting to try different things at different times throughout their career—that's what we like about them, that they're not stagnant. They don't play the same thing over and over again monotonously like some bands—that's not Rush.

And so I love *Vapor Trails*. To me it was a celebratory kickass return. We didn't know we were going to have that again. There was some acceptance that they may never play again and that might've been the end of Rush. So *Vapor Trails* holds a special place in our hearts. It meant they were back, that they weren't done, and we got thirteen more years of Rush.

POPOFF: What's a deep track highlight on the record beyond the known singles?

MAXWELL: "Peaceable Kingdom" I thought was interesting. Especially when I found out that originally it was going to be an instrumental, which would've been a fabulous instrumental. But then it now means so much. *Talk of a time without fear / The ones*

"Secret Touch" spoke of the need to look within amid difficult circumstances.

Vapor Trails **tour, Shoreline Amphitheater, Mountain View, California, September 20, 2002.** *Tim Mosenfelder/Getty Images*

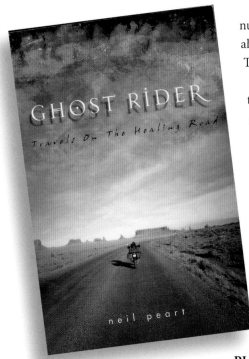

"Ghost Rider" was essentially the soundtrack to Neil's hit book about his long and meditative motorcycle trips.

we wish would listen / Are never going to hear. I think that's pretty global; that's a pretty universal feeling that we all have. And I remember when this album came out, there was a bunch of us Rush fans that got together for a little listening party, and we listened to the songs and talked about them. And I believe that this was one of the songs we talked about the most. You could talk to somebody for an hour about that song, about what it means, and actually what it meant then. You know, who were the big players in the world then? Who are the big players now?

IRWIN: I'd say the heaviest song on the album is probably "Freeze"—they go nuts on that. And it's kind of funny how many albums later, *Grace Under Pressure* all the way through to *Vapor Trails*, they do a part four, and it's not the "Fear Trilogy" anymore, right? [laughs]

"Earthshine" is interesting because that song is apparently the only Rush song that was completely deconstructed and reconstructed as a completely different song. It was changed and changed to the point where there was nothing left. And I'm curious to find out whether the original song was written into another song on that album or if it was something that was just tossed out.

And a couple more . . . it's interesting, both "Ceiling Unlimited" and another favorite song on that, "Out of the Cradle," both start off with a similar sort of lyric. "Ceiling Unlimited" has *It's not the heat / It's the inhumanity,* while "Out of the Cradle" starts with *It's not a place / It's a yearning.* "Ceiling Unlimited," the title came from Neil watching the weather one day, the weather report, as he often does. I love those two songs. A lot of Neil's writing at that time was coming from a place of terrible pain. And I think a lot of it was just him looking for sort of a shift in perspective, like you could look at something one way, but if you look at it another way, maybe you can see a more positive outcome.

PLEWS: I would like to talk about "The Stars Look Down" a little bit. Besides the layered vocals on it, I love how it talks about how we can't control our own fate, sometimes. It's kind of an interesting juxtaposition to the song "Freewill." You know, we always have a choice, but sometimes you don't have a choice. Sometimes your fate is just handed to you and you've got no control over it. Obviously you have a choice in how you react to it, but I think this song is saying that sometimes your free will is taken out of the mix and you've just got to deal with it. And you are wondering, looking up to heaven, is anybody up there? Is anybody listening? That you can't believe. Like the song says, *Like the rat in a maze.* So I think we all try to find meaning in disasters or traumas or losses; it's a human need to ascribe meaning to events, and I think that song says sometimes there is no meaning and there is no answer. Sometimes there is just no answer why things happen.

MAXWELL: "Out of the Cradle" is another favorite because it's typical Rush, very positive, and it's about looking forward. And then *Endlessly rocking.* It was a great way to end the album, because I felt that it was saying, "We're here, we're going to stay for a while," which they did. And so *Endlessly rocking,* I'm thinking as a big music fan for most of my life, that feeling of, okay, I'm in my forties now, I'm still rocking. The band is a little older than me and they're still rocking. And it's all good—we're all good.

PLEWS: Oh, I agree. That song inspires a lot of hope for me. That *Endlessly rocking, endlessly rocking* will always be about Rush. Rush will be endlessly rocking. They may not tour anymore, and they may not have any shows, but to me, they'll be endlessly rocking. So "Out of the Cradle" is a big song for me and has a big place in my heart. And it talks again about how you can live life right on the edge. You can fall right off the edge of the knife. And yet it really is kind of a life-affirming song.

Hope is a big theme in Rush's songs. Like the end of "Ceiling Unlimited": *hope is like an endless river / the time is now again.* I like that the song and the lyric is there, but the melody is also there. It's like after all this, it inspires hope. Like, now is the time; hope is endless. And that's a recurring theme.

"Sweet Miracle" served as the third and final single from *Vapor Trails*, releasing in September 2002.

POPOFF: In terms of the more famed songs, "Secret Touch" was the record's second single.

IRWIN: Yes, I like that one. *The way out is the way in.* Just the whole idea of looking at things one way or another. Are you going out of the situation or are you going into the situation? Although it's also about Neil having a hole in his heart.

PLEWS: "Secret Touch," just like the first four lines, *The way out is the way in.* Which is, you know, man's search, woman's search for happiness, and what is the meaning of life? And how do I become fulfilled? You can't look outside yourself. You have to look inside yourself. So that is a philosophy that is obviously a tenet of psychology, and as a therapist, I know that, and it speaks volumes. And I think, again, that's an overall theme of the whole album. It's what's going on with Neil, internally, what goes on with people, internally, interpersonally, when they go through something like he has been through. What is grief and loss about?

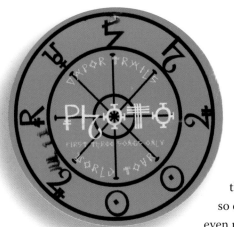

Photo pass from the *Vapor Trails* tour foreshadows *Clockwork Angels* imagery.

POPOFF: And "Earthshine" is of course the big one on here.

MAXWELL: "Earthshine" is more poetic, a little more abstract. The way Geddy sings it, where he goes high, it's just lovely. It's almost like haiku. It has that kind of feeling, very visual.

PLEWS: "Earthshine" is another one of my favorite Rush songs of all time, really. I like the vocal layering on it. It almost sounds like there's a choir at times in the song. The lyrics . . . when you've been through losses like that, you certainly feel so empty. We probably have all felt that way. The idea that you're invisible, you're not even real, or that people can't see you. At the time, my mother was going through chemo and died a little after, about a year after this came out. And so some of those songs at the time are very meaningful to me, and those lyrics in particular.

IRWIN: I'll always remember "Earthshine" because it was used in the Rush episode of *Trailer Park Boys*. Which, by the way, I don't know if you know this, *Trailer Park Boys* did not approach them to join in—Alex approached the *Trailer Park Boys*. Coincidence, we lived in Dartmouth, Nova Scotia, and my brother went to high school with the actor that plays Ricky. Anyway, what happened was, on the *Vapor Trails* tour, as the band would set up and tear down, they would play on the screen the first two seasons of *Trailer Park Boys*, just because they liked them. And Alex got hooked on them. The crew kind of turned him onto them.

And he liked it so much that he approached Mike Clattenburg, who actually was a drummer in a punk band . . . [and] asked if he could do a cameo. And they said, "Well, how about instead of a cameo, we'll write an entire episode around you?" "Cool, let's do it." And so "Earthshine" was used in the episode. Over the radio, Bubbles wins Rush tickets to their show in Halifax because he knows that Alex's real last name is Zivojinovic. So Randy overhears that and he gets on the phone and he beats him to it.

And as Trevor and Corey are out in front of the arena there, they end up playing "Earthshine" on the radio.

POPOFF: "Earthshine" is another example of one of these driving, wall-of-sound tracks on the album, an album that feels more about chords than riffs. And with Geddy's aggressive bass, again, it feels much more about texture.

PLEWS: Yeah, it is a very textured album. That's a good way to put it.

POPOFF: How much of this would be due to Paul Northfield? He's an engineer elevated to producer, and he's a close associate.

PLEWS: I think in this case it was more up to the guys. Paul had been working with them for twenty years or so. Nick Raskulinecz—they called him Boougjzhe—has a very different style than Paul. For them at that time, Paul's what they needed. They didn't need somebody to come in and shake them up, which Nick would do. They didn't need somebody to come in and ask them to be different. They needed to be with somebody they knew and somebody they trusted. And because this was going to be a lengthy process and it was going to be very personal and deal with sensitive issues, they needed a safe place to come back together. And I think Paul gave them that—that's what they needed at the time.

POPOFF: One other important track is "Ghost Rider," essentially the soundtrack to Neil's hit book and his grieving process, his long and contemplative and even meditative motorcycle trips.

PLEWS: Yes, "Ghost Rider" really is Neil's story, of him coming back, and obviously he wrote that book with the same name. The song offers an incredible visual of his travels and his journey and

what he had been through. The rhythm of the song matches the mood, and Geddy's voice really portrays the emotion. I've found other people who feel the same way and have seen it in reviews. And I believe even Neil has said how much he felt Geddy captured the spirit of the song. And I love the ending too, *Nothing can stop you now*. So, really, it ends with hope. It's so inspiring that he can get through that. Can't you just see Neil riding down the road on his motorcycle and looking in his rearview mirror? It's so descriptive.

Performing for 400,000-plus (including the author) at "SARS-Stock," Downsview Park, Toronto, July 30, 2003. *Roger Bacon/ Reuters/Alamy*

POPOFF: Finally, we should address this powerful image of a vapor trail—on the cover, in song—the overarching theme of the entire album, perhaps.

IRWIN: The things from the past are going to be in the past, and there's nothing you can do about them, and they're going to fade away. It's funny, I was thinking about the title the other day, and I happened to look up to the sky and I saw a jet fly by, leaving a long vapor trail, and slowly it fades away and there's really nothing you can do about it. You can just kind of plow on and strive to move forward. That was the whole thing with Neil. I forget where the quote is from, but somebody said, "You can get busy living or get busy dying."

PLEWS: A vapor trail, of course, is the trail a plane leaves behind, but Neil was imbuing it with more of a spiritual meaning than that, the idea that we all leave a trail behind. We leave a mark on the world, even if it's seemingly temporary. As in the song, *Atmospheric phases make the transitory last / Vaporize the memories that freeze the fading past*. There are things, you know, *footprints in the rain, the oceans drain away . . .* all those things say that everything is temporary. But we leave a trail, and the trail has an impact. So maybe, even though what we've done is temporary, what we leave behind has a lasting impact. As for the cover of the album, the visual I get is that it's them coming back, making their mark again, it's them being shot out like a rocket.

Feedback

with Pete Koza, Douglas Maher, Mary Jo Plews, Chris Schneberger, and Ray Wawrzyniak

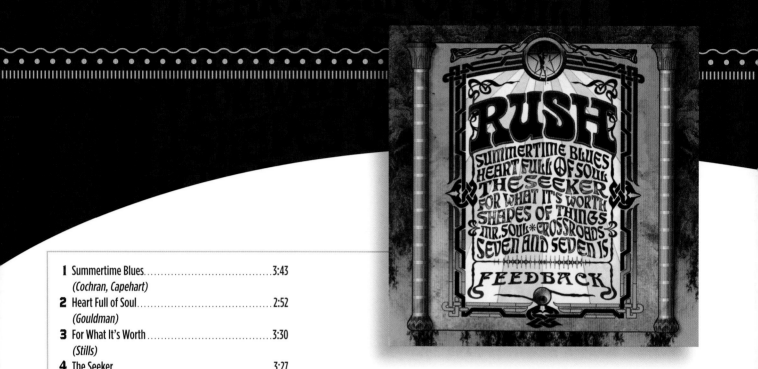

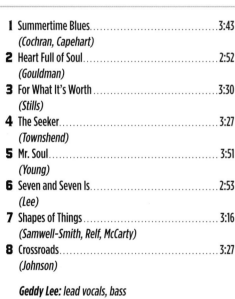

1 Summertime Blues.....................................3:43
   (Cochran, Capehart)
2 Heart Full of Soul.....................................2:52
   (Gouldman)
3 For What It's Worth...................................3:30
   (Stills)
4 The Seeker..3:27
   (Townshend)
5 Mr. Soul..3:51
   (Young)
6 Seven and Seven Is....................................2:53
   (Lee)
7 Shapes of Things......................................3:16
   (Samwell-Smith, Relf, McCarty)
8 Crossroads..3:27
   (Johnson)

Geddy Lee: lead vocals, bass
Alex Lifeson: guitar
Neil Peart: drums, percussion
Released June 29, 2004
Recorded at Phase One Studios, Toronto
Produced by David Leonard and Rush

(opposite)
After decades of straight-laced original recordings and setlists, Rush suddenly bashed out eight beloved oldies. R30 tour, Wembley Arena, London, September 8, 2004. *Pictorial Press Ltd./Alamy*

Because of a little asterisk of inconvenience called *Feedback*, declaring Rush a band of twenty (studio) records necessarily requires additional clumsy wording, involving add-ons like "nineteen of original material" or "nineteen plus one EP," plus "it's a long EP and even a short album," bolstered by "it's got eight songs and it's twenty-eight minutes so in the land of Van Halen, yeah, it's an album!" Well, we can be thankful that we don't have to talk about the breakup then reunion album, the one record with a different singer, or the half live/half studio record.

In any event, the reality is, Rush made a long covers EP, and we have to deal with it. And so enough about the affront to tidiness, a tacit expectation that Rush themselves have bred in their fan base, but now shattered. Into the music, and guess what? It's just kind of cool that Rush, after straight-laced decades of no covers in the studio or live, suddenly bashed out eight oldies beloved by the guys as teens, whacked it into a digipak, and then bashed out on stage, much to the surprise of the trained faithful.

Highlights perhaps are Love oddity "Seven and Seven Is," due to its proto-prog; "The Seeker," due to its *Who de vivre*; and "Summertime Blues," due to its topical and tropical freshness tied into the Rush tour to come, a celebration of thirty years on the job, built off the inspiration of these songs in their original nascent and naïve rock form.

POPOFF: What was your initial reaction upon hearing *Feedback*?

WAWRZYNIAK: I was completely surprised that they were doing such a record. I never thought that they would ever do anything like that. And I know in some interview years earlier, Geddy said they would never do something like that. And here they were. I understand them doing it. They were going out and doing the R30 tour, thirtieth anniversary, and I think at that point they just weren't comfortable going out without some kind of new product to promote.

(opposite)
R30 tour, Tweeter Center, Tinley Park, Illinois, June 5, 2004. *Matt Carmichael/Getty Images*

Inspirations for *Feedback*. Some of the songs from *Feedback* would occupy key slots in R30 setlists.

And this way they didn't have to worry about lyrics or song structure; they could just go into the studio and bang out a few songs. They worked with a producer called David Leonard, who has an extensive resume, but had also worked with Geddy on his solo album, *My Favorite Headache*. The sessions were quick and short and easy. Again, because they weren't slaving over song structure and putting a song together, crafting a song from floor to ceiling, it was easy. They just went in and paid homage to these songs they played all these years ago.

SCHNEBERGER: I agree, that's exactly how I felt—surprised [laughs]. I didn't think Rush would ever do covers of any kind. But then Rush is always challenging expectations. And when I listen to the songs, a lot of them are just big strong hits. It was interesting to hear them go back to get these tunes, but I would've just as soon had them create a new album for doing that tour. It was the prelude to R30, and I think they wanted to have something to tour for. And it does give a little insight into their musical background and influences.

KOZA: I liked their take, and I guess because I'm such a big Rush nut, those kind of became the standards for me! I knew some of the songs, but I didn't know "Seven and Seven Is," the Love track, until I heard Rush do it. And then I went back and have since grown to like that band.

POPOFF: One supposes the theme to the whole idea is represented by the heaviest and most joyous track, opener "Summertime Blues," correct?

SCHNEBERGER: Yes, and there were some great little accents, some additional little rhythmic moments from Neil there. "Summertime Blues" is incredible because it was essentially a mixture of The Who and the Blue Cheer versions. Plus "The Seeker" is great, as was "For What It's Worth." And "Crossroads," that's totally in their wheelhouse.

WAWRZYNIAK: I really thought they were just perfect choices. Rush doing "The Seeker" was just fantastic. Geddy's vocals suited that track perfectly. And they had, for so many years, given a nod to The Who, all three of them, as being a band that influence them so greatly. Alex as well, having mentioned so many times about how he loved Cream. So them doing "Crossroads," the Cream version, good God, that song was just an Alex Lifeson tour de force. That is so representative of his ability as a lead player—great guitar solo, and that translated so well live.

They really believed in that project. They put some of those songs in some real key slots on the supporting R30 tour. To come out in the encore, with all these songs in their pocket, and they pull out "Summertime Blues" and "Crossroads," followed by "Limelight," that to me showed their conviction in the project. It was something they were proud of. They ended up putting "Heart Full of Soul" in the set right after "Resist," during an acoustic-ish moment in the show. "Summertime Blues" was a great way to open the record and a seminal song to open up the encore, them going out on a summertime tour. That was a no-brainer.

So, you know, it surprised me, but once I realized, okay, they're going out on tour, they are going to want to have something to promote—fine. Even the album cover was so different for something by Hugh Syme. Everything about that project was different. Nobody expected it. Actually, here's a small little nugget: they released "Seven and Seven Is" as a seven-inch single on Record Store Day in 2014.

PLEWS: I have a brother who is about Rush's age, and I actually gave him that as a Christmas gift one year, and he loved it, because it was all the music he grew up with and that he was inspired by. It was a great nod to their influences, and I think it introduced some of their younger fans to maybe some older music. But yeah, those songs were of my brother's generation. I knew them, but I liked them better when Rush covered them.

POPOFF: That's a good point. Let's face it, these are not exactly the songs Rush fans would have wanted to hear from the boys.

MAHER: No, it was awful! [laughs]. But seriously, basically, when you're at that thirty-year point in your career, celebrating at least from '74, they weren't at a stage when they were going to go in and do an album of original material. Rush's formula is, once we start something, we can't stop. And they were afraid they were going to go and get in there and love what they were doing so much that it was going to wind up turning into an album, and then there would've been no R30 tour.

Ray Danniels was the one who really pushed R30, pushed the idea of paying homage to the music that they grew up on and that they loved, and it was something that was going to be quick, something that they could tour for, or tour with. Just like *Snakes & Arrows Live*, on the 2008 tour, when they toured for that.

Feedback wasn't well received. It's not well liked. It's maybe appreciated by people who grew up in the '60s. But I can tell you one thing: Rush fans had to endure decades of classic rock radio and rock radio in general, sitting through those

The all-covers affair *Feedback* took many longtime fans by surprise. Of course Rush had a history of cover songs going way back.

songs by the original artists, waiting to hear Rush. And those were not Rush fan songs at all. You know, I can remember numerous times, "Crossroads" and "For What It's Worth" and "Summertime Blues," whether it was by The Who or Blue Cheer or whatever, I would hear those songs on classic rock radio, and I was thinking, I cannot friggin' wait for Rush to come on. Oh geez, how many times am I going to hear this? Especially "Crossroads." Still, it would be cool if they released their shelved '80s cover project or what was to be *Feedback II*.

POPOFF: What about hearing some of those songs played live? Did that go over better than the EP itself?

KOZA: I would say I'm in the minority, but when I think back to that tour, I really enjoyed it, I loved it and thought it was cool. I respect that it was something they did, as they usually do, for themselves first and foremost, that they revisited those songs that inspired them back in the day. I think back to my friends and peers, and a number of them were a little put off that they played those songs in the concert setting.

And perhaps they were looking at it from a more rigid point of view: "Oh, I would rather have just heard a few more Rush songs as opposed to that." But all the great recordings from that R30 tour, I enjoyed them immensely. And even from that release's point of view, I thought it was a breath of fresh air for them to do it, and as quick as they did, pounding it out. Yeah, it's recorded a little hot, still, but after *Vapor Trails*, and the issues sonically over that, I thought this had a little bit more of a live feel. And so I like that they went in and banged it out, without all that thought that they tend to put into production.

Record Store Day split single, 2004.

And I thought they ripped them up live too; they really wailed. I was really cool with that. But it just seems like for the most part, people weren't down with it. I thought it was better than nothing, better than just going out touring without something. I wish there was more stuff on it, and they were a little conservative in their approach. "Well, we don't want to do too many, if it's not going to represent." But I like all of the textures that Alex is doing. He's still throwing in a lot of guitar stuff that he's done these last couple of decades, guitar layering and so forth. And again, it's a little on the hot end, but that makes it organic, for lack of a better word.

R30 tour, Wembley Arena, London, September 9, 2004. *Brian Rasic/ Getty Images*

CHAPTER 19

Snakes & Arrows

with Mary Jo Plews
and Ray Wawrzyniak

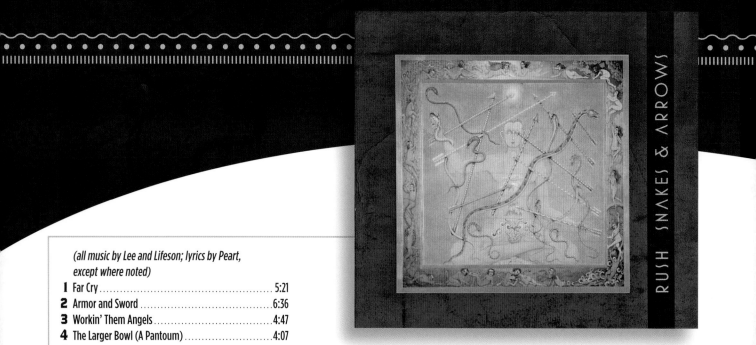

Geddy Lee: *vocals, bass, mellotron, bass pedal*
Alex Lifeson: *electric and acoustic guitars, mandolin, bouzouki*
Neil Peart: *drums, percussion*
Released May 1, 2007
Recorded at Allaire Studios, Shokan, New York, and Grandmaster Recorders, Hollywood, California
Produced by Nick Raskulinecz and Rush

(opposite)
Promoting and performing a strange new record. *Snakes & Arrows Live* **Tour, Pavilion, Concord, California, May 4, 2008.** *Jerome Brunet/Zuma Press/Alamy*

Alive the band most definitely were, running the business of Rush, which meant promoting their strange new record and then performing it live. But what felt subtly different as Geddy, Alex, and Neil gingerly picked their way as pensioners over the cracks in the sidewalk was this noticeable swell of legendary status that they themselves helped fuel, through covering the songs of hoary old '60s rockers (thereby looking old themselves), through the celebration of anniversaries (R30), and through the seismic conquering of new territories, namely Mexico and, most impressively Brazil, which resulted in the mania that was *Rock in Rio*.

Tear-dropped at the end of all this was the energy and enthusiasm for making a set of new songs that might distance the band from the events that comprised the emotional flashpoints for the intense *Vapor Trails* album. *Snakes & Arrows* would be the result, with three dynamics pressing upon its curious making. One, Neil, found himself reflecting philosophically on the subject of faith and his own placement in the world as faithless but morally indignant. The outpouring of thoughts had been the result of a mind race to match his motorcycle chase and the chastening of as many of the memories to which he wanted to let go, a purging of the bad against a desperate cling to the good. Ergo, essentially, the lyrics of *Snakes & Arrows* ask, "What now?"

The R30 anniversary tour and the conquering of new territories, notably Mexico and Brazil, helped create a noticeable swell in Rush's "legendary" status.

Adding to the slant of the new record from a musical standpoint would be Alex taking heed of Pink Floyd guitarist David Gilmour's suggestion that he try to write more on acoustic guitar. Alex had met Gilmour when he performed a solo show at Toronto's venerable Massey Hall, and the helpful comment was subsequently taken to heart. The result is an eccentric batch of songs o'er which Alex added to the compositional methodology by baking the resulting acoustic root of the songs he was writing right into the cake, whether the song was balladic and sensitive or whether it represented the band's blustery and almost tribal new take on loud rock.

Third, for no good reason, and while not really looking hard, the band had found themselves a gem of a new friend and producer in Nick Raskulinecz, who, as a professed fan of a generation younger than the boys, brought an enthusiasm to the project that had the guys fired up and working quickly, and ultimately very pleased with the results, judging from how many songs from the record were introduced into the subsequent live show. The numbers don't lie, nor does the fact that it was never in question that Nick would be back to record another record for the band, the immense *Clockwork Angels* opus of five years hence.

POPOFF: Contrast what kind of record we got with *Snakes & Arrows* versus *Vapor Trails*.

PLEWS: Right, well, obviously, *Vapor Trails* was the comeback album, and it was very personal and introspective and intimate, and I think *Snakes & Arrows* is increasingly outward-looking in comparison, with themes about religion, spirituality, relationships, the government, specifically the American government, and some of the religious extremes you get in the Middle East. So I think it's a very different look at the world, *Snakes & Arrows*. *Vapor Trails* was more internalized, while *Snakes & Arrows*

Snakes & Arrows tour, Wembley Arena, London, October 9, 2007.
Matt Kent/Redferns/Getty Images

SNAKES & ARROWS

Snakes & Arrows tour book. The outward-looking new album marked a return to heavy.

was looking out at the world, what's going on in the world, and how one survives in it.

POPOFF: Ray, how about musically? Should we consider this a heavy Rush record? I'm really on the fence about the nature of its heaviness, although I wouldn't question its energy.

WAWRZYNIAK: Well, I lean toward heaviness, I think. Don't forget, the band did the *Feedback* record, just to have new product out for the tour, to have something to say. . . . But all that is important in knowing that the making of the *Feedback* record really ended up parlaying itself into the energy in some of the songs on *Snakes & Arrows*. Some people maybe thought, oh, I can't believe Rush is doing an anniversary with just a cover album. They're not that kind of band to do that. Well, it really ended up paying dividends, because when they went back and did some of those songs on *Feedback*, and just discovered a lot of spirit and energy in playing those songs, plus the spirit and the energy that the band had when they first played those songs all those years ago, it really recharged their batteries and affected how they approached this new batch of songs that they were going to be making.

And so *Snakes & Arrows* was intended to be just a heavy rock record, and it really did translate that way. A lot of times artists have these notions of what they're shooting for, but ultimately they never quite get there. I think Rush nailed it in so many ways with what they ended up producing, and right from the first track, "Far Cry" . . . a seminal 2000s-representative Rush track. It's a perfect leadoff track for an album. It was the perfect first single too, released to radio. It had the famous elements that clearly identified the band, and in fact there's a complete rip off of the big chord from "Hemispheres." We're just going to put it in there intentionally. They were plagiarizing themselves, almost, which was just a great way of them having a nod to who they were and are, including the energy of who they were, and proposing that they still had.

PLEWS: I think the band itself framed the record as heavy, or agreed it was heavy. Alex was okay with not having any synthesizers or organs or any kind of keyboards involved. And so I think they were thrilled to kind of get back to where they were, where they started, and in fact you hear a lot of bluesy guitars, which I think was intentional, or a statement of sorts.

"Far Cry" proved the perfect lead-off track and great representation of 2000s-era Rush.

RUSH FAR CRY

Catchy ballad "The Larger Bowl"—a lyrical masterpiece?

POPOFF: "Spindrift" is a fairly heavy one, and I guess they liked it enough to issue it as the album's second single after "Far Cry."

PLEWS: Yes, and "Spindrift," really, is one of my favorite Rush songs of all time. I liked the discussion and the challenge of the way it describes how you're trying to reach out to somebody that you care for. How do you reach out to somebody who is maybe in peril, somebody who you love, and find that you can't get to them despite your best efforts. That's the picture I get from that lyric. And the music, I can almost feel the sand and the wind and the sea spray on my face. The tone of the music really is very atmospheric, and I love its heavy textures.

POPOFF: "Spindrift" failed to chart, with "The Larger Bowl (A Pantoum)" getting put out as the record's third and last single. A fairly catchy ballad, this one did a bit better at radio.

WAWRZYNIAK: Yes, and I think "The Larger Bowl" is a lyrical masterpiece. When the record came out, in the booklet, there it is, "The Larger Bowl," and underneath in parentheses it says "a pantoum." I had no idea what the heck a pantoum is. So, of course I had to look it up. It's a structure for the lyrics that are so unique. First verse has lines one, two, three, and four. Verse two then begins with lines two, three, and four from the first verse, followed by a new line. Verse three begins with lines two, three, and four from verse two, and a new fourth line. Oh, it's just fascinating. It's something that Neil said he had been toying with for a while, and was a little hesitant to present to Geddy and Alex. But he was much relieved when it was received by the two of them so well. The presentation of that song live was really, really strong. Some of the rear screen graphics they had married to the lyrics . . . it was really emotional, really strong and powerful. I don't think the song itself ended up going over as well live, but the presentation sure did.

POPOFF: It's not one of the album's three singles, but "Armor and Sword" is as important to the record as any of the marquee tracks. Would you agree?

WAWRZYNIAK: I guess "Far Cry" is probably the most representative Rush song here, but I think "Armor and Sword" might be the thematic centerpoint to the record, yes. Snakes and arrows being a metaphor for the armor that we wear, or the swords that we wield, in regards to faith, relationships, love, et cetera. Sometimes we wear armor to protect ourselves, or sometimes that same kind of armor is used as some sort of weaponry. And within some of the lyrics, especially on "Armor and Sword," appears what I think is the heartbeat of the entire record, thematically. The opening lines there, *The snakes and arrows a child is heir to . . .* , Neil made the point in his piece introducing the record that appeared in all print media and in the tour book, about how children are just kind of given a lot of their values by what they see in their parents, that they're going to be raised

to believe this or raised to believe that, not by their own choice. Just because that's what they're given by their parents. Whether positive or negative energy, the impression that we leave on our children is just immense.

PLEWS: Exactly. "Armor and Sword" really struck me as a social worker, and me being a therapist, I work with children that have been abused. And so "Armor and Sword," the lyrics jumped out at me, and it made me think about some of the children I had worked with. . . . Similarly, there are some kids that are abused, and as they grow up to be adults, they might re-create that trauma and become abusers themselves. That's a coping mechanism. But some kids, it makes them more sensitive, and maybe they want to grow up and be foster parents if they have been abused, and be more caring and compassionate toward people. And so it was interesting to me how he portrayed those childhood scars. You have two different reactions, and the two different paths that you can take.

Rush would continue to enjoy a surge in popularity thanks to a key role in the feature film *I Love You, Man* (2009) and the feature-length documentary *Beyond the Lighted Stage* (2010).

POPOFF: But isn't "Faithless" more the centerpoint of the album? Here we've got all these satellite issues distilled down to a very personal and unadorned statement from Neil. And of course it sounds perfectly reasonable coming out of Geddy, because we know they line up pretty closely on the subject of faith.

PLEWS: I think a lot of people were upset with Neil about that. That he was rejecting religion; and yet he was, I think, more embracing a spiritual side. And I think some really long-term fans and even newer fans that are very religious really were offended. I'd heard a little bit about that. So yeah, there was kickback with that. And there are some lyrics in there that reference, to me, the Bible, like the temple and marketplace, and preaching voices. But don't we all . . . we've all [known] people that are empty vessels, and they usually are the ones that yell so loud.

Snakes & Arrows Live tour, Pavilion, Concord, California, May 4, 2008. *Jerome Brunet/Zuma Press/Alamy*

I remember seeing, too, in philosophy, that one of the highest levels of moral compass or consciousness is your own. You have these levels that your parents have to impose on you, what's good and bad. And as you get older, you learn from the church or from the police or from laws what is right or wrong. And eventually, as you evolve higher, you have your own spirit level and your own moral compass, that you may say that even though the law says I can do that, or it's okay that I can do that, I don't feel comfortable with that. So I think that's what Neil was going for. I think it was misinterpreted by people who really, you know, count on their religion to guide their morals.

WAWRZYNIAK: There's a lot in the record about spirit, about faith, about wisdom. But nothing is overtly religious. "Faithless," that song was a bit controversial amongst some fans, just with regard to what he was kind of saying, almost religiously. And I'm not sure that's why that song wasn't played on its corresponding tour. Although it was brought back out a tour later—two tours later—on the *Time Machine* tour.

POPOFF: Mary Jo, you mentioned the Middle East earlier . . .

PLEWS: Right, well, the song that comes to mind is "The Way the Wind Blows." Strangely enough, I think, from an American perspective, we're hearing some of these themes again about are we going to let people in the country, are we going to build a wall, are we going to start wars again? So I think those issues are kind of raised in "The Way the Wind Blows," where Neil talks about how we can only go the way the wind blows, and the way that others perceive the rest of Americans. How are we supposed to head in another direction if our leaders aren't going to take us there? So it's kind of scary that we're starting to see some of the same things happen.

WAWRZYNIAK: I must add that the opening lick that Alex plays in that song, after the opening little drum fill, is as close to Alex Lifeson playing the blues on a Rush record in a long time. I mean, it's just a bona fide blues passage, before they go into the proper Rush riff. To hear him playing the blues like that is so new and just so different.

POPOFF: "Bravest Face" is interesting, because it subtly reminds us of the end game of all this faith talk, right? I mean, it seems like Neil is back to informing us about our own moral compass.

PLEWS: Right, and more, I suspect. There's the idea that we have this dual nature within us and it's not always recognized by people, and I like how the lyrics reflect that. And I think he was . . . we just talked about religion and spirituality, and I think Mother Teresa once said we all have a little bit of evil in us. I'm not sure I'm quoting her exactly right, but that's interesting to me. So Neil kind of lays it out that you don't really know what you're dealing with, sometimes, with people. They may seem all pulled together, but you get to know them a little bit better, and their life is just as much of a mess as anybody else's. So you can't really judge a book by its cover. That's basically the message I get from that song, and I appreciate that there is recognition that there is good and bad in all of us, yin and yang in all of us. Nobody is all good, nobody is all bad.

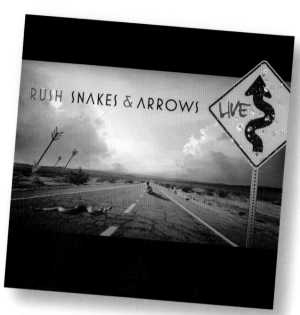

POPOFF: And then, weirdly, Neil puts aside the pen and paper, and the band gives us fully three instrumentals!

PLEWS: I get a kick out of "The Main Monkey Business." It's just kind of weird song, isn't it? It's got a lot of changes in it. I like where Geddy got the title, from his mom. There is a joke about that. Geddy's mom was talking about one of Geddy's cousins, and he was up to no good, doing some kind of business, and Geddy said, "What kind of business?" And she said, "The main monkey business." I guess it was a euphemism for something. So I get a kick out of that. But "Hope" is probably my favorite Rush instrumental. Which is kind of interesting to me, that I would pick a song that just features Alex as my favorite instrumental. I like the fact that the album has three instrumentals, but I don't know if everybody feels that way.

WAWRZYNIAK: Yeah, how about the first ever Rush record with three instrumentals? I'm trying to think, is there even a Rush record with two instrumentals? They come out with "Hope," which is just an Alex Lifeson solo acoustic piece. Even just the title "Hope" is phonetically connected to "Faithless" and others on the record. Which, "Faithless," by the way, features one of my favorite all-time Alex Lifeson guitar solos.

"Malignant Narcissism," a really short instrumental, features Neil playing just on a four-piece drum kit. Only a guy like Neil could record this track and have a four-piece drum kit sound as big as it does. However, "The Main Monkey Business" is the best instrumental Rush has ever recorded, and it was recently voted Rush's best live song ever. It should be noted, by the way, that myself and a friend of mine were the only two people voting in that little poll [laughs]. Yeah, "The Main Monkey Business" live is an absolute Rush tour de force. It's everything that represents grand, pompous, indulgent, in-your-face Rush. It's a masterpiece, everything they had hoped any of their previous instrumentals could be. It's not a great song—"YYZ" is a legitimate song, which just happens to be instrumental without lyrics—so I don't think it flows as well as a song. But for pure indulgent Rush, it's perfect.

Rush Time Machine tour, Molson Canadian Amphitheatre, Toronto, July 13, 2010. *Darren Eagles/Zuma Press/Alamy*

POPOFF: What is the story concerning this album cover?

WAWRZYNIAK: Okay, this is the first album cover since *Fly by Night* that is not a Hugh Syme design. This game board that adorns the cover of the record is something that Neil found. He was looking up snakes and arrows, and the band decided on *Snakes & Arrows* as an album title. He did his due diligence, thinking, "Hey, I want to make sure no other rock band's used this title recently." And in looking for it, in looking up *Snakes & Arrows*, the only thing he found was this Leela game, at it was called. And this Leela game, his continued research ended up leading him to this image that ended up being on the front of the record. This Leela game being a game of snakes and arrows, and this was the game board that this Leela game offered its users. He liked it, he wanted it for the cover, presented it to Hugh Syme, who was disappointed, because he'd already come up with his visual graphic to represent the record, which ended up being used inside the record on the booklet, the picture of the baby on the road with the arrows and the snake and the signpost on the side of the road. Which . . . parts of it I thought were interesting, but there are elements inside that I didn't think were him pushing the boundaries much. It's not my favorite album cover by a country mile; it might be in my bottom third.

POPOFF: Finally, now that the excitement of it being a new album has worn off, what generally do the serious Rush fans say about this record?

PLEWS: *Snakes & Arrows* might get a little lost because it doesn't have a continuous theme like *Clockwork Angels*, doesn't present a continuous story. It's not a comeback album, or an album after five years like *Vapor Trails* was. So

I wonder if *Snakes & Arrows* gets a little lost in the shuffle. Of course, they still play "Far Cry"—it's a big live hit—and I think "Malignant Narcissism" and "The Main Monkey Business," the two main instrumentals, maybe get played more than the other songs.

You know, *Snakes & Arrows* was a lot easier than it was making *Vapor Trails*. I think it was done in less than two months. They had a fresh new producer and there was not the heaviness and the trauma that was reflected in *Vapor Trails*. So it kind of got them back to more of their pattern of singing about the world and being within the world, along with some songs about relationships. So I think that's probably why they themselves would embrace it more than some others.

Rush Time Machine tour, Bayfest, Sarnia, Ontario, July 9, 2010. *Gene Schilling/Zuma Press/Alamy*

WAWRZYNIAK: That's true, so yes, putting aside what the fans think, the band definitely is fond of it—that record was very well represented live. They had more songs from a new record played live, on its supporting tour, than any other previous Rush tour for a long time. I mean, some of the tours from years gone by, they would put out records with eight songs on them, and oftentimes they would play seven of the eight songs. But on this tour, I think their sincere love of the record and their belief in the record was manifested in the live show. Just the sheer number of songs that they played from that record can help you connect the dots there.

Plus, the tour in support of that, they didn't play an old show. It was a brand-new show that they were playing. Oftentimes they'd been criticized for using a template from the previous tour. And they even admitted this. This is how they would do it. They would take the template from the previous tour, they're gonna start with that, and then they would just highlight, delete, and insert song A; highlight, delete, insert song B. So a lot of the songs would not only stay the same, they would even stay in the same place in the set.

Snakes & Arrows live was a brand-new show from beginning to end, with songs that had not been played either ever or in forever. It was just an incredibly successful tour for the band, in terms of where they were playing and the attendance at all the respective shows. At that point, Rush, in 2007 and 2008, they were really enjoying a huge spike in their career. Not necessarily popularity-wise—that came a few years later, with *Beyond the Lighted Stage*, *I Love You Man*, a great book written by successful author Martin Popoff [laughs], the Hall of Fame . . . all of those things hadn't quite reared their head yet. It was just the band enjoying being back on the road and being Rush, after the hiatus that they had to take. But, yes, I do have a great affinity for that record. I really do think it's a late-career masterpiece.

Clockwork Angels

with Eddy Maxwell and Chris Nelson

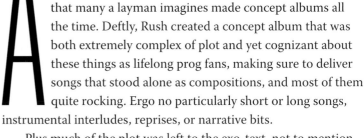

(all music by Lee and Lifeson; lyrics by Peart)

Geddy Lee: *bass, bass pedals, vocals, synthesizers*
Alex Lifeson: *electric and acoustic guitars, additional keyboards*
Neil Peart: *drums, percussion*
David Campbell: *string arrangements and conductor*
Jason Sniderman: *piano on "The Garden"*
Released June 12, 2012
Recorded at Blackbird Studio, Nashville, and Revolution Recording, Toronto
Produced by Nick Raskulinecz and Rush

A nd so we arrive at Rush's twentieth studio record, and a grand statement it was, the first concept album by a band that many a layman imagines made concept albums all the time. Deftly, Rush created a concept album that was both extremely complex of plot and yet cognizant about these things as lifelong prog fans, making sure to deliver songs that stood alone as compositions, and most of them quite rocking. Ergo no particularly short or long songs, instrumental interludes, reprises, or narrative bits.

Plus much of the plot was left to the exo-text, not to mention the novelization of the whole enchilada embarked upon after the fact by bestselling sci-fi author Kevin Anderson. *Clockwork Angels* seemed to just expand and unfurl, in the imagination once immersions begin, and even over time—before, after, during, beneath, between, and behind.

Indeed, there was the book, the expanded liner notes version, the magazine version, the *Clockwork Angels* tour (with reduced string section, but a string section, nonetheless, sawing away faithfully at songs from the album), and of course the attendant live album. And there was even the backward-in-time echo of what was to come during the steampunk-inspired *Time Machine* tour, which provided a taster with advance tracks "Caravan" and "BU2B." These were followed well after the 2010–2011 tour but still before the album release by "Headlong Flight," and through that trio, fans balanced on the arms of their theater seats, expecting a swirling, noisy bashfest of a record from their heroes.

Geddy, Neil, and Alex didn't disappoint, delivering an album that pointedly ran up against concept album rules in yet another sense, namely through the raw, organic, almost casual and jammy flow of the songs, melodic and sensitive or pounded with bass. Returning producer Nick Raskulinecz captured the band at their most live-off-the-floor since, well, arguably *Vapor Trails* and before that, er, *Rush*.

"Finding My Way," indeed.

POPOFF: As we arrive at the end of our journey, surprise, Rush finally delivers a concept album. How did the fans receive *Clockwork Angels*?

NELSON: What Rush fan wouldn't like that, right? Yeah, that was just such welcome news. And a beautiful story for Rush fans to follow. Really, when I first heard the news, I thought it might've been more like *2112*, or even *Tommy* by The Who, where you had reoccurring elements like that B sustained chord that is a signature in

Clockwork Angels . . . prog with a raw, jammy feel. Snakes & Arrows Live tour, Pavilion, Concord, California, May 4, 2008. Jerome Brunet/Zuma Press/Alamy

"Pinball Wizard" and some other tracks on that album where it reoccurs. But it's interesting that Rush gave us like entirely different tracks.

MAXWELL: Well, we all had the advance of "Caravan" and "BU2B," which was just massive. But when the album arrived, it was just what I'd been waiting for for years. And that was the consensus of just about everybody that I talked to. They just loved the theme of it, the music was strong, and everybody was going, "Oh, did you hear 'Clockwork Angels'?! Oh my God, what about 'The Anarchist'?" Like every song—people were going crazy for "The Wreckers." When my husband heard "Headlong Flight," and he's been a huge Rush been since he was sixteen, he was like, "Oh my God, I have to hear this over and over again." I think we played "Headlong Flight" a dozen times in a row when I first heard it.

POPOFF: Eddy, you mentioned the music was strong. I mean, the first thing that comes to mind is the word *lively*.

MAXWELL: Yes, and spontaneous—it feels very spontaneous; it's fresh, like a jam. "All right, let's go see what we're going to do today." As opposed to, "Okay, we're going to plan out this part; now we have to go create this part over here." It was very much like a jam. And then Nick Raskulinecz, he brings some of that crunch, a kind of twenty-first century freshness. This doesn't sound like a record by a band that's been around for forty-five years. It sounded very modern, but he let the band be the band. He brought out the best in them, and brought out the guitars. The guitars are just so beautiful on this album. And of course that's also Alex's playing. But he isn't getting lost in the mix. So Nick's bringing that modern sensibility, some crunch, some depth. There's a lot of depth and layers to this album, but it's not mushy.

Alex hams it up at Rush's long-overdue Rock and Roll Hall of Fame induction, Nokia Theater, Los Angeles, April 18, 2013. *Kevin Winter/Getty Images*

NELSON: I think Nick's like a hybrid between Kevin Shirley and Terry Brown. It sounds like they have the rawness that The Caveman wanted on *Counterparts*, but the arrangements are just so lush. But Nick retains that rawness. If you heard Rush twenty-five years ago, and said, "Okay, I wonder what this band is going to sound like in twenty-five years," I think they're right on par. I think their ears and songwriting ability have expanded, their lyrics continue to be beautiful, thoughtful, and they're still absolutely monster musicians.

And nothing was mailed in on this record. Analyzing this stuff and doing it in our tribute band, there are elements, particularly in the vocals . . . when people say Geddy doesn't sing the high stuff anymore, I know what they're saying with the screeching stuff, but he is singing so high and powerful on *Clockwork Angels*, it's amazing. For example, "Headlong Flight"—those notes, they're no joke. And listen to the harmonies in "Wish Them Well," the background track where he's screaming in the chorus, that is super-high—and deceivingly so. People don't realize it. And of course his voice has changed a little bit—they all do as they get older—but it's so beautiful.

POPOFF: Before we get any further, we should address the issue that this is indeed a concept record. First, what is the overarching theme and then perhaps a little more specifically, give me a sense of the plot.

MAXWELL: Thematically, it's definitely a journey, starting with "Caravan," moving all the way to "The Garden." That's handled in the book also, but even if you didn't know about the book, if you just read the lyrics and listened to it, you can hear the overall

Clockwork Angels was a concept record supported by two books: a novel released in 2012 and later a graphic novel published in 2015.

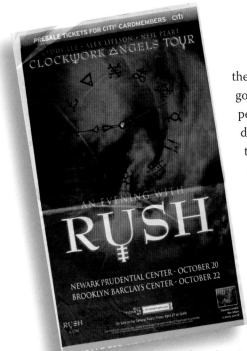

Rush supported *Clockwork Angels* with a 72-date jaunt in North America and Europe.

The *Clockwork Angels* tour was documented in a three-hour film described as "voyeuristic."

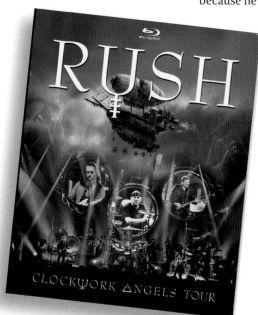

theme of starting out as a young man, or young woman, starting her adventure, going through, you know, dangers, lost love, finding love again, meeting crazy people along the way, and then at the end kind of releasing all the negativity, demonstrating that sense of maturity, finally let go, doing the "wish them well" thing of letting go of the anger and the resentment. Like, "Oh, this person really made me angry in high school." That doesn't matter anymore. And then into "The Garden" and finding that point of love and respect. That's what life is about, and that's what makes a person valuable.

But okay, if you want more [laughs], so I would say it's about Owen Hardy, our hero persona, who has a very comfortable life but then kind of wants to do something else. He takes a chance for adventure, which, you know, a lot of people don't want to do. They're comfortable in their lives, and they just want to keep living them, and that's okay. But he had a sense of adventure; he says I want to do something more.

So he just disappears, takes off one day and goes to the big city—like a lot of us do from small towns—goes to the big city, meets people, falls in love, sees some crazy and wild miracles as in "Clockwork Angels," seeing those miraculous things like we've always heard about, and then comes across somebody who wants to destroy all that is good.

And then he gets framed for being the anarchist, which of course he isn't—he's the good guy. But everybody thinks he's the bad guy, so he takes off, has some more adventures, just living a free life, a traveling life. You could obviously kind of compare it to being on tour, the road life, as he sees some more wonderful places. Goes out on a personal adventure as in "Seven Cities of Gold," goes out into the desert, risking his life because he was out there on his own and anything could've happened.

But it was worth it because he found not what he expected, but what he needed to see. And I think we all have those kinds of points of going, "I'm going where I want, not where I should." And sometimes it turns out good, and sometimes it doesn't turn out so well. So it works out for Owen, but when he was coming back, he encountered The Wreckers, and he encountered . . . kind of had a big battle, I would say. The big battle of the book and in the storyline is that The Wreckers are the anarchists, and then you have the watchmaker people who are total control. So you've got total control and total chaos.

And these two forces are fighting, but he sees that and goes, "No, I reject that. I'm going to go and take off. I'm going to do my headlong flight and I'm going to get out of here. I'm getting away, because that battle of chaos and total control, anarchy and fascism, whatever you want to call it, it's constant, and it's been part of our world for thousands of years."

So he says, "I'm going to find that third path. I'm going to take a headlong flight—I'm going to leave. I'm getting out of here. I wish you well," you know, "take care, I'm going to go somewhere else." And then he gets to the point where he reunites with his love and they settle down and have a family. He spends time in the garden, and he finds peace at the end.

POPOFF: Wow. And of course the cool thing is, while all this is going on, Rush is being the mad power trio Rush. Neil is just flowing track to track, Geddy is aggressive on bass, and guitars have won the battle over keyboards.

NELSON: Yeah, that's a good point, and also, because so many strings are applied to these tunes, as far as keyboards, it's certainly not like *Signals*—they're back to like supporting parts. They are pads in the background. The sounds have come so far since 1982, so they are beautiful sounds; they're gorgeous.

And you're right. There is something about Neil on this record . . . last night, I played our drummer this one fill Neil has in the record, which almost sounds like that Buddy Rich tribute stuff he did, where the snare is constantly buzzing and rapidly alternating with these toms and it happens so quickly. He's definitely not lost anything. I love the feel, the change, in "Clockwork Angels." It's fast and almost sounds like "2112," coupled with that kind of triumphant guitar riff that Geddy and Alex are playing together, and Neil is doing the toms like in "2112" to start the tune. And then they go into a section, which is like a completely different feel, just mind-blowing, really.

It's funny, because I wasn't that familiar with the record when I saw that tour. So I kind of saw that song live for the first time, before I'd heard it. And that was a great experience, because that time change blew me away. And I don't mean time change as an odd time, but the feel, the feel change. And just hearing it beautifully done. And then yet another part in the middle, after the guitar solo, they come out with that strange acoustic guitar part, where the whole band is still rocking, but Geddy sings over it with that kind of wacky EQ effect on his vocals.

That's the trifecta. That's why it reminds me of, say, "Natural Science," where there are three completely different parts. I know it sounds nothing like it, but in the sense that it's almost three tunes in one. It's drastically different parts, but they go together beautifully. Rush always make this stuff work like a charm.

POPOFF: Eddy, what are a couple of highlights on the album for you?

MAXWELL: "BU2B" is one of the most rocking, grungy, powerful songs they've done. That's one that every time I saw it on tour, I was headbanging. I don't know what the band was doing on stage because I was headbanging the whole time. And that song just really spoke to me. When it was released, we didn't know how "BU2B" related to the Owen Hardy story and the way it fits into *Clockwork Angels*, because it hadn't been made yet. And so some people were taking that lyric as kind of a slam on Christianity.

Clockwork Angels **tour, O2 World, Berlin, June 6, 2013.** *Frank Hoensch/Redferns/Getty Images*

And it was kind of a negative. Not everybody, but there were people who were like, that comes across as kind of a slam on my belief system—which was not where Neil was coming from at all. It wasn't until we saw the book and the album, oh, okay, this is not about that. Not to say that Neil doesn't have those views—we saw that a bit with *Snakes & Arrows*, in "Faithless," and some of the other songs on there, like "Armor and Sword."

"Caravan" was also very refreshing, because people were very excited. *Snakes & Arrows*, that's a big album. There's a lot of songs and it's a lot to digest. And when they sneak in "Caravan," okay, they're rocking and they're keeping it good. "Caravan" was actually the inspiration when I was resigning from a job that I was miserable at. I wanted to do something better, and so when I was filling out their resignation form, where it says what's the reason? I actually put, "I can't stop thinking big," which is from "Caravan."

And then the third advance song was "Headlong Flight"—driving music, very powerful but beautiful; it was like Rush is back with a vengeance. The lyrics were great, because with *Some days were dark / I wish that I could live it all again / Some nights were bright / I wish that I could live it all again*, you have a little bit of nostalgia. Because we've been fans for so long, we're looking back at Rush's career and we're looking back at our lives and seeing where we're moving forward. But then it's, you know, "I wouldn't trade tomorrow for today," and I think a lot of people were just saying, yeah, this is how I feel—they could really relate.

NELSON: Yeah, love that one, and when we did it live, sometimes it's "Headlong Fright" [laughs]. That song is crazy involved to play. That's just good ol' Geddy there. It is very note-y, vocally speaking. That tune, in particular, those notes are no joke. He's got a lot of breath in him, to get those notes out. And his bass playing under that, I mean, that's what he does. It's reminiscent definitely of "By-Tor," with the jam in E they do in the middle. And also "Bastille Day," when they come in with their little drum and bass accents under the guitar, on the intro—that's basically a quote from "Bastille Day." And Alex takes that big solo in the middle, which, again, that's "By-Tor"—old-school Alex.

POPOFF: Again, there's a thickness and fullness to the sound all over this record. There's more power and electricity here and, dare I say, bottom end even over and above *Snakes & Arrows*, which Nick also produced.

NELSON: Yes, I agree, and I have to reference *Counterparts*. Around that time, Geddy started what he calls "my flamenco way of playing the bass." I'm sure you've seen it, where the right hand executes a kind of strumming move. If you position your wrist like you would, between the two pickups . . . and this is all right-hand technique, it all has to do with the right hand. And it's pretty much his first finger, his index finger, that he is using as a pick, really. So he's doing downstrokes and upstrokes and back and forth. He's got great strength, believe me, from somebody who studies the stuff. He has great strength and he's very precise, with his string skipping. It really sounds like he's using a pick and he's not. It's something to marvel at, really amazing.

And that technique is all over this record, starting right in with "Caravan." There's like a minute-and-a-half jam they do in the middle of the tune, and it's like all that technique. And it's just rocking and busy and vicious and aggressive, and yet it's beautiful and there's grace to it. It all makes sense; it's not just pounding the instrument.

Find the drummer. *Clockwork Angels* **tour, Bridgestone Arena, Nashville, Tennessee, May 1, 2013.** *Frederick Breedon/Getty Images*

POPOFF: This no doubt results in a chordal feel, further filling out the bottom end.

NELSON: Yes, and some of that is in "Caravan," for example. He's doing what you would call double stops, where he's doing a fifth, kind of. He's doing like a chordal . . . almost like a power chord—not almost, it is. It's a power chord he's applying that technique to. And yeah, it's really cool. And obviously, he does more chordal stuff on other tracks in that record too. You can tell, his ears are huge. He's used to writing . . . he's even said this, that a bass is a lonely instrument by itself. And he can play also what they call triple stops, which is like a root and a third note at the same time, for a chord, but then you have a major or minor distinction, and he can play those. When I hear him do that chordal stuff, it sounds like he would write in that fashion, because that's the basis of writing: you hear major and minor chords, and it moves along accordingly. It's tough, because when you're playing a singular note on a bass, there's no major or minor distinction. So it can be taken any way.

Also with respect to the bass, something we've been doing lately is "The Anarchist," and it's funny, I hear Chris Squire in that bass line. And something else about that bass line, it's deceivingly hard to sing over even though it's not superfast. One part in particular, *The lenses inside of me that paint the world black*, that point where he's playing that line and singing over that, the bass accents are all on the upbeat, which is a little departure for him. But I marvel at his ability to sing straight, over that upbeat phrasing that he is playing. It's really amazing.

POPOFF: And one other highlight on the album, it seems, with really serious Rush fans is "The Wreckers."

MAXWELL: For sure—that is just musically beautiful. But I wasn't sure about the storyline, what it really meant at first. I had my original vision for "The Wreckers," thinking about Hurricane Katrina in New Orleans, and thinking about all the destruction of a terrible storm coming into a city and wrecking everything. So that was my original imagery. But then looking at the lyrics, it's like, oh, this is about people who harm others who are in danger. They aren't rescuing them. They're killing them. They're taking their stuff. And so it's a beautiful song with a dark theme to it lyrically.

NELSON: Sure, oh, I agree, "The Wreckers" is really beautiful; that resonated with me. And there's a tune that proves what you can do with just a handful of chords. They can write just amazing, amazing songs with these traditional chords. It's like D, C, E minor, just basic stuff, and especially for Rush. And you just get lost in it. You forget they're not playing these mind-blowing notes, fast notes, or whatever. I love Alex's guitar parts in that song. Right after the opening riff, when the music dies down and the vocal comes in, listen to the

guitar on that, where Alex is strumming sixteenth notes. They're not syncopated or accented; they're just very balanced and beautiful. It's almost like an egg shaker, really soft and present.

POPOFF: And finally we arrive at "The Garden." When we think about this record outside of the power of the guitar, bass, and drums, it's refreshing not to think about keyboards, but instead strings, and "The Garden" is the boldest and most memorable example of strings being used on the record, and live, for that matter.

MAXWELL: Yes, the strings—I loved it. I was a music major in college, and I have a very big appreciation for classical music. And so for me, I was just thrilled and excited. I know people who were not, because, oh my God, there's somebody else on stage. Oh, Rush has changed; this is the wrong direction. And I would say ninety-five percent of them or more [now say], "Oh, this is fabulous. I'm so glad we hear this." They love the strings now, but they had to go see it. They weren't confident in what the guys were trying to do. And then when they saw that, they went, oh, okay, this is fabulous. But I loved it from the beginning. "The Garden" would not be "The Garden" without the strings. It was just a plush and gorgeous and even brave way to end both the story and the album.

Contributors

ABOUT THE INTERVIEWER

At approximately 7,900 (with more than 7,000 appearing in his books), **Martin Popoff** has unofficially written more record reviews than anybody in the history of music writing across all genres. Additionally, Martin has penned fifty-six books on hard rock, heavy metal, classic rock, and record collecting, including 2004's *Contents Under Pressure: 30 Years of Rush at Home and Away* and 2013's *Rush: The Illustrated History*. He was editor-in-chief of the now-retired *Brave Words & Bloody Knuckles*, Canada's foremost heavy metal publication in print for fourteen years, and has also contributed to *Revolver*, *Guitar World*, *Goldmine*, *Record Collector*, bravewords.com, lollipop.com, and hardradio.com. Martin has been a regular contractor to Banger Films, having worked on the award-winning documentary *Rush: Beyond the Lighted Stage*, the eleven-episode *Metal Evolution*, and the ten-episode *Rock Icons*, both for VH1 Classic. Martin currently resides in Toronto and can be reached through martinp@inforamp.net or www.martinpopoff.com.

ABOUT THE INTERVIEWEES

Ralph Chapman scripted the very first official feature documentary on that "little ol' band from Texas," ZZ Top, in collaboration with Banger Films. Previously, he served as writer and associate producer on the VH1 series *Rock Icons*, which included a Geddy Lee episode. Prior to that, he served the same roles on the critically acclaimed eleven-part series on heavy metal, *Metal Evolution*. Ralph was also part of the creative team behind the Juno Award–winning documentary, *Rush: Beyond the Lighted Stage*, which took the Audience Award at the Tribeca Film Festival in 2010. Ralph also continues to work with Iconoclassic Records as a project producer, notably overseeing the reissue campaign of The Guess Who catalog. He continues to develop projects with Banger Films and on his own with his production company, Wesbrage Productions, while contributing to various music-related websites in his spare time.

Platinum "shredder" **Paul Gilbert** is one of the world's most respected "guitarist's guitarists," having played with Racer X and Mr. Big and notching fourteen solo albums and dozens of guest appearances to his name. Mr. Big supported Rush on both the *Presto* and *Roll the Bones* tours. Gilbert's celebrated Rush covers with Dream Theater's Mike Portnoy on YouTube are head-scratchingly perfect.

Ian Grandy was Rush's first roadie, working with the band since they first set up in his parents' garage as kids, prompting a thanks to his parents on the original Moon Records issue of the first album. Along the way, working through the ranks, Ian was Neil's drum tech, managed the road crew, and performed front-of-house sound for the band through the end of 1980.

Kirk Hammett is guitarist for Metallica, appearing with the band on every album since their 1983 debut, *Kill 'Em All*. He was a featured commentator in feature the documentary *Rush: Beyond the Lighted Stage*.

As **Chris Irwin** says, "The surreality of being a huge Rush fan and living in the Niagara area where Neil Peart grew up has become a weird kind of normal. Neil's former manager, Rick Jones (The Majority 1968–1969), parks next to me at work. Neil's next manager, Brian O'Mara (J. R. Flood 1970–71), is my backyard neighbor. It is not uncommon to go into the local Starbucks and see former bandmate Terry Walsh (The Majority) sitting with Neil's first drum teacher, Don George. Look to the next table and there's two of the *Moving Pictures* red suits Mike Dixon and Bob King, Bob also being the *Hemispheres* gentleman and original nude model for the Rush Starman." Irwin, a full-time advertising salesman and part-time semi-professional historian with fifty published articles to his name, has attended every Toronto RushCon and has had the pleasure of sharing many of his discoveries with other Rush fans, including a photo of Neil's first live performance, at his high school talent show, the earliest known recordings of Neil in the above-mentioned bands, Geddy Lee's grade-eleven class photo, and a 1972 Halloween photo of Neil dressed as a *Clockwork Orange* droog.

Sean Kelly is a Toronto-based guitarist, songwriter, author, educator, music director, and producer. Sean has toured the world as lead guitarist for Nelly Furtado and has recorded and/or toured with a number of award-winning artists, including Lee Aaron, Alan Frew, Helix, Gilby Clarke, Carole Pope and Rough Trade, Honeymoon Suite, Emm Gryner, Howie D, Coney Hatch, The Canadian Brass, The Kenyan Boys Choir, Wild Strawberries, and many others. He was recently cast in Dee Snider's *Rock & Roll Christmas Tale* and authored the book *Metal on Ice: Tales from Canada's Hard Rock and Heavy Metal Heroes*. Sean has fifteen years' experience as a vocal music teacher with the Toronto Catholic District School Board, and is a graduate of the University of Toronto's Music Program, where he studied classical guitar under Eli Kassner.

Collector and respected Rush historian specializing on the band's concert career, **Pete Koza** has seen Rush 183 times in 11 countries, most with his buddy, UK Steve.

Michel "Away" Lanvegin is lyricist and drummer for Canadian conceptual progressive thrash legends Voivod, who supported Rush on four Canadian dates in May 1990. The band's 1991 album, *Angel Rat*, was produced by longtime Rush producer Terry Brown.

Douglas Maher has been a well known and highly regarded Rush historian and archivist since 1980. Having attended nearly one hundred Rush concerts in his lifetime across the continental United States, Maher has worked with various authors and filmmakers on Rush information and authentication of film, audio, and print. Quite often regarded as the walking encyclopedia of Rush, Maher has researched the band in months'-long archival exploration projects at the Library of Congress and hundreds of other institutions across the United States and Canada. He is credited in the documentary, *Rush: Beyond the Lighted Stage*.

Jillian Maryonovich has been a "beyond medically appropriate" Rush fan since high school, first seeing the band on the *Roll the Bones* tour. She is currently creative director for RushCon, the extremely professional convention for Rush fans that is an annual pilgrimage for

fans from around the world, and was creative director at the Obama White House. She lives in Washington, D.C., with her two cats, who live on top of many piles of unwashed Rush T-shirts.

Massachusetts native **Jim Matheos** is guitarist extraordinaire with progressive metal legends Fates Warning, who have issued twelve studio albums since their pioneering *Night on Bröcken* album issued on Metal Blade back in 1984. Matheos has also issued solo guitar albums, collaborated with myriad prog giants, and is a principal in OSI, greatest damn prog band on the planet.

Eddy Maxwell started RushCon in 2000, holding the first one in 2001, and has been an organizer ever since. Says Eddy, "The goals of RushCon have always been meeting fellow fans, celebrating Rush's music, and raising money for a worthwhile charity. As of 2015, we've raised $100,000 for charity. I've spent many evenings discussing Rush with friends new and old, how their music has helped us through difficult times, and the joy it's brought to our lives." Maxwell, who grew up in South Dakota and has called Houston, Texas, home for twenty-five years, majored in music and broadcasting, worked in audio-visual, educational technology, and multimedia communications, and is currently in training administration. "It's a running joke that Rush fans are science fiction–/fantasy-loving techno-geeks," Eddy notes, "and I proudly match that stereotype to a T."

Chris Nelson's Rush tribute band, Lotus Land, has won RushCon's battle of the bands twice (as many times as entered) and were selected to play AXSTV's World's Greatest Tribute Bands, live from the Whisky a Go Go in Hollywood. Chris has seen approximately twenty Rush concerts since signing on at *Power Windows*. Previous to Lotus Land, Chris toured for fifteen years with Rock Hall inductee Herb Reed from the original Platters, having also played with members of The Coasters and The Drifters.

Mary Jo Plews has seen Rush seventy times, including the Rock and Roll Hall of Fame induction ceremony/performance in 2013, and the last R40 show in LA in 2015, currently on the books as the last Rush show ever. A master's degree holder in social work, Plews is executive director of a Tampa Bay, Florida, nonprofit serving mothers-to-be, newborns, and their families. She is one of the original group of women who cofounded RushCon in 2000 and remains active in organizing it. Since 2007, she's had a *Snakes & Arrows* tattoo on her ankle, which was unadorned when Mary Jo went out on Halloween dressed as Alex while still in high school.

A drummer since he was ten years old, **Jason Popovich** had his first professional gig was with a band called Profile, although for the last four years, he has drummed for Rush tribute act My Favorite Headache. Adds Popovich, "I'm also selling Mercedes-Benz vehicles at Mercedes-Benz Newmarket and have previously sold Ferraris and BMWs. I actually got to meet Geddy Lee on his driveway when we delivered a new 750Li to him just after the *Vapor Trails* tour. By selling high-end cars all over Toronto and living just north of the city, I have come into contact with so many people who are actually friends with members of Rush, and there's always an interesting story or two there."

Storied percussionist **Mike Portnoy** is probably the first name that comes to mind when people think of an heir to Neil Peart's "drummer's drummer" throne of distinction. Through his work with Adrenaline Mob; The Winery Dogs; myriad, multiple progressive acts over the years; and most notably Dream Theater, Mike has vaulted to the ranks of the handful of the most celebrated drummers in the media and drum community, certainly in the last twenty years, at least. In terms of Rush, Portnoy's fandom is unquestioned, with Mike having covered the band extensively across many band and project situations. Mike also appeared in *Rush: Beyond the Lighted Stage*, extolling the virtues of the band that most inspired Dream Theater.

Chris Schneberger is a photographer and musician living in Chicago and currently drumming in the band Moon.

His friend Dean owns "Chromey," Neil's first drum kit with Rush, and Chris helps out with showing it at charity events, acting as Chromey's drum tech. Chris has seen Rush exactly fifty times (including in Puerto Rico) and has attended RushCon many times over the years. A knowledgeable Rush expert, Chris was interviewed for the documentary, *Rush: Beyond the Lighted Stage*.

One of the "fan-scholars" cited in the book *Rush, Rock and the Middle Class*, **Robert Telleria** had his own encyclopedic Rush biography, *Merely Players*, published in 2001, thirteen years after the previous official bio. While privately restoring Neil's red Tama drums, he researched, compiled, and verified Rush's complete tour history for a possible future book, developed an unreleased Rush trivia game, and finished a book on Tama. Robert also contributed statistics for the first two official Rush calendars and is credited in *Rush: Beyond the Lighted Stage*. As an editor, he can spell merely. His first publisher couldn't.

Jeff Wagner's favorite album of all time is Rush's *Moving Pictures*. He is the author of *Mean Deviation: Four Decades of Progressive Heavy Metal* and *Soul on Fire: The Life and Music of Peter Steele*, and he contributed three essays to Martin Popoff's *Rush: The Illustrated History*. He lives in Greensboro, North Carolina, where he bikes around wearing a *Fly by Night* cycling jersey. When not studying music, cycling, or watching Washington Nationals baseball, Wagner works for prog rock record label InsideOut Music. He never uses 2112 as a password. Ever.

Ray Wawrzyniak first saw Rush perform live on April 5, 1983, and has gone on to see the band more than 110 times since. Ray was a contributor to the *Rush: Beyond the Lighted Stage* documentary, Martin Popoff's *Rush: The Illustrated History*, and numerous other Rush-related releases over the years. Ray has a basement-dominating Rush collection summarized in an absurd ninety-plus-page document. Ray disguises himself as an elementary school teacher by day and lives happily at his home near Buffalo, New York, with his wife Lisa and their three kids, cheering on his beloved Buffalo Bills and Sabres.

Author Bibliography

Rush: Album by Album (2017)

Rock the Nation: Montrose, Gamma, and Ronnie Redefined (2016)

Punk Tees: The Punk Revolution in 125 T-Shirts (2016)

Metal Heart: Aiming High with Accept (2016)

The Deep Purple Family: Year by Year (2016)

Wind of Change: The Scorpions Story (2016)

Agents of Fortune: The Blue Öyster Cult Story (2016)

From Dublin to Jailbreak: Thin Lizzy 1969–76 (2016)

Ramones at 40 (2016)

Time and a Word: The Yes Story (2016)

This Means War: The Sunset Years of the NWOBHM (2015)

Wheels of Steel: The Explosive Early Years of the NWOBHM (2015)

Swords and Tequila: Riot's Classic First Decade (2015)

Who Invented Heavy Metal? (2015)

Sail Away: Whitesnake's Fantastic Voyage (2015)

Live Magnetic Air: The Unlikely Saga of the Superlative Max Webster (2014)

Steal Away the Night: An Ozzy Osbourne Day-by-Day (2014)

The Big Book of Hair Metal (2014)

Sweating Bullets: The Deth and Rebirth of Megadeth (2014)

Smokin' Valves: A Headbanger's Guide to 900 NWOBHM Records (2014)

The Art of Metal (co-edit with Malcolm Dome, 2013)

2 Minutes to Midnight: An Iron Maiden Day-by-Day (2013)

Metallica: The Complete Illustrated History (2013)

Rush: The Illustrated History (2013)

Ye Olde Metal: 1979 (2013)

Scorpions: Top of the Bill (2013)

Epic Ted Nugent (2012)

Fade to Black: Hard Rock Cover Art of the Vinyl Age (2012)

It's Getting Dangerous: Thin Lizzy 81–12 (2012)

We Will Be Strong: Thin Lizzy 76–81 (2012)

Fighting My Way Back: Thin Lizzy 69–76 (2011)

The Deep Purple Royal Family: Chain of Events '80–'11 (2011)

The Deep Purple Royal Family: Chain of Events through '79 (2011)

Black Sabbath FAQ (2011)

The Collector's Guide to Heavy Metal: Volume 4: The '00s (co-author with David Perri, 2011)

Goldmine Standard Catalog of American Records 1948–1991, 7th Edition (2010)

Goldmine Record Album Price Guide, 6th Edition (2009)

Goldmine 45 RPM Price Guide, 7th Edition (2009)

A Castle Full of Rascals: Deep Purple '83–'09 (2009)

Worlds Away: Voivod and the Art of Michel Langevin (2009)

Ye Olde Metal: 1978 (2009)

Gettin' Tighter: Deep Purple '68–'76 (2008)

All Access: The Art of the Backstage Pass (2008)

Ye Olde Metal: 1977 (2008)

Ye Olde Metal: 1976 (2008)

Judas Priest: Heavy Metal Painkillers (2007)

Ye Olde Metal: 1973 to 1975 (2007)

The Collector's Guide to Heavy Metal: Volume 3: The Nineties (2007)

Ye Olde Metal: 1968 to 1972 (2007)

Run for Cover: The Art of Derek Riggs (2006)

Black Sabbath: Doom Let Loose (2006)

Dio: Light Beyond the Black (2006)

The Collector's Guide to Heavy Metal: Volume 2: The Eighties (2005)

Rainbow: English Castle Magic (2005)

UFO: Shoot Out the Lights (2005)

The New Wave of British Heavy Metal Singles (2005)

Blue Öyster Cult: Secrets Revealed! (2004)

Contents Under Pressure: 30 Years of Rush at Home & Away (2004)

The Top 500 Heavy Metal Albums of All Time (2004)

The Collector's Guide to Heavy Metal: Volume 1: The Seventies (2003)

The Top 500 Heavy Metal Songs of All Time (2003)

Southern Rock Review (2001)

Heavy Metal: 20th Century Rock and Roll (2000)

The Goldmine Price Guide to Heavy Metal Records (2000)

The Collector's Guide to Heavy Metal (1997)

Riff Kills Man! 25 Years of Recorded Hard Rock & Heavy Metal (1993)

See martinpopoff.com for complete details and ordering information.

Index

MARTIN POPOFF has been described as "the world's most famous heavy metal journalist." He has penned 7,000-plus album reviews and more than 40 books on hard rock and heavy metal, including Voyageur Press's *Rush: The Illustrated History* and *Metallica: The Complete Illustrated History*. Martin has also worked in film and television, notably on the documentary *Rush: Beyond the Lighted Stage* and VH1's *Metal Evolution*. He lives in Toronto with his wife and son.